THE
ILLUSTRATED HISTORY OF
TEXTILES

THE
ILLUSTRATED HISTORY OF
TEXTILES

Edited by
Madeleine Ginsburg

Foreword by
Charles Saumarez Smith

PORTLAND HOUSE
NEW YORK

THE ILLUSTRATED HISTORY OF
TEXTILES

This 1991 edition published by Portland House,
distributed by Outlet Book Company, Inc.,
a Random House Company,
225 Park Avenue South
New York, New York 10003

Copyright © 1991 Studio Editions Ltd, London.

Project Editor: John Taylor
Designed by Malcolm Preskett

ISBN1 0–517–05031–5

8 7 6 5 4 3 2 1

Printed and bound in Hong Kong

CONTENTS

Illustration Acknowledgements

Abegg collection, Bern: pp. 14, 23, 176 bottom. Alte Pinakothek, Munich: p. 23 top. Courtesy G.P. & J. Baker, London: pp. 61, 80. Bauhaus Archiv, Berlin: p. 72. Bern Historical Museum: p. 130 bottom. Bodleian Library, Oxford: pp. 30, 32, 48 bottom. Boughton House: p. 114. Bridgeman Art Library, London: pp. 28 top, 28 bottom, 35, 40, 49 top, 79 top, 79 bottom, 136 bottom, 173, 191 top. Trustees of Chatsworth: p. 121. Chicago Art Institute: pp. 62 top, 62 bottom, 64 bottom, 131 top. Courtesy Christie's, London: pp. 41, 51 top, 67, 124 bottom, 127 bottom, 131 bottom, 135, 139, 142, 163 top, 163 bottom, 165, 166 top, middle & bottom, 168, 170, 171 top, 171 bottom, 185 top, 185 bottom, 186, 190. City of London Polytechnic, Fawcett Collection: p. 77 left. Cleveland Museum of Art: pp. 20, 78 top, 174. Courtesy Clifton Textiles Ltd.: p. 106 top. Coke Estates: p. 33. Courtesy Collier & Campbell: p. 101. Cooper-Hewitt Museum, New York: 141 bottom. Courtesy Crane Gallery, London: p. 181. Detroit Institute of Art: pp. 103 top, 132 middle, 134 bottom, 140. Edimedia, Paris: pp. 36, 85 left, 85 right, 115, 168 top, 177, 179 top, 180, 183. English Heritage, London: pp. 52 top, 133 bottom, 154, 155. Courtesy Guy Evans, London: pp. 37, 45, 48 top, 54, 55, 56. Courtesy the Fan Museum, Greenwich: pp. 65 bottom, 191 bottom. K. Finch, London: pp. 192, 197, 208, 209. Courtesy S. Franses Ltd., London: p. 119. Courtesy Cora Ginsburg, New York: pp. 53, 138 top, 187 top, 187 bottom. Giraudon: pp. 12, 13, 31, 161, 169, 178, 179. Sonia Halliday: p. 194. Hamburg Kunsthalle: p. 147. Courtesy Heals, London: p. 94 bottom. Historical Museum, Stockholm: 131 middle, 198, 199. Michael Holford, Loughton: pp. 49 bottom, 68, 138 bottom. Angelo Hornak, London: 64 top, 83 top. Kunsthis-

torisches Museum, Vienna: p. 160. Courtesy Maison Lesage, Paris: p. 144. Courtesy Liberty's, London: p. 94 top. Courtesy Marimekko, Finland: p. 91. Metropolitan Museum, New York: p. 137 top. Musée des Etoffes, Lyon: pp. 21 bottom, 136 top. Museum of London: p. 151. The National Trust, London: pp. 50, 132 bottom, 133 top. Norsk Folkemuseum, Oslo: pp. 146, 157 top right. Philadelphia Museum of Art: pp. 46, 52 bottom, 60, 95 bottom, 99 bottom, 188. Private collections: pp. 38, 47, 71, 78 bottom, 81, 84 top, 92, 93, 95, 96 top, 96 bottom, 97 top, 97 bottom, 100, 102 top, 104 top, 104 bottom, 105 bottom, 105 top left, 107 bottom, 108 top, 109, 112, 116, 123, 126 bottom, 126 top left, 126 top right, 141 top, 158, 159 top, 159 bottom, 201, 203 top. Courtesy Rentokil: pp. 204 top left, 204 top right, 204 bottom. Royal Collection: pp. 103 bottom, 124 top. Royal Ontario Museum, Toronto: p. 15. Courtesy Sanderson, London: 98 top, 98 bottom. Photo Slunk-Kender: p. 108 bottom. Courtesy Sotheby's, London: pp. 175, 189. Courtesy Spink's, London: pp. 22, 34, 42 bottom, 43, 44, 46 left, 63, 69, 117, 127 top, 128, 132 top, 153 left, 167, 182, 184. Courtesy the Textile Conservation Centre: pp. 193, 196, 200 top, 200 bottom, 203, 205, 206 top, 206 bottom, 207. Courtesy the Board of Trustees, Victoria & Albert Museum, London: pp. 17, 18, 24, 39, 59, 65 top, 76, 77 right, 80 top left, 80 bottom, 87, 88 top, 88 bottom, 89 top right, 89 bottom, 99 top, 118, 122, 125, 134 top, 143, 148 top, 148 bottom, 149, 150, 156, 157 top left, 162, 172. Visual Arts Library, London: pp. 21 top, 25, 26, 27, 29, 42 top, 57, 66, 73, 74, 82, 84 bottom, 86, 89, 90, 105, 106, 107, 113, 129, 130 top, 137, 145, 152, 153, 157 bottom right, 164, 176, 195. Whitworth Art Gallery, Manchester: pp. 16, 51 bottom, 70, 75, 83 bottom.

FOREWORD

by Charles Saumarez Smith

THIS NEW INTRODUCTION to the history of textiles has a particular use and value, since, of all the applied arts, I have found this subject the most difficult to which to gain access. There are a number of reasons for this. Firstly, the material which is being studied is often very fragile and, of necessity, stored in conditions under which it is not easily retrievable for purposes of examination. Secondly, it is obvious that what has survived is almost invariably only that which was most remarkable, so that there is a disconcerting disparity between the beauty of the few fragments which one is able to inspect and the immense bulk of everyday fabric which used to exist. Finally, in attempting to read the history of textiles as it has frequently been written, as one of the most important industries of Asia and Europe, I have found it frustrating that it is hard to visualise the weight and weave of the textiles which were produced in such gigantic quantities. More problematically than in the history of paintings or even of furniture, the history of textiles is suspended in awkward territory somewhere between the expertise of museum curators, who are capable of dating a bed-hanging to a precise year on the basis of a sharply developed and experienced eye, the number-crunching of economic historians, who can provide statistical tables of annual exports of different types of cloth, and the stores of museums where row upon row of textiles are stored in a taxonomic system which ranges geographically from the Andes to the Yangtze, and by type from tapestries to pocket handkerchiefs.

Because of all these difficulties, I was delighted to hear that a group of former students of the MA Course, run jointly by the Victoria and Albert Museum and the Royal College of Art, and other specialists were collaborating in providing a straightforward, up-to-date, well-illustrated and (so far as is possible within the confines of a single volume) comprehensive introductory study of the history of textiles. Under the guidance of Madeleine Ginsburg, a former member of staff at the Victoria and Albert Museum, who was invariably helpful to students, the contributors have assembled a combined theoretical and historical survey which will provide for those who know nothing or only a little about the subject some knowledge of the basic fabric types and how they evolved through history.

Even those who are well acquainted with the field are in for some surprises and the opportunity to extend their knowledge. I have enjoyed reading about the different centres of medieval silk production, about the earliest wool tunics which survived in Coptic graveyards and the different types of silk produced in Mozarabic Spain, including *dibaj*, *mulham* and *lolol*. I had not known that the Bayeux tapestry is a secular companion to more elaborate ecclesiastical embroideries, the so-called Opus Anglicanum. Nor did I realise the extent to which the paintings of Trecento Italy coincided with the dispersal of silk weavers to provincial centres following the sack of Lucca in 1314, so that the emergence of a highly visual culture may have coincided with the replacement of wool by silk as a dominant industry.

When it comes to changes in production in the sixteenth and seventeenth centuries, I am more familiar with the innovations in furniture type which were introduced as a result of changes in the pattern of demand, including the desire for new types of floor-covering and more comfortable chairs; how consumer goods spread into the households of the merchant and administrative élite, as recorded in inventories; and the visual stimulus which was provided by the bulk import of chintz, including calico to line Mrs Pepys's study, which her husband thought was 'very preety'. Yet even in this chapter I learned things I had not previously known, for example the fact that Boucher became director of the Royal Gobelins tapestry factory, and the relationship between the physical appearance of mid-eighteenth-century silks and the development of the *point rentré* technique. What emerges very clearly is the extent to which changes in the technology of production at the end of the eighteenth century were preceded by innumerable developments in design, fabric type, and the distribution of different types of textile throughout the preceding century and in countries other than England. For example, William Sherwin, a portrait engraver, took out a patent for a new method of printing calico in 1676 and twenty years later employed 200 people in his calico-printing factory.

Although the changes in the technology of production at the end of the eighteenth century were clearly a development of what had come before and should not be regarded as revolutionary, the pace of change around 1800 is undeniable. There was a multiplicity of innovations associated with the introduction of new machinery, including changes in advertising, the proliferation of women's magazines, and perhaps a degree of standardisation in fashion. Indeed, one of the great benefits in looking at technical changes from the point of view of the finished product is that it shifts the emphasis away from famous inventions, such as the spinning jenny, towards less well-known aspects of manufacture – the production of a turkey red dye, the mechanisation of cylinder printing, the introduction of a prototype sewing machine by a cabinetmaker in 1790, and the development of the Jacquard loom. Equally, by concentrating the focus of historical examination on a particular medium of production such as textiles, it becomes possible to see familiar events of history in a new light. How many people associate the Great Exhibition with the display of Mr Charles Mackintosh's invaluable new product? And how many people think of William Morris in terms of a highly-developed disgust against aniline dyes?

Just as in previous centuries, in which the close associations between textiles and other aspects of the fine and applied arts are too little known, so in the chapters on the twentieth century I was fascinated to learn that Gustave Klimt designed kaftans, that batik made an important contribution to art deco, that the hammer and sickle was a prominent motif at the 1925 Paris exhibition, and that Paul Nash had written a book about interior decoration. I also found fascinating the way that recent history begins to be constructed with such a cavalier disregard for what the period appeared to be like at the time: it is perhaps worth thinking about the disparity between what the vast majority of people buy and wear all the time and the way that it is made to seem as if everyone in 1966 was shopping in Mary Quant and wandering round the streets of London in mini-dresses made of see-through PVC.

What this book sets out to do is provide a narrative summary of the key developments in the history of textiles from the Copts to David Hockney. I very much hope that it will make people who are not familiar with the history of textiles more aware of the gaps in their knowledge. It should encourage students who are embarking on a degree course in some aspect of practical textiles to think more carefully about the history of the discipline, at the same time as they learn about its contemporary practice. It will serve as a useful primer for those who want to learn about basic developments in technology. Perhaps most importantly, it should make readers think about different ways of studying textiles. For the text necessarily weaves together different elements of an historical narrative, including the examination of conditions of manufacture and the visual inspiration provided by individual fine artists; these familiar aspects of historical study need to be counterbalanced by what may be described as the weft, such as the involvement of women in embroidery, the manipulation of fashion, and what causes changes in popular taste.

I would like to think that this volume might act as a starting-point and encourage people to investigate more deeply the history of textiles, to go off to museums and examine not only the major works of textile art which are out on display, but, also, to consult the relevant specialist literature, and to make an appointment to see the many thousands of textiles which are kept in museum stores. For it is necessary always to remember that illustrations in books, however excellent, are only extremely inadequate approximations of the physical appearance of what has survived; and that the beauty of textiles lies in the quality of individual objects, their combination of colour and feel and texture, as well as the characteristics of their design reproducible on paper.

EDITOR'S PREFACE

TEXTILES, THE CLOTHES for our backs, covers for our beds and a source of beauty and comfort in the home, are so integral a part of a civilised life that we tend to take them for granted. We rarely see them as unique and complex products with their own aesthetic, a range of techniques and a history reaching back at least 2,000 years with crucial implications for the wealth of nations.

One aim of this book has been to build a bridge between those concerned with the 'How', the museums of science and technology, and the 'Why', the museums of fine and applied arts. The story which stretches from earliest times to the microchip is recounted here by a team of specialists in the applied arts. In the first part of the book they provide a chronological account summarising the development of the different types of textiles, their methods of manufacture, their appearance and aesthetic, their designers, and the life style of those who bought them. The range is wide: it encompasses Louis XIV's glorious court setting at Versailles as well as the unknown eighteenth-century purchaser of a new-fashioned printed cotton marked ten pence a yard.

Charles Saumarez Smith, Head of the Research Department at the Victoria and Albert Museum, London, and formerly head of the joint Victoria and Albert Museum and Royal College of Art MA course in the History of Design, who has encouraged so many to undertake work in this field, has been kind enough to write a foreword which sets the work in context.

The volume concentrates on the United Kingdom, which between 1500 and 1900 became the textile workshop of the world, the United States, which took over its role, France, which for so long set the standards of design, as well as the contributions of Italy and the Low Countries. Another theme is the way in which designs and techniques have travelled around the world, for this is the most international of industries. It can be no accident that in the first English travellers'

phrasebook in the fifteenth century, William Caxton's *Ryght good lernyng, for to lerne shortly frenssh and englyssh*, readers were taken on a bilingual shopping trip, and instructed on buying themeselves cloth for a new suit of clothes. Ever-practical Caxton provided them with phrases on striking the bargain and measuring the cloth. Short length, faulty fabric and end of roll defects have a long history it seems!

According to legend the manufacture of luxury textiles in the West began in the sixth century when Byzantine monks, concealing contraband silkworm eggs in their walking staffs, brought the closely guarded secrets of the silk industry from the Orient. It is perhaps poetic justice that many European countries have now yielded their primacy in the textile trades to the east from which the knowledge originally came. If on the one hand there are unscrupulous manufacturers slapping false designer labels on their products with cosmopolitan abandon, on the other we have a galaxy of designers whose work has a truly worldwide appeal.

But, despite its constant experimentation with new technology, this is an industry which cherishes and constantly re-creates its past. Even the full frontal views of neat vases filled with gaily coloured flowers so popular with the makers of modern embroidery kits have a history which goes back to Coptic tapestries, to motifs which have travelled to the Far East and back several times in the intervening centuries. Many patterns have great longevity: William Morris textiles, for example, are just as desirable today as they were a hundred years ago when they were created. Older textile firms cherish their pattern books, and designers are the most faithful of customers in the antique textile trade, constantly searching either for inspiration or an as yet undiscovered design classic with an appeal which transcends time. Its rich historical repertoire is the industry's great resource and perhaps this book will suggest further archives worthy of explanation. Three-dimensional Fibre art is, however inimitable, an artistic creation of our own time.

The second half of the book deals with the 'What', in sections intended for connoisseurs, collectors, designers and students. The writers, five from one of the great London auction houses, demonstrate the close links and parity of standards between the established antiques trade, academics and museums. There is an equal awareness of scholarship in the preparation of their catalogues, and the advice given to clients is none the less scrupulous for being applied in the pursuit of commerce. The chapters examine the most popular textiles on the art market today – carpets, knitting, embroidery, lace and tapestries – and give advice on how to select and buy antique textiles and know the best value. The last section, by a conservator with long international experience, analyses the causes of the degeneration of these attractive and deceptively fragile survivors and suggests ways in which they can be protected from the further perils of pest and pollution in the future.

The final section is a glossary, a ready-reference guide to terms, techniques, designers, firms, material and motifs. A select bibliography and an international list of relevant collections offer help to those who wish to make further study of their specialist subjects. Those who wish to follow up the necessarily brief references in the text to the pioneers of the industry may find themselves in an encouragingly Samuel Smiles world in which talent and effort as well as luck are signposts on the road to fortune. Some pioneers might verge on the unscrupulous, like the eighteenth-century Earl of Pembroke who is said to have transported his clandestine French carpet-weavers concealed in a barrel. There are also the undutiful, like Samuel Slater, founder of the industrialised American textile industry, so anxious to conceal his departure for the New World that he failed to inform his family until

actually on board the ship. Richard Arkwright, founder of the English textile industry, barber turned inventor, financed his experiments with a new type of hair dye, suspected of witchcraft by neighbours perplexed by the strange noises emanating from his secret workplace, still rose early to practise his writing and spelling at the age of fifty. And in an age which respects precocity, how encouraging to realise that William Perkin was only nineteen when he created the searingly vivid aniline purple which is the hallmark of popular high Victorian taste. For factual background to the picturesque legends culled from the older books, there is an ever growing body of 'hard' academic research on the realities of the trade from economic and business historians. The story is never-ending and it is one that we can ourselves update from the news and city pages of our daily newspapers.

The colour illustrations have been specially selected to amplify the text and provide a visual reference for designers and collectors as well as showing the textiles in the decorative context of their period.

We would like to thank our authors who have willingly worked towards a common goal, telling a story so varied and complex that it has never before appeared in one volume; all who responded so kindly and generously to our questions; the dealers and collectors who helped us to try to find the most appropriate objects to illustrate; the editorial team, illustration researcher and designer who brought together the many diverse elements that it was decided to try and include.

The patchwork album quilt became a symbol of friendship and cooperative achievement in the pioneering days of the United States. In this book, a composite of contributions from specialists in the applied arts, museums, experts in antiques and conservators, we have a similar aim. We hope we have achieved a unity from diversity and that readers will find the result useful.

PART ONE

The History of Textiles

Samite, silk of Imperial factory weaving. Byzantine,
10th century. A relic of St Germain now in the church of
St Eusebius, Auxerre, France.

The earliest times to 1550

Clare Phillips

The Duke de Berry at dinner, about 1410. An illustration for the month of January from the *Très Riches Heures du Duc de Berry* by the Limburg Brothers. There is great variety of rich textiles, the tapestry with a battle scene, possibly the Trojan War, which can be seen behind the Duke, the rich clothing and the damask tablecloth.

WEAVING is one of the oldest of crafts, with fine and sophisticated textiles being produced from early times. A fine linen shirt preserved in the tomb of Tutankhamun and now in the Victoria and Albert Museum, London dates from around 1360 BC, but such early survivals are extremely rare and depend on favourable archaeological conditions. The fragmentary and discoloured state of most excavated textiles makes literary references and visual evidence such as the depiction of fine garments on Pompeiian wall paintings particularly valuable. Another indirect clue for early textiles is the weave impression sometimes left by a fabric on corroded metal or clay which can preserve the weave structure after the complete decay of the actual cloth.

Many more textiles from the medieval period have survived, primarily in shrines, royal tombs and ecclesiastical treasuries. But here again the random nature of what has been preserved presents a rather distorted

Cythar player, tapestry woven. Coptic, 5th–6th century.

view of what was typical at any time.

Textile manufacture throughout the period relied on natural dyes and the four basic fibres of wool, silk, linen and cotton. Fabrics were commonly left plain, or dyed a single colour. With more costly fabrics decoration was applied in the weave either by tapestry or later by the drawloom, by embroidery, or more rarely by simple printing methods. Although most everyday cloth was produced locally, an international market in luxury textiles developed, and it is these more precious textiles that are usually the ones to have survived. Information on their making often comes from guild regulations which often stipulated standards of size, content and method.

The movement of textiles was extensive within Europe, as they were part of an international trade network in luxury goods which reached even to the Far East. As early as the first century BC, Chinese goods in-cluding textiles reached the Mediterranean, brought by camel caravans. Within Europe goods were transported by ship across the Mediterranean or to the Black Sea and then up the system of rivers that lead to Russia and Scandinavia. The trade was in the hands of merchants with a widespread international clientele.

Fairs played a vital part in the trade of Medieval Europe and the distribution of textiles. There were hundreds of local fairs but the most famous were the Champagne Fairs, at their height from 1150 to 1300, and those of St Denis, Cologne and Venice.

Coptic Tapestries and the Textiles of Christian Egypt

Coptic textiles may be defined as those produced in Egypt from the introduction of Christianity to the conquest by the Arabs in AD 640. Egypt had been a Roman province since 30 BC with a strong and long-established Greek presence. Pharaonic elements had long since disappeared to be replaced by more international influences and styles of ornament, and it is as examples of Graeco-Roman and then early Christian art that Coptic textiles are significant. Representative of the state of textile art throughout the Mediterranean region, they are particularly important since almost nothing as early has been preserved elsewhere.

The vast number of surviving textiles were discovered thanks to the systematic excavations of late nineteenth-century archaeologists working on the Christian burial grounds in Egypt. Only land not suitable for cultivation had been used for graveyards: this arid land, beyond the area flooded each year by the Nile, provided ideal soil conditions for the preservation of buried cloths and garments. Bodies were generally buried in the clothes worn in daily life which usually consisted of one or two tunics, a cloak and footwear. Sometimes other garments and cloths were also added. The site which yielded the greatest quantity of textiles was at Akhmîm in Upper Egypt which had been one of the greatest centres of linen production. The other major site was at Antinoë, an

Linen tunic with wool tapestry decoration. Coptic, 4th century. Tunics complete with tapestry decorations rarely survive.

extremely wealthy city founded in AD 140 by the Emperor Hadrian.

The principal garment worn by both men and women in Egypt was the tunic, a simple shape usually woven in one piece with a slit at the neck. Its basic shape remained constant, although sixth-century examples often have an oval neck opening rather than a horizontal slit. Decorative panels were frequently added, most commonly a patterned stripe descending from each shoulder at the front, with matching cuff bands. On early tunics these shoulder bands (or 'clavi') usually continue to the hem whereas on later ones they reach only as far as the waistband and have a roundel at each end.

Although by the sixth century there are some tunics of wool, locally produced linen in plain weave or 'tabby' was the most important fabric being used, and the commonest decorative technique was tapestry weaving. Areas to be decorated were first differentiated on the loom. In such parts the warp and weft would not be interwoven but left to lie in two layers one on the other. The decoration would then be added by hand using different coloured weft threads usually of wool with a finer undyed linen thread outlining the pattern. This would be beaten down or compressed to make a firm panel using a comb beater. Alternatively tunic decorations could be woven or embroidered separately and applied afterwards. When silk tunic decorations appear in the sixth century this was the technique used. Decorative panels of all types were frequently cut out and transferred from an old garment to a new one.

Large rectangular textiles have also been found, cloths that could be used either as cloaks, blankets or hangings. Of the earlier examples some of these have decorative areas of looped tapestry giving greater bulk and warmth, while some are tapestry woven throughout allowing all-over patterning. By the sixth century, decoration of these cloths is simpler, typically consisting of parallel stripes.

Development from a pagan to a Christian society was gradual and initially patchy. As a result, although the corresponding iconographies are represented in textile design, any clear classification of different stages is problematic. However, three general and overlapping categories do emerge: first, the Graeco-Roman period, followed by the Transitional period, and finally the Coptic period proper.

Characteristics of the Graeco-Roman period probably stretch back to the first and second centuries AD but examples that can be securely dated only start in the third century. Motifs are classical and pagan, finely executed with pleasing use of colour – either soft polychrome or a single colour, most typically dark purple. Mythological, hunting and vineyard scenes were popular in addition to animals, birds, fish, trees, fruit and flowers.

The Transitional period covers roughly the fifth and sixth centuries, a time of change and of decline in both quality of material and technical skill. Colours are brighter and less successful, figures appear somewhat flatter, and ornament haphazardly scattered. Paganism predominates but Christian motifs are often incorporated inconspicuously on otherwise Graeco-Roman decoration. Christian emblems commonly used at this time are the cross, the traditional Egyptian cross or 'ankh', the Chi Rho monogram of Christ, and the letters Alpha and Omega.

During the sixth century, Christian iconography, biblical scenes and figures of the Saints replace pagan themes, and any inscriptions now appear in Coptic rather than Greek. Some scenes required little adaptation: a figure on horseback could easily be either a pagan huntsman or a saint, and of course motifs such as fruit, flowers and animals combine through each of these stages. The Christian period tapestries suffer a little from confused delineation where too much detail is attempted with bulky woollen threads, and the finer silk embroideries which date from this period are much more successful.

Textile crafts gradually diversified and silk weaving also began to be practised in Egypt in the sixth century. Much of it is two-colour work, usually drab or yellow on purple, woven in decorative strips that were to be cut and applied to linen tunics like the tapestry ornament already described. Silk weaving was to increase in Egypt following the Arab conquest of AD 640.

Coptic burial grounds have also preserved a few examples of the different technique of resist style printing. Although the process was known in Egypt as early as the first century AD these pieces dating from the fifth or sixth century are among the earliest to have survived. A technique similar to batik, the pattern was created by a resist of either wax or clay being painted on the linen before it was dipped into indigo dye. A group of four such fragments decorated with biblical scenes is in the collection of the Victoria and Albert Museum, London.

A wool and linen tapestry roundel, probably a decorative motif detached from a tunic. Coptic, 4th century.

16

Taming wild animals: a figured
Byzantine silk, 6th–7th century.

The Byzantine Silk Industry

Constantinople, the Byzantine capital, was well placed to become the centre of silk cloth production for the late Roman Empire and for early Medieval Europe. The city was sufficiently close to Persia for supplies of raw silk from China to be available, and the Empire had a climate in which silk-worms and the mulberry trees on which they fed could flourish. Being placed between Europe and Asia the Byzantine Empire was to a certain extent able to block the route further west and carry out all trade with Christian Europe itself. Aware of the power and prestige this monopoly conferred, the Empire actively promoted the idea of exclusivity, and exports were carefully restricted to prevent any other city rivalling the splendour of Constantinople.

According to legend it was in about 552 that two Byzantine monks smuggled silk-worm eggs out of China in bamboo canes, enabling sericulture to commence in the West. Silk weaving had been established in Constantinople long before this date, but it had relied on large quantities of raw silk being imported from China. This had always been problematic: even in times of peace, high customs duties particularly at the Persian frontier considerably increased the basic price, and in times of war the supply inevitably dwindled. Therefore, in order to develop a strong industry that could compete with Persian and Syrian silk production, home cultivation of silk became essential for the Byzantines.

The development of the Byzantine silk

Linen, printed with wood-block in an imitation of an Italian pattern. German, 14th century. Printed linens were often used as room decoration.

industry owed much to that already existing in Persia. In terms of design it is often impossible to distinguish between Byzantine and Persian silks, and in terms of manufacture they both relied on the invention of the drawloom to create their elaborate patterns and accurate repeats. The highly versatile drawloom became known to weavers of the Near East around AD 500. It was mechanically complex, requiring a constantly changing combination of warp threads to be lifted in order to create the design. Symmetrical designs halved the number of strings that were required to lift the warp threads at any one time and so were more commonly used. Motifs included human beings, animals, plants and inanimate objects, and occasionally woven inscriptions were added. Typically these designs were framed in roundel borders. The silk was a substantial

'compound' weave which had a structure requiring both binding and pattern warps and used various colours of weft threads.

Three grades of workshop co-existed in Constantinople. At the highest level were the Imperial workshops housed within the palace and whose employees had once been a hereditary caste. They provided the most magnificent silks for the Emperor, the Church and the Court and also produced the silks used as diplomatic gifts or tribute to foreign powers. Below them came the public workshops made up of independent craftsmen organised into guilds. They manufactured and sold second quality precious silks and their fabrics were available to the public and to foreign merchants. Their activities and the silks that they produced were closely scrutinised and were controlled by the detailed regulations set down in the *Book of the Prefect* (issued in 911–12). This document also contains a list of 'Kekolymena' or forbidden cloths, silks which because of their quality, colour or size could not be bought by foreign merchants. Constantinople maintained the system of 'hierarchy through clothing' through the Imperial workshops, but citizens were allowed unrestricted purchases of fine cloth made by the public guilds. As a result the wealth and splendour of the city became famous and was admiringly described by foreigners. The third type of workshop was found within the households of wealthy citizens, producing on a small scale for private consumption.

Foreign merchants dealing in silk were subject to particular scrutiny and restrictions. The length of their stay in Constantinople was strictly limited to three months and while there they had to live and carry out all business in the purpose-built *mitata* or hostels. According to the *Book of the Prefect*, being caught with forbidden cloth resulted in a merchant being whipped and shaved, having all goods confiscated and being expelled from the city. Specific trading treaties were drawn up with individual nations detailing the varying degrees of privilege in terms of quality and quantity of silk cloth allowed.

Most of the Byzantine silk arriving in Western Europe came through Italy, and in particular, Venice which as a Byzantine vassal state was allowed to buy great quantities of fine quality silks. A second route particularly relevant to the Anglo-Saxons was through Russia and Scandinavia (via the River Dnieper and the Baltic) both of whom had generous trade agreements with the Byzantines. Many precious textiles were also removed from the city in 1204 when the Fourth Crusade sacked and plundered Constantinople. So portable and of such great value, silk was an ideal form of booty.

Examples that have survived are those from ecclesiastical rather than secular use. Connected with the cult of relics and often placed in tombs of medieval saints or royalty, fragments have been preserved in church treasuries throughout Europe.

Silk Weaving in Spain

One consequence of the Islamic conquest of almost the whole of the Iberian peninsula in 711 was the early introduction of fine quality silk weaving and sericulture to Spain. The invasion had been led by the Berber tribes of Africa, and as they were Muslims, Spain then became a part of the Oriental world. Settlers including weavers arrived from distant parts of the Caliphate, also bringing cotton plants and sugar-cane, and Spain developed culturally and politically in isolation from the rest of Europe.

Ornate silks had reached Visigothic Spain as early as the seventh century. Greatly treasured and used mainly for vestments it is not known whether they originated in Constantinople or Baghdad. They were certainly imported, for in common with everywhere else west of Byzantium silk weaving was unknown in Spain at this date. It was to be introduced during the eighth century following the sophisticated Persian techniques and designs. Initially the raw silk had to be imported, but the mulberry trees necessary for silk worms were soon planted and local cultivation of silk began. By the tenth century, sericulture was fully established. The planting of cotton was also extremely successful particularly in Oliva and Candea.

Cordoba was the seat of government and also became the first centre for silk production in Spain. As silk was always amongst the most prestigious of manufactures, the weaving pavilion or *tiraz* was usually under the control of a nobleman. By the tenth century there were many silk factories in Spain, some of which were independent although most were controlled by royal interests. Most of the silk was woven for domestic use but a substantial amount was exported primarily to other Muslim lands.

The most distinctive type of silk fabric was known as *tiraz*, a Persian word which referred to the prominent arabic inscriptions woven into the silk, often in gold thread. These were usually religious texts or the names of sultans and noblemen. *Dibaj* was a high-quality dress silk; *lolol*, a striped silk;

Lampas woven in silk and metal thread with a design based on Kufic lettering and animals. Almeria, Spain, 12th century.

mulham, a cloth used for scarves, woven with a silk warp and cotton weft; fine patterned velvets were also produced. An enormous variety of silk fabrics were available, the names of which are known but their distinguishing characteristics no longer fully understood.

The designs woven into the silks are oriental in inspiration and are characterised primarily by their geometric style. Angular designs are well suited for woven ornament but the main reason for their popularity in this case is the Islamic avoidance of pictorial representation of living things. However, figurative elements are present in many of the designs, notably plants and animals, often integrated into the more prominent geometric ornament.

By the tenth century, the city of Almeria was the major centre for silk and a port from which cloth was exported to Christian Europe as well as other Muslim countries. It is described as having eight hundred looms for *tirazi* silk and one thousand for brocades. Malaga, the other famous silk-manufacturing town, in the early twelfth century rivalled Almeria in its production of costly and intricately woven silk cloth.

The political situation in Spain had changed considerably during the eleventh century. Civil war between the Berbers and the Arabs prompted the Christian states in the North to attack, and gradually the frontier was pushed south. By the second half of the thirteenth century only the small area of Granada remained under Muslim control and the Muslims had lost this too by the end of the fifteenth century. However, these changes had no visible effect on the silk industry, which by this time was sufficiently well established and dynamic to survive a change of culture and government. Despite its origins in an infidel culture the Christian rulers realised the value of what they had inherited and were determined to encourage it. The desirability of silk remained the same, and the demand even grew as the number of centres of power increased. Weaving spread further north to towns such as Toledo, which in the middle of the sixteenth century had an estimated five thousand looms, and designs came more closely into line with those of Italy and European taste.

Coronation mantle of Roger II (1130–1154) which became a coronation mantle of the Holy Roman Emperors. Made by Arab embroiderers in Sicily with exotic motifs, palms, and tigers attacking camels.

Silk brocade, Venetian, early 15th century.

Norman and Renaissance Silks in Italy

The Norman kingdom of Sicily and Southern Italy was the first area of Italy to achieve successful cultivation of silk. As was the case in Spain, it had been introduced by the Arabs along with cotton, sugar-cane, indigo and henna. Mulberry trees were planted at the latest by the tenth century and a census of 1050 shows Calabria to have well-established plantations totalling twenty thousand trees. Much of the raw silk was exported, the rest being woven in Sicily. The Sicilian silk industry centred on Palermo was at its height in the late twelfth century, although it still remained a small concern. It had been considerably improved by Roger II's rather drastic measure of capturing silk-workers from Thebes during his attack on Greece in 1147. Designs, not surprisingly, were Byzantine in style. Even at this point, though, it concentrated almost entirely on luxury textiles for the palace and the court rather than on cloth for export. Finished textiles played a very minor part in the Sicilian economy and exports were almost entirely confined to bales of raw silk.

Although Lucca in northern Tuscany be-

Silk velvet, with a gold ground, Italian, probably Florentine, late 15th century.

gan to develop silk weaving as early as the thirteenth century, silk production in northern Italy was primarily an activity of the Renaissance. After the sack of Lucca by the Pisans in 1314, many silk weavers fled and their skills were dispersed to cities such as Florence, Venice, Genoa, Bologna and Milan. Lucca remained pre-eminent and in 1531 had an estimated sixteen hundred silk looms. For many of these northern cities, and for Florence in particular, the problems that would have accompanied the decline of the wool industry in the fifteenth century were largely averted thanks to the timely

growth of the silk industry. Aware of the changed status of Italian wool, Filippo Maria Visconti of Milan offered privileges to Florentine silk workers to come and settle in the city in 1442. This was emulated elsewhere and the silk industry successfully replaced that of fine wool throughout Italy.

Like the woollen cloth before it, much was destined for export, and by the sixteenth century Lucca and Florence controlled the important silk market of Lyons. However, Renaissance Italy itself was a major consumer of the silk it produced. Although the authorities periodically

The Angel of the Annunciation wears a cope of Italian silk with embroidered hood and orphreys. Detail from The Annunciation by The Master of Mary, Flemish, mid 15th century.

attempted to restrict the weaving of silk to the upper classes, their efforts never achieved much success and silk was worn by even the wives of shopkeepers.

There was a small amount of specialisation between the cities. Venice was noted for ribbons and Naples for decorative trimmings, but a wide variety of textiles were produced in each city. Heavy brocades with gold and silver thread, damasks, patterned velvets, satins and taffetas were all typical products. Plants and animals were often represented on patterned silks and with a greater degree of naturalism than on medieval textiles. New patterns such as the flower-vase motif, the pomegranate and the acanthus were introduced. The decorative possibilities of velvet were explored, and different textures and effects were created by varying the height of the pile or the method of cutting the loops of silk. The Genoese developed a method for crimping the threads of the pile, and these techniques when combined with the possible use of different coloured silks and metal thread enabled extremely sophisticated and expensive textiles to be produced. The most famous, *altobasseo*, was a velvet with varying heights of pile against a gold background.

Silk velvet with voided cut design. Italian, late 15th century.

The Birth of the Virgin, an embroidered motif from an alb, German, early 14th century. The pillowcase and the baby's swaddling bands in the vignette illustrate other domestic uses for embroidery.

The Finest Embroideries – Opus Anglicanum and the Tradition of English Needlework

The work of English embroiderers was known and sought throughout Medieval Europe by the wealthiest members of Church and State. Embroidery is a highly versatile means of decoration which could be practised at varying levels of complexity and magnificence, using materials ranging from cheap locally produced wools to costly silks, gold thread and precious stones. Both were being made, but it was for subtle and skilled use of the latter materials, work regarded as being closer to that of the goldsmith than a traditional textile craft, that English needlework, or Opus Anglica-

num, was particularly famed.

As either commissions or diplomatic gifts, many such textiles found their way to far-flung destinations. Well over a hundred pieces are recorded in the Vatican inventory of 1295, outnumbering all other types of embroidery mentioned. Collections of Opus Anglicanum have also survived in church treasuries in Austria, Belgium, France, Germany, Italy, Spain and Sweden. Although much has perished through continued use, embroideries on the Continent were at least spared the destruction which took place during the English Reformation when much ecclesiastical embroidery was lost.

The earliest reference to Anglo-Saxon needlework is an account of St Etheldreda, a seventh-century Abbess of Ely, embroider-

Relic of St Cuthbert, from Durham Cathedral. The maniple embroidered in silk on a couched gold ground, from integral inscriptions, was commissioned by Aelfled (909–913) probably in Winchester for Bishop Wulfstan.

work that has survived, embroidered hangings often commemorated secular events and were found in wealthy domestic interiors rather than churches. The eighth-century poem *Beowulf* describes tapestries decorated with gold on the walls of a palace banqueting hall. Much later, the deeds of the East Anglian hero Byrhnoth who was killed fighting the Vikings in 991 were embroidered by his widow on a hanging given to the Abbey of Ely. Around this date, secular embroideries began to appear in wills and were often bequeathed to the Church. A further example of fine secular work was King Harold's banner at the Battle of Hastings which, according to William of Malmesbury, was of a man fighting and was embroidered in gold and precious stones.

Mention of the Battle of Hastings leads inevitably to the remarkable embroidered hanging, the Bayeux Tapestry, thought to have been commissioned by the French from Anglo-Saxon embroiderers shortly after the Norman Conquest and still to be seen in the Abbey of Bayeux, in France. Although it is now undoubtedly the best-known early embroidery, its origins are rather obscure. Mentioned first in the inventory of 1476 for Bayeux Cathedral, where it decorated the nave on certain feast days, it was not until its rediscovery at the beginning of the eighteenth century that it became known to scholars. There are a total of seventy-nine scenes, accompanied by Latin inscriptions and showing very much more than scenes of battle. Over six hundred figures and seven hundred animals are embroidered, with scenes of farming, cooking, feasting, boat-building, and hunting among the activities shown. Thus it portrays many levels of society and is an excellent source for costume, furnishings and buildings.

The tapestry is worked in eight shades of wool on a banner of coarse linen over 70 m (230 feet) long and 50 cm (20 inches) deep. It now enjoys much greater fame than it would ever have achieved in the Middle Ages, when embroidered hangings narrating secular events were less rare and only work made of silks and gold was considered of

ing a stole and maniple in gold and precious stones for Saint Cuthbert. Unfortunately no needlework of such an early date has survived, and the oldest example of Anglo-Saxon embroidery is mid ninth-century work, preserved on a chasuble belonging to the collegiate church of Maeseyck in Belgium. The decoration consisting of several bands of embroidery is made up of interlacing and animal ornament worked in gold and coloured silks. It appears that pearls were also attached but these are now missing. Magnificent embroideries from the beginning of the tenth century were found in the tomb of Saint Cuthbert and are now in the treasury of Durham Cathedral: a stole and a maniple embroidered with figures of prophets and saints, thought to have been made in the Saxon capital, Winchester.

Although it is almost entirely ecclesiastical

The Normans set sail for England, embroidered in wool on linen, a scene from the
Bayeux tapestry, Anglo–French, about 1070.

primary importance.

In terms of technique, the outline of the design to be embroidered would first be drawn onto a stretched canvas by an artist or draughtsman. Choice of colours was probably a matter for the embroiderer. The stitches used were simple and widely known: split stitch was used for the silk threads, and the gold thread was applied by a method called underside couching. This involved looping a second thread usually of linen over the metal thread which had been laid in place on the surface of the cloth. The loop was then pulled tight from behind, so that no trace of the linen was visible, and the line of the gold thread was broken up at frequent intervals. An economical method, as no gold was wasted on the back of the piece, the regular indentations in the metal thread could be used decoratively and also made the cloth much more flexible than would otherwise have been the case.

An alternative method initiated by Continental embroiderers was Burgundian or lazur technique. Here, the metal thread was laid on the canvas and coloured silk stitched over it. The silk thread was not pulled tight but remained on the surface, creating a wonderful woven effect. This allowed subtle variations in the balance between the colour used and the underlying metal thread. Vestments embroidered in this way can be seen in the Rijksmuseum in Amsterdam and the Schatzkammer in Vienna.

Rich heavy embroidery was of course extremely time-consuming work and it was common for a group of craftsmen to work together on each piece. It is recorded that during Henry III's reign four women embroiderers worked for almost four years on an altarpiece for Westminster Abbey. Most of the costliest work was carried out in professional workshops. Both men and women were employed and a seven-year apprenticeship was required. But amateur needlework also accounts for much of the embroidery of the time, particularly that done in convents and noble households. A nun, Johanna Beverlai, embroidered the only surviving signed piece, and, in 1314, nuns in Yorkshire were forbidden to let their silk embroidery take priority over attendance at divine service.

Not surprisingly a progression of styles

Chasuble of brocaded velvet, the orphrey embroidered with scenes from the life of St Stanislas, and now in Wawel Castle, Poland. The silk is probably Italian and the embroidery, needle painting in silk and gold thread with raised detail, probably Flemish, 1501–05.

that mirrors developments in architecture and manuscript illumination is evident in Opus Anglicanum. In general, there is a liveliness about the Anglo-Saxon work which in the twelfth century is replaced by more solid Romanesque. In the case of the latter much surviving work is in gold thread and the figures are contained in rectangular, circular or round-arched panels. The thirteenth-century work is influenced by the Gothic style, with more graceful designs and more extensive use of coloured silks. In gold-thread work, a chevron pattern replaces the earlier blocks of stitching, and such examples mark the beginning of the greatest period of Opus Anglicanum. Fourteenth-century work, influenced by the

Decorated style in architecture, can best be seen in the wonderful arrangement of designs on surviving copes (large semi-circular vestments). Superb examples are the Syon cope and the Butler Bowden cope now in the Victoria and Albert Museum, London. At the beginning of the fourteenth century, the Tree of Jesse scheme was popular; compartments are formed by branches of a vine which emanates from a sleeping figure of Jesse and grows to fill the whole cloth. Concentric bands of arcading are also typical of the first half of the fourteenth century and can be seen at their best in the copes of Piacenza, Bologna and Toledo. Velvet was introduced as a new ground material for embroidery around this time. By the mid

Cope and detail of the hood from the Vestments of the Order of the Golden Fleece,
designed in the style of Rogier van der Weyden and probably embroidered in Brussels,
early 15th century. It was commissioned by Duke Philip (the Good) of Burgundy,
and is now in the Imperial Treasury, Vienna.

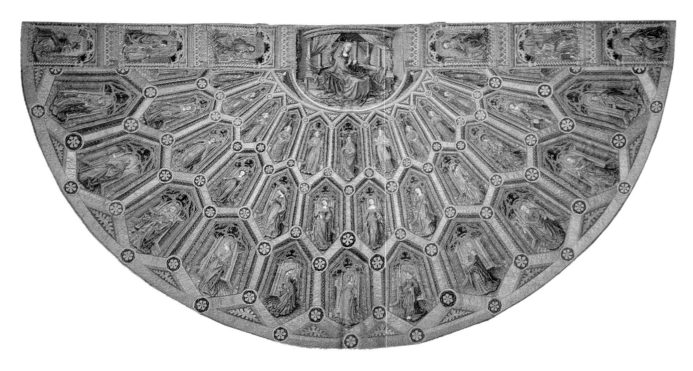

fourteenth century, the influence of the more rigid Perpendicular style becomes evident: gold backgrounds are given angular lattice rather than curved patterns, the arcading becomes wider and flatter, and the figures stiffer.

The late fourteenth century saw the decline of Opus Anglicanum and the increase in competition from foreign workshops. English techniques were simplified with a corresponding reduction in quality, and originality in design was gradually lost to the workshops of the Netherlands. An aspect of a general decline of the arts in England, it was in part due to factors such as the Black Death and the continued strife at home and abroad.

The Continental embroiderers developed the realism of needle painting, and their work illustrates the interdependence of the artist and the craftsman. The varied stitching combined with subtle use of padding and skilled blending of the colours and textures of the silks give a three-dimensional effect, and the high artistic quality is enhanced by the lively expressions and graceful animated poses of the figures. Backgrounds in *Or Nué*, Burgundian gold or lazur technique gleam like embossed metal. By the late fourteenth century, Florentine work had an international reputation. There are mentions of painters in the role of embroidery designers and the partnership of artist and embroiderers is well illustrated by the embroidered pictures, commissioned by the Guild of Merchants, made between 1466 and 1489, designed by Antonio Pallaiuolo and now in the Cathedral at Florence. The culmination of this style are the mass vestments of the Order of the Golden Fleece, commissioned by Philip the Good of Burgundy between 1425 and 1477 and now in the Schatzkammer in Vienna. They were designed in the style of Rogier van der Weyden and probably made in Brussels. In pristine condition, they still retain their additional embellishment of seed pearls and semi-precious stones and are a revelation of the skills and artistic aspirations of the embroiderers and their patrons.

Finishing a piece of cloth, a drawing from the *Zwölfbruder Stiftung Mendelschen Hausbuch*, Nuremburg, about 1540. The craftsman is raising the nap of the woven cloth with teasels mounted on a frame.

The Medieval Wool Trade

Most of the woollen cloth used in Medieval Europe was produced as an everyday commodity using locally produced raw materials. Design was not an issue, although colour available from natural dyes was important. In England, at the cheapest end of the market, low-grade wool was woven into fabrics such as bure and kersey, coarse cloths used for clothing by servants and the poor. Camelin was a woollen fabric of slightly better quality and above this came the worsted cloths such as say and fustian produced primarily around Norfolk. These textiles supplied the general need but did not prevent an international luxury trade developing with particular strength in the twelfth and thirteenth centuries.

A woollen cloth called camlet was imported into England from as far afield as the Near East, prized because it was made from the soft wool of the angora goat. However, this was an exception and the trade in luxury woollen cloth was primarily a European phenomenon.

The most important manufacturing centres were the towns of the Low Countries, initially Arras, St Omer and Douai, to be followed by Ypres, Ghent, and Bruges, which on its own had 40,000 looms in the thirteenth century. Florence with its two cloth guilds known as the Calimala of the Arte della Lana was the other major centre of production. Neither area used local wool but relied primarily on English imports. Florence, which had been using English

Dyeing the cloth, by boiling it in a vat. From the *Chronicles of Jesus*, English manuscript, mid 14th century.

wool at least since the Norman conquest, also used much wool from Burgundy. Spain, with its merino sheep introduced by the Berbers in the twelfth century, was the only other country able to supply wool of sufficiently high quality. But most of the wool used came from England – from Shropshire, Herefordshire, the Cotswolds and Yorkshire. In these areas sheep farming was an activity practised by all levels of society: bishops and monasteries, noblemen, tenant farmers and peasants. The scale of the larger flocks indicates considerable investment and the large profits to be made from the wool trade: the Bishop of Winchester owned 29,000 sheep in 1259, and about fifty years

later the priory of St Swithun, Winchester is recorded as having a flock of 20,000. These large wool producers would sell their fleeces directly to the exporting merchant whereas the small producers relied on the services of woolmen or middlemen. In both cases the trade was ultimately controlled by the Wool Staple, a company of English wool merchants through which all exported wool had to be directed, a system which enabled the highly lucrative tax on wool to be levied effectively. In 1421 wool tax accounted for 74 per cent of the entire customs revenue.

However, not all the fine wool was destined for foreign looms and, as native competence improved, England's role changed from that of supplier to manufacturer. Under Henry I, guilds of weavers were established in London, Winchester, Oxford, Lincoln and Huntingdon, augmenting the more homespun domestic production of woollen cloth, but their autonomy gradually came under challenge by merchant middlemen or clothiers. In the mid thirteenth century there was an attempt to forbid the export of all English wool to Flanders and to promote the use of English cloth among the wealthy. A more effective means of improving the home industry was the importing of specialised labour, and invitations to settle in England were issued to foreign weavers, dyers and fullers at various times after 1271. In the 1330s there was an influx of such artisans keen to escape the unrest in the Low Countries and receive the privileges and protection offered by the English Crown. They settled throughout the country and, although initially resented by the guilds, they had a critical effect on the scale and quality of the English cloth industry.

From the 1330s until the first half of the sixteenth century the quantity of cloth produced in England for export increased at least twentyfold. The weavers of Flanders were unable to compete, and indeed were no longer even able to obtain sufficient quantities of raw materials. The 30,000 sacks of wool sent abroad each year in Edward III's reign had decreased to about 5,000 as the capacity of English looms had increased.

The Sense of Hearing from the tapestry series The Lady with the Unicorn. In the mille fleurs
style, associated with the La Viste family, the series commemorates the five senses and
was made in France, probably in the Loire Valley, about 1500.

Jousting scene from a mid 15th-century manuscript of Froissart. Textiles, woven, printed, and embroidered were much used as decorations for outdoor festive occasions.

Their source of wealth disappearing, the great weaving centres of Flanders went into decline as England replaced them as the most important manufacturer of woollen cloth in Europe, though to some degree their decline was compensated by linen weaving.

Contemporary references to textiles are mainly to be found in accounts and business documents. They are not easy to assimilate into the total picture of a time when gradations of society were abrupt. For those at the top of the social pyramid there was a plenitude of material possessions, and an almost complete lack of creature comforts for those at its base. Some documents, however, do have a general appeal, are accessible, enjoyable and help us to relate people to their possessions and the industries to the supply and the demand. The pilgrims in Geoffrey Chaucer's *Canterbury Tales* (1389) wear clothes suitable to station, evocative of personality and their stories are enacted against fully furnished backgrounds. Caring for a

household and its furnishings is described by the Goodman of Paris, who in 1394 instructed his young wife in all aspects of housewifery. The international business practice of a very successful Italian merchant with an international clientele, between 1350 and 1410, sometimes considered the founding father of the small textile town of Prato outside Florence, can be discovered from Iris Origo's *Merchant of Prato* (1963), based on his complete business archive, left to the town. His English equivalents may be the Cely family, Merchants of the Staple, whose letters between 1477 and 1488 have been published.

Examples of most of the finest textiles of the period can be found in museums and treasuries throughout the world but it is only in the household accounts and inventories of a family such as that of the Dukes of Burgundy that we can appreciate the scope and scale of top-level consumption and demand at its most discriminating.

Among the richest rulers of their time, their life style described as one of 'magical luxury', they exchanged superlative gifts and had ritual changes of splendid clothes and furnishings on every conceivable occasion. For a visit of the King of France in 1389, there was an official issue of red and white livery, the Royal colours, to Court and retainers, satin for the lower ranks, and velvet for their superiors. The tent specially erected for the occasion required 30,000 ells (22,500 yards) of linen, though the material was subsequently ruined by bad storage. For the birth of John, a son of Philip the Good, there was a cradle covered with ermine and cloth of gold, and for the mother, a State bedroom with silk-covered walls, brocade bench pillows and a bed canopy embroidered with a golden sun.

Philip the Good was said to be the richest man of his age, and in the 1467 inventory of the goods left to his son, later Charles the Bold, there are many textiles among the thousands of precious items listed. There is table linen; 22 sets of voluminous bed curtains; brocade, samite, satin, damask, velvet and camlet; 15 pieces of gold brocade with several 39 and a half ells long (as the Flemish ell measured 27 inches, these were nearly 90 feet long); 15 sets of vestments, the mitres laden with jewels and the copes and chasubles gleaming through the ages encrusted with gold and precious stones, bordered with gold work and embroidered with saints, angels and inscriptions. The Golden Fleece vestments are there, described with what can only seem to us as a degree of understatement: they are termed 'well and richly' embroidered. Finally, there are the pride of the Duke's collection, the tapestries. There are 86 sets, battle scenes, myths, legends, emblems, bible stories. There is something for every mood and occasion, from the 'Battle of Ronceveaulx', 1382, five years in the making, 56 ells long by 7½ ells wide (126 feet by nearly 17 feet) and too big to transport, to a lighthearted pastoral with children playing among rose trees. After the end of the Burgundian dynasty in 1489, the collection was dispersed but in its prime it was the culmination of the textile arts and crafts of the period and set standards that in many technical and aesthetic senses were never surpassed.

Ladies weaving tapestries on upright looms, from a Flemish manuscript of the *Metamorphoses*, about 1497.

Brocaded silk, English (Spitalfields), about 1738,
designed by Anna Maria Garthwaite.

TWO

The dawn of the modern era
1550–1780

Andreas Petzold

'A Reading from Molière', by Jean-François de Troy, 1728, illustrates dress silks, upholstery
and wall hangings, all in the height of French taste.

THE PERIOD 1550–1780 was one of considerable change and development in the textile arts. Established industries in wool, linen and silk developed in response to an expanding market at home and in new territories across a wider world. From India and the East came increasing quantities of silk and cotton. The demand for both grew as well as pressure for renewal of the design repertoire. New European colonies, of which the most considerable were to be the Americas, gradually evolved from the beginning of the sixteenth century to become enthusiastic purchasers of European fabrics, and fashions, until such time as their own resources and initiatives led them to seek independence and attempt to achieve selfsufficiency.

From this period also, the sources relating to the history of textiles become more accessible. Paintings record the splendid opulence and conspicuous expenditure on dress and furnishings which were a feature of the period, our experience of which is enlarged

'Louis XIV and Colbert visiting the Gobelins tapestry workshop, October 1667', a design by
Charles Le Brun for the series 'The Story of the King'. The series was widely reproduced,
and this is from the set rewoven 1729–34.

by the quantity of woven fabrics, embroideries and laces which have survived and which provide a continuing inspiration for designers. The crafts and methods of manufacture also become more comprehensible to us, with the availability from the late eighteenth century onwards of patent information, and the work of the didactic publishers, the encyclopedists, in what was to be known as the Age of Enlightenment. From the middle of the eighteenth century, encyclopedias, especially those published by the French Académie des Sciences, made a conscious effort to explain and illustrate techniques and the conditions of the industries. Other useful documents are news sheets and journals, advertising and commenting on new styles and types of material.

Mercantilism

Because the textile industry played such an important part in the European economy, it inevitably became, in the context of the prevailing political and economic philosophy of the time, sometimes termed 'mercantilism', a target for government intervention. Mercantilism was concerned with conserving national wealth by encouraging self-sufficiency and exports, and discouraging imports. Home industries were fostered by protective legislation and by punitive import levies. Restraints were often placed on skilled artisans to dissuade them from emigrating though bribes and temptations were placed in their way, and industrial processes were sought and stolen. There are many instances of international skulduggery in all the textile crafts. The secrets of Lee's revolutionary knitting-machine were stolen in the mid-seventeenth century and accurate drawings found their way into Spanish government archives; in the 1740s Lord Wilton is said to have imported French carpet weavers concealed in wine barrels; during the American War of Independence, John Hewson, father of the American printed cotton industry, had a high price on his head, dead or alive, because of his skill in a branch of manufacture 'which the home country sought to suppress'. Nor did the traffic end with men and machines. During an embargo on the import of Flemish lace in the eighteenth century, dogs in lace overcoats dodged customs patrols at the border.

Any depression in the textile industry could cause widespread unemployment and the dislocation of trade in Europe during the Thirty Years War, 1618–48, in which England had no direct involvement, caused a slump in the English woollen industry. An interruption in supplies could, on the other hand, encourage enterprise and a search for alternatives. The disruption of trade with England during the 1640s prompted the General Court of Massachusetts first to import cotton from Barbados and then to encourage the manufacture of fustian, a hard-wearing fabric with linen warp and cotton weft which had been introduced into England by Flemish weavers in the sixteenth century.

Stamped moreen, a wool furnishing fabric, third quarter 18th century.

The English Woollen Industry

The English woollen industry, described by Daniel Defoe in 1723 as 'The richest and most valuable manufacture in the world', was seen as the key to England's prosperity. According to Sir Edward Coke in the 1680s, 'there are more people employed and more profit made and money imported by the making of cloth than by all the manufactures of England put together'. It was an industry already very well established by the beginning of the period, and technological changes were soon to improve productivity. The spinning wheel which had replaced the spindle in the fourteenth century was in the eighteenth century to be improved with a bobbin or flyer. The horizontal treadle loom, in use for three hundred years since the thirteenth century, was not changed, but the Dutch and Walloon weavers who emigrated to England during the Spanish invasion of the Low Countries in the sixteenth century, increased the repertoire of weaves with their experience of the drawboy loom as well as introducing different types of cloth. The 'New Draperies' with which they were associated involved a lighter weight textile with a long-staple combed worsted weave and a short-staple carded weft. There were concentrations of weavers in the East of England, especially Norwich and Colchester, and the West Riding of Yorkshire, while the restrictive practices of the guilds became progressively' weaker as the trade moved outside their territorial limits. Much work was contracted to small outworkers responsible to middlemen clothiers but some establishments were factory sized. The two hundred looms controlled by Jack of Newbury (John Winchcombe) had by the late sixteenth century been immortalised in popular doggerel by Thomas Deloney.

> 'Within one room being large and long
> There stood two hundred looms full strong:
> Two hundred men, the truth is so
> Wrought in these looms all in a row'

By the end of the eighteenth century, government fostering of the wool industry had occasioned no less than three hundred statutes of the realm. The most important was the prohibition by James I on the export of raw wool, which remained in force until the nineteenth century. Even the dead were pressed into service: from 1667 all shrouds had to be of wool, unless an exemption was obtained. There were also restraints on the development of a textile industry in the North American colonies: hardly surprising, since one third of the wool which England produced was, by 1760, exported to North America. These were restrictions much resented and, as with other trade restraints, they were a contributory cause of the War of Independence. The 1731 Board of Trade Enquiry into the Domestic Manufactures of the American Colonies is thought to have been more complacent than accurate in concluding that the colonists were content with mere self-sufficiency and home-spun and depended on England for their luxuries.

Luxury fabrics and France

The general rise in the standard of living of a broad spectrum of the population had great repercussions on the fabric industries. There was an increased consumption of domestic textiles and, between the late sixteenth and eighteenth centuries, and a dramatic change in the appearance of domestic interiors, with a greater emphasis on luxury and comfort. By the latter part of the seventeenth century, France, through the patronage of Louis XIV and the policies of his minister Jean Baptiste Colbert, tended to set the fashion for this transformation of interior design. At Versailles, Louis XIV had built a palace of unsurpassed magnificence and furnished it with luxury items which were made at accredited Manufactures Royales, overseen by artistic directors, most notably Charles Le Brun and Jean Berain. Colbert aimed at establishing France's pre-eminence as producer of luxury artefacts and to make the country economically more self-sufficient. He was following in a path already pioneered by Louis XI who, in the late fifteenth century, had invited Italian silk weavers to settle in Lyons and stimulate the

silk industry, and Henry IV who, in 1604, had sponsored the carpet factory at Savonnerie. Colbert's mercantilist policy has been categorised by economic historians as encouragement, regulation, protection and promotion. Royal charters, important commissions and financial grants, were given to Savonnerie for carpets, Gobelins and Beauvais for tapestries, to Alençon for lace and Lyons for silks. At Abbeville he established one of the largest factories for woollen goods in Europe.

The demand for luxury fabrics was not confined to royalty and the nobility, but extended to increasing numbers of the middle classes, who were enjoying steadily growing prosperity during the period. This was reflected not only in their dress but also in their homes. William Harrison, in his *Chronicles of England*, published in 1577, observed that 'in the houses of knights and gentlemen, merchantmen and some other wealthy citizens it is not so geson {rare} to behold generally their great provision of tapestry, turkey work . . . and fine linen . . .

Chair with Turkey work or pile woven upholstery, English, about 1620.

38

The tapestry room at Osterley House, designed by Robert Adam, 1775. The tapestries and upholstery were woven at Gobelins after a design by François Boucher.

many farmers and skilled tradesmen garnish their joined beds with tapestrie and silk hangings, and their tables with carpets and fine naperie whereby the wealth of the country doth infinitely appear'. In the 1660s, Samuel Pepys, a middle-class government official, was to record in his diaries many purchases of fashionable furnishings and clothes.

Upholstery, beds and interior design

One new use to which fabrics were put was as covers for upholstered chairs and settees which were introduced at the end of the sixteenth century. Examples from this early period can be seen at Knole, the Sackville family home in Kent, which has given its name to many variants on the original design. Previously, chairs had wooden seats, the hardness of which was only relieved by cushions, though these provided the opportunity for the display of elaborate embroidery, as may be seen, for instance, in the set of Elizabethan long cushions from Hardwick Hall. Some were tapestry woven and the tapestry works at Sheldon also made covers

for cushions as well as larger pieces. The most sumptuous fabrics were used for furniture upholstery, the designs similar but usually more conservative than those used for dress fabrics. Washable loose covers had always been used as protection and by the eighteenth century cotton with printed patterns became the vogue. Soft furnishings were often made en suite with room hangings. A superb example of this may be seen at the tapestry room in Osterley Park House, Middlesex, where the designs on the upholstered chairs match the set of Gobelins tapestries dated 1775 on the walls.

The bed, a prestige item of furnishing since medieval times, was the item which required textiles in the greatest quantity, for the curtains, the canopy, valances for the head and foot board, and the coverlet and decorative pillow cases, as well, of course, as the sheets and blankets. The trimming of a state bed was usually very elaborate. One of the earliest beds to have survived with its original trimmings is the King's Bed at Knole, made by a French artificer for James II. The hangings are of gold and silver tissue

The Spangle Bedroom at Knole House. The bed curtains and fittings are early 17th century, made from satin with an appliqué strapwork pattern outlined in gilt spangles. The tapestries which can be seen behind the bed are Brussels, with scenes from Ovid's *Metamorphoses*, marked HR, the initials of the weaver Hendrik Reydams.

lined with salmon pink satin and embroidered with silver and black thread. Often the hangings and other trimmings made it most expensive. In the reign of Elizabeth I, the Countess of Salisbury is reputed to have had a bed with white satin-embroidered hangings decorated with silver and pearls costing £14,000. This, however, must have been exceptional. Less elaborate are the lively products of the amateur, such as the set of late seventeenth-century bed hangings in the Victoria and Albert Museum marked with the name of their maker, Abigail Pett. They are embroidered with a charming and naïve collection of animals birds and flowers culled from printed design books. Another set from the same collection disposes these very English motifs against luxuriant tropical foliage, perched on Chinese-style cloud-like hillocks. They are examples of crewel work, embroidered in worsted wool, on a creamy white cotton and linen twill ground. Hangings of this type were fashionable from the early seventeenth century but most surviving examples are from the late seventeenth and

early eighteenth century. The designs derive from the luxuriant background of the fifteenth-century Flemish verdure tapestries, with an admixture of oriental floral motifs from imported Indian palampores, themselves probably influenced by Western motifs. Crewel work was made in North America as well as England, and there too was sometimes purchased with the pattern ready drawn. In the main, such curtains were intended for beds: at this period window curtains were usually utilitarian and comparatively plain.

Another innovatory use of textiles in interior designs involved carpets. In the sixteenth century they were usually of Eastern origin and were regarded as general coverings, especially for tables: they were not often used on the floor. There was a small European woven pile carpet industry but some of the finest European carpets of the period are embroidered not woven. The sixteenth-century Gifford Table carpet now in the Victoria and Albert Museum illustrates the link with the East and its motifs recall those on Turkish carpets, but the Bradford table carpet, from the same collection, is embroidered with lively country scenes. By the second half of the seventeenth century, the small industry established at The Savonnerie was experienced enough to respond to Louis XIV's commission for prestige furnishings for the Louvre and Versailles, an accolade for a product soon to be in international demand. A carpet industry was a valuable state asset, it made an expensive item for which there was great demand, it was labour intensive, and it made use of wool, which, in the case of the cheapest form of carpet, 'foote cloths', was unsuitable for any other purpose. By the middle of the eighteenth century, England was developing her own carpet industries with expatriate French workers. Official recognition came from the Society for the Encouragement of Arts, Education and Manufactures (later the Royal Society of Arts . . .), founded in 1757, which awarded prizes for the best English-made carpets. Its concern for the textile industries within the period was constant and in 1763 it was to award a prize for an improvement in wool-spinning methods.

Trade with the Orient

The second major development was the opening up of trade beyond Europe, particularly with India and China, which provided not only raw material such as silk and cotton but also finished goods. Trade with the East had been in the hands of the Turkey Company but, in 1601, the English East India Company was founded, and there were similar trading companies in France and the Netherlands. Among the artefacts that were brought to Europe were Indian painted and printed cottons, the so-called chintzes. These appealed to Europeans because, unlike the home products, they were both brightly patterned and the dyes were fast, a quality achieved with mordants so that they could be washed again and again: indeed, it was thought that their appearance was improved by repeated washing. These chintzes were used as furnishing fabrics, particularly as bed hangings and coverlets,

Chinoiserie-style embroidered hanging, early 18th century.

and were also used for clothes. Samuel Pepys, for instance, noted in his diary in 1663 that he had bought his wife 'a chinte . . . that is a painted callico for her to line her new study which is very preetie'; another entry records the purchase of 'an Indian gown for myself'.

These chintzes were so popular in Europe by the late seventeenth century that their importation led to a decrease in the demand for the woollen and silk productions of the European weavers. In order to combat this, protectionist policies were introduced. In France, in 1686, the wearing of Indian chintzes was prohibited and similar laws were passed in England in 1701 and in 1720,

The Bradford table carpet, late
16th century, detail from the border.
Professionally embroidered in tent stitch
with people in a landscape.

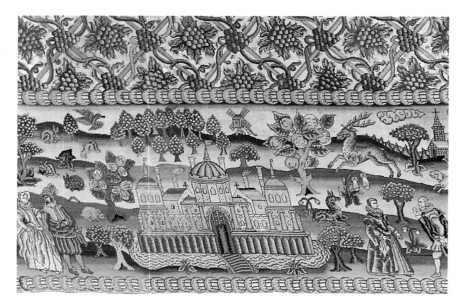

though they were frequently flouted. The actor David Garrick, for instance, is recorded in 1775 as having been sent from India a 'chintz bed and curtains'; on its arrival in England it was detained by customs, but Garrick, by using his influence, eventually succeeded in acquiring it. This bed still survives and may be seen in the Victoria and Albert Museum.

How far these Indian chintzes influenced European design is a matter of dispute. The so-called 'bizarre' silks, with strange exotic plant shapes and disintegrated background patterns which were fashionable at the beginning of the eighteenth century, were once thought to be Indian but are now considered to be the response of the Western mind to a plethora of Eastern designs flooding into Europe.

Raw silk was imported from China, as well as a small number of finished silks often painted with flowers and used for dress or furnishing. Madame de Pompadour, for instance, is shown wearing a dress made from Chinese silk in a painting by François Drouais now in the National Gallery, London, which was completed in 1764, shortly before her death.

A fantastic vision of Chinese life was conjured up in the European imagination and encapsulated in the style referred to as Chinoiserie. This typically consisted of designs incorporating figures with a vaguely Chinese look, often holding sunshades or engaged in drinking tea or standing on bridges or clouds. The style was an offshoot of the Rococo, with its lightness and frivolity, and initiated in France: it had as its main exponents Antoine Watteau and Jean Baptiste Pillement. Pillement is particularly in-

Brocaded silk in Bizarre type pattern, English (Spitalfields), about 1715.

The Tree of Life printed on a Mezzara (bedcover) of mixed silk and cotton. Italian, about 1840. An 18th century-type design with 19th century floral features.

teresting because he executed a series of engravings of Chinese subjects which were widely circulated. They were adapted for silk designs from Lyons, printed cotton from Jouy and England, as well as for tapestries, embroideries, fans and many types of decorative objects.

The vast demand for textiles increased pressures on the means of production. There was a constant striving towards technological innovation and a gradual switch from the workshop to what was almost a factory. The textile industries were to be in the forefront of the Industrial Revolution. The development was initiated by the invention of the knitting frame by William Lee in 1589. This made possible the making of knitted fabric, especially stockings which were then in great demand, by machine rather than by hand, using needles. Lee did not find official support for his invention in England because it was feared that it might lead to social unrest as a result of unemployment among the hand knitters. He therefore took it to France where, under the patronage of Henry IV, it was to form the basis of the French knitting industry.

Technical developments

The great period of technical innovation was, however, the eighteenth century, with its enormous increase in demand from home and overseas. The preparation of woollen yarn was improved by the replacement of hand carding with a stock card and table and, in 1733, John Kay invented his 'flying shuttle'. This speeded the making of broadcloths, that is, fabrics over 36 inches wide. By using the device, one man at a loom could do the work which had formerly needed two. This aroused great hostility among weavers who almost killed Kay when they mobbed his house.

The great need, however, was for yarn which the spinners with their single wheels could not supply in sufficient quantity. In 1764, James Hargreaves invented the 'spinning jenny' (jenny was a local diminutive for engine). This involved multiple wheels which could be worked from a single power source and which could be used in the home. One person could spin eight, then sixteen and, finally, over one hundred threads at once. It was suitable for both wool and cotton and made a soft yarn strong enough for weft, but not for warp. James Arkwright's spinning machine, patented in 1769, which, since it could also be powered by water was known as the water frame, made coarse cotton yarn which was, for the first time, usable as a warp, but the cost of patent rights and its mechanical complexity restricted it to factories. The advantages of the two devices were combined in Samuel Crompton's spinning mule, invented in 1779, which, since it was capable of producing a yarn which was strong yet soft and fine, was also known as the muslin wheel. It could be used for this fabric, which had hitherto been an Eastern import, but which was to become very fashionable by the end of the eighteenth century. Manchester and surrounding areas of Lancashire had a long tradition of cotton and cotton-mixture weaving for which their moist climate made them suitable. Lancashire's natural advantage of water power was by the last quarter of the eighteenth century to confirm its position as the centre of the new, mechanised textile industry.

The silk industry

Despite these technical developments, silk continued to be the fabric for formal dress and the highest quality furnishings, and the techniques of silk weaving had changed little since medieval times. At the beginning of the period, the main centre of European manufacture was Italy, with Genoa, Milan and Florence as the principal centres of production. Their damasks and velvets with patterns of graded depth combined with a gold ground have never been surpassed. By the end of the sixteenth century small symmetrical patterns had become popular. They were gradually enlarged, reaching their greatest size in the 1660s, and thereafter shrinking, fragmented and partitioned by the late seventeenth- and early eighteenth-century vogue for vertical stripes. Furnishing fabrics tended to be influenced by the formal baroque of Daniel Marot.

In the second half of the seventeenth century, France began to succeed Italy as the main producer of high-quality patterned silk, with important centres at Tours and Lyons. It was a development stimulated by Colbert's reorganisation of the French silk industry in the 1660s. Despite the emigration of Huguenot French weavers after the revocation of the edict of Nantes in 1684, the silks of Lyons retained their European supremacy and were to continue to earn the admiration of Europe through to the twentieth century. The persecution of the Huguenots had as a direct result the stimulation and founding of silk industries in other parts of Europe. That of England, centring on Spitalfields in the East End of London and its sequence of silk patterns during the eighteenth century, has been studied in detail and its fabrics and designs are typical of those current in the rest of fashionable Europe. There are many examples of the bizarre pattern silks already mentioned as being fashionable from about 1706–12 and these are succeeded by those based on lace

Brocaded silk with unusual Indo-Chinoiserie design, featuring elephants and a Buddha. French about 1740.

Italian brocaded upholstery silk about 1680: an accurate period reproduction.

motifs and, in the 1730s, by large-scale luxuriant floral designs. They have a striking three-dimensional quality, the result of an initiative by Jean Revel, a Lyons designer who had trained as a painter and who developed the *point rentré* technique which permitted colour transitions to shade into one another. In the 1740s, the size of the motifs diminished, naturalism is a feature and the motifs began to echo the contrapuntal Rococo rhythm. In the last quarter of the century, a small floral spray was the most popular motif, sometimes combined with vertical stripes.

A further stimulus to the English silk industry was the introduction to England of the silk-throwing machine which was largely based on, indeed plagiarised from, an Italian model. This facilitated the production of high twist yarn called organzine, necessary for warps which previously had to be imported at great expense from Italy. The value of this invention was indicated by the very large government payment of £18,000 made to Thomas Lombe, the inventor, upon his relinquishing his patent rights, and he

established a very large water-powered silk mill at Derby. There was an increased supply of silk yarn, though the fabrics were still expensive, since, in addition to the yarn, there was the high cost of weaving. Setting up a drawboy loom to weave a complicated pattern could take several weeks. A simple patterned silk could cost 6 shillings per yard, a low average week's wage for a woman, and a dress could use 23 yards. In the middle of the eighteenth century, there are said to have been 17,000 silk looms in operation at Spitalfields, and much of the product was exported, especially to North America, where many collections hold silks datable by and associated with the English sources. During the 1760s the trade began to decline, partly as a result of the fashionable preference for light plain silks and printed cottons. In 1766, an act prohibited the importation of French silks, though the demand for these had always been restricted by high duties.

The designs commissioned by the silk mercers from the Spitalfields weavers owed a strong debt to France, but those of Anna Maria Garthwaite (1690–1763), a professional designer and the daughter of a Lincolnshire parson, though clearly responsive to French trends, represent a very real original contribution by England to the Rococo style. The types of silks for which she was responsible, as well as others typical of the English upper middle-class market wardrobe, are represented in the Barbara Johnson Album, her dress fabric scrap-book now at the Victoria and Albert Museum.

The cotton industry

By the last quarter of the eighteenth century, cotton was beginning to replace silk as the fabric of fashion, underlining the contemporary preoccupation with a new ideal of rural simplicity rather than wealthy ostentation. The fashion for patterned cotton had been growing since the importation of chintzes from India, the popularity of which inspired the European manufacturers to compete. Printing with wood blocks had been practised since medieval times and was a development of the methods used for

Brocaded silk with luxuriant pomegranate design illustrating 'point rentrée' technique, French, Lyons, about 1735.

Cotton, copper plate printed by Francis Nixon, about 1765–75, and used for a bed hanging.

printing on paper. Colours were limited and not fast until, in 1676, William Sherwin of West Ham patented his new way of printing broad calicos, based on the Indian method of madder dying with metallic mordants. His colours were washable, his fabrics cotton, fustian, a linen cotton mix, or linen on its own. Although his colour range was limited, and indigo and yellow weld were added later to the dye range, such fabrics were popular enough to pose a threat to the wool and silk weavers, who by concerted lobbying succeeded in placing restrictions on

their manufacture in each of the countries – England, France, the Netherlands and Germany – where the new techniques were being used. In France, as early as 1686, Indian chintzes were prohibited, as well as European printed fabrics; this law was not rescinded until 1759. Printed cottons were prohibited in England in 1720, though printing on linen and fustian was permitted and, most importantly, cottons could be printed for export, which explains why so many have found their way to America. However, the restrictions do not seem to have been very effective and were frequently evaded. Barbara Johnson's Album of fabrics from her wardrobe, compiled between 1745 and 1825, contains two of the earliest dated specimens of printed cottons, 1746 and 1747 respectively, and this series has been regarded as conventional for the period. The restrictions were finally removed in England in 1774, partly as a result of Arkwright's promotion of all-cotton fabric, the product of his water-frame and cotton mill. In order both to distinguish and encourage home manufacture of cotton, the Act of 1774 stipulated that three blue threads should be woven into the selvedge of each piece of home-produced cotton which was charged at a lower rate of excise duty than those printed on imported cotton. It was not rescinded until 1824.

An important innovation originating in Britain was the use of copper plate printing, which facilitated a larger repeat unit with finer engraved detail. The process was pioneered by Francis Nixon at the Drumcondra Printworks near Dublin in 1752 and introduced into England by 1756. Various factories were set up, particularly in the East End of London, such as that of Robert Jones of Old Ford and Talwin and Foster at the Bromley Hall printworks on the River Lea, while John Munn established the Wallis printworks at Crayford in Kent. The price of these attractive cottons could be reasonable and on one is the inscription 'Country Village, 10 pence per yard Talwin and Foster'.

When the law prohibiting the wearing of printed cottons in France was rescinded in 1759, Christopher Oberkampf established at Jouy what was to become the most famous printed cotton factory: its products are usually referred to as *Toiles de Jouy*. Such fabrics became fashionable as dress materials. So popular were their striped designs at the court of Louis XVI, that a contemporary described the courtiers as zebras! Other important centres of production in France were at Nantes, Rouen, and in Alsace, where Mulhouse was to become one of the most notable producers of printed cloth in the nineteenth century. If a fabric was of a fast or durable colour it would be stamped '*bon teint*' to distinguish it from the possibly brighter but less fast '*petits teints*'. The end of the piece was sometimes stamped with the maker's name: the '*tête de piece*'.

By the last quarter of the eighteenth century, in addition to the floral subjects which had always been very popular, there was a

Central motif from a bedcover, copper plate printed by John Hewson, USA, about 1790.

great variety of narrative subjects, including Chinoiserie, scenes from the theatre and scenes portraying an idealised view of rural life. One of the most interesting, by J.B. Huet, dated 1783, illustrates the manufacture of printed cotton at Jouy. Interesting are the printed handkerchiefs, very varied, topical or commemorative, and popular as gifts and even love tokens.

The United States

In America in the eighteenth century there was a vast importation of French and English printed cottons. The founding father of the American printed cotton industry was an Englishman, John Hewson, who had been a cotton printer in England and was encouraged by Benjamin Franklin to emigrate to Philadelphia, where he and his son operated a printworks from 1773 to 1810. His pro-

Copper-plate printed cotton, John Baptiste Huet's first design for Oberkampf's printing factory at Jouy-en-Josas, France, 1783–4.

ductions are of high quality and initially in the English style, and he is recorded as producing printed handkerchiefs, bedspreads, and 'a variety of nankin waistcoat shapes and breeches, as neat as any imported from England or elsewhere' as well as 'gown patterns'. Several examples of his work still survive, including a series of bedspreads, somewhat Neo-classical in style. Martha Washington is reported to have worn dresses made of fabric printed by Hewson.

Needlecrafts and embroidery

The status of the traditional needlecrafts changed during the period and became largely secular in orientation. This was particularly marked in England, where the Roman Catholic church was disestablished by Henry VIII in 1533, as well as in other European Protestant countries. Ecclesiastical embroideries had in any case begun to lose their impetus by the end of the preceding period though bible covers remained popular, and the techniques merged, via the professional embroiderers, with those of high-class secular work. The characteristics

An embroidered bible binding made for Queen Elizabeth I, 1584.

Handkerchief with design 'The Gambols of Greenwich Park in Holliday time', copper plate printed by B. Warren, 1770s.

Chasuble, heavily embroidered in gold thread, worn at the funeral of Philip II of Spain, 1598, and now at the Escorial Palace, Madrid.

of professional ecclesiastical work are splendidly summarised in an embroidered panel representing the Adoration of the Shepherds, now in the Victoria and Albert Museum. Its visual effect is close to that of a painted picture, and it is executed in the *Or Nué* technique and needle-painting. It is inscribed 'Edmund Harrison, imbroderar to King Charles made this 1637'. Edmund Harrison was a member of the Embroiderers Company and embroiderer to James I, Charles I and Charles II, and the panel is from a series made for one of the English Catholic families. Other examples of the professional embroiderers' skill are hangings, large prestige furnishings and items of formal dress. In addition to skill in needle-painting, which by the late seventeenth and eighteenth centuries was applied increasingly to floral rather than pictorial designs, there is metal thread embroidery of virtuoso quality, with varied often three-dimensional effects.

A very large number of the surviving pieces of embroidery are not only secular, they are also the work of amateurs. Where attributions are available it seems that although many amateurs were capable of professional skill, they also had the help of

'Virtue grows by wounding'
(Virescit vulnere virtus), a motto and
emblematic device of the pruning of a
vine, embroidered by Mary Queen of
Scots about 1569. The tent-stitched
panel was applied to a hanging which is
from Oxburgh Hall, Norfolk.

professional embroiderers. They also made use of an increasing number of published designs and motifs, a product of the new and growing printing industry. Most books with designs for motifs, flowers, birds, animals and emblems went into several editions. Both of these features can be observed in the work of the best known pieces of British embroidery of the period. These were worked by Mary Queen of Scots during her exile in England as the enforced houseguest of another skilled embroideress, Elizabeth Countess of Shrewsbury, and can now be seen at the Victoria and Albert Museum and Oxburgh Hall, Norfolk. The most personal and poignant is the hanging which has at its centre the embroidered motif of a knife cutting a dead branch from a vine, accompanied by the Latin motto 'virescit vulnere virtus' (virtue flourishes by wounding): the inference is that the unfruitful branch of the royal family (Elizabeth I) was to be cut off, while the fruitful branch, Mary, would live and bear fruit. A number of Mary's and Bess of Hardwick's motifs have been traced back to their pictorial sources, as have those of the skilled but unknown English

embroideresses who made the many surviving coifs and jackets and small household furnishings characterised by flower, animal and insect motifs in curving trails.

The work and training of the amateur embroideress can be studied in samplers introduced within the period, the earliest dated example of which is that of Jane Bostock who, in 1598, as a gift for two-year-old Alice Lee, embroidered a piece of linen with a series of exquisite interlace bands and animal and floral motifs as well as the inscription. There are many such charming examples which illustrated how a useful domestic craft, needlework, can develop into an art. They were undeniably effective as an educational technique, and it has been alleged that through their inscriptions they also functioned as moral and on occasion even as male chauvinist didactics. Shape and design changed within the period and technique became stereotyped and less impressive, but such work was a convention of female education. It must have been with some relief that the skilled youthful needlewoman graduated to the stumpwork pieces, trinket boxes and mirror frames fashionable in the middle of the seventeenth century. *Pièces de resistance* of three-dimensional embroidery, they are also based on printed sources, and contemporary inscriptions suggest that many of these were the work of youthful embroideresses.

These techniques were brought to America by the colonists, and the dearth of professional embroiderers necessitated that the lady of the house did her own embroidery. Crewel work was popular, and many examples are to be found in museums: stylistically these follow their English counterparts but with greater spaciousness of pattern and much more work showing on the surface these were economical in time and technique. Martha Washington is but one lady known to have made crewel-work cushions.

Embroidery was just as important in the American girl's education, and a well-known series of canvas work pictures, the so-called Fishing lady pictures, were made in Boston girls' schools, the earliest in 1748. Several of the embroideresses have been identified as well as the embroidery sources, in English and French prints, though some have in the background the house of John

Workbag embroidered with pattern-book motifs by IS, aged 19, 1669.

Hancock, the first signatory of the Declaration of Independence. The motif of fishing, it has been suggested, may conceal a reference to eighteenth-century courtship patterns, with women fishing for men rather than having their marriages arranged for them by parents as in the seventeenth century.

Lace

Lace was a textile art which developed within the period after 1550, bobbin lace and needle-point growing from the existing needlecraft techniques of drawn thread and openwork. Italy was to become particularly associated with needlepoint lace and Flanders with bobbin lace. The techniques began to emerge in the sixteenth century and the earliest known embroidery pattern book (1527) has designs for laces in its second edition, the first printed needlepoint pattern appearing in 1558, and for bobbin lace in 1594. Lace pattern books were produced steadily through the early part of the seventeenth century, suggesting that the craft was domestic as well as professional.

By the middle of the seventeenth century, Italy, where there were centres for lace-making in Venice and Genoa with Milan

A stump work casket worked by Hannah Smith, 1656. The earliest dated and attributed example.

'Mary Countess Howe' by Thomas Gainsborough, 1763, wears the plain crisp silks and lightly embroidered nets and laces which had become fashionable by the 1760s.

flecting the influence of Le Brun and Berain, but after 1673, with the standard established, the craft was free to develop its own designs.

Flanders continued to be the main centre for bobbin lace, with important industries in Brussels, Mechlin and Antwerp, from which as early as the 1640s the technique had been brought to Valenciennes. English bobbin lace is said to have been introduced by Catherine of Aragon, first wife of Henry VIII, but probably owed more to the Dutch and Flemish emigrés in the middle of the sixteenth century. Although there was consistent production in the counties of Buckinghamshire and Bedfordshire and, subsequently, in Northamptonshire and Devon, and there were fine laces and occasional royal patronage, it never attained the prestige of imported laces from France or Flander. It tended to remain a cottage industry with no pretension to serve a fashionable market. A constant problem was the difficulty in obtaining linen thread as fine as that used in the Low Countries.

The prestige laces were those from France and Flanders, and they were in universal demand throughout Europe and in fashionable America, despite restrictions on imports and crippling customs duties. Lace smuggling was as flourishing a trade as lace dealing and, in the eighteenth century, Flemish bobbin lace became known as *Point*

specialising in braid or *passementerie*, had begun to cede its dominating position to France. There had been lace-making in the Auvergne region since the late sixteenth century, but the fashion at the court of Louis XIV for expensive raised relief lace from Venice, prompted Colbert to persuade Italian lacemakers to move to France. The new craft was protected by a state subsidy, a monopoly, and an embargo on imports. Initially it was centred on Paris, but by 1665 it had spread to provincial workshops at Alençon and Argenton. Early patterns were developed under state guidance, many re-

Embroidered picture, American, about 1740. Note the red-coated British soldiers and the Anglo-Dutch colonial house.

d'Angleterre in an attempt to become acceptable in its most important market.

With the trend towards less ostentatious dressing in the third quarter of the eighteenth century, lace became simpler in style and began to be overtaken by whitework, always the fashion for informal occasions. Nevertheless, the demand was sufficiently strong to persuade the lace manufacturers to begin to experiment with machine-made substitutes, though these would not be successful until the early nineteenth century.

The growth of the market

By the end of the eighteenth century, there was a growing conviction that the textile crafts were making the kind of goods to which most people could aspire. The growth of a larger market was beginning to democratise design, though this trend would not be fully apparent until the middle of the nineteenth century.

The rise in living standards had been noticed by Edmund Harrison as early as the late sixteenth century. By 1720, Daniel Defoe in *The London Tradesman* was describing his country grocer and his wife, the archetypal English consumers, as clad and furnished almost completely from English sources:

'For his clothing . . . the cloth comes from Wiltshire and his stockings of Worsted from Nottingham . . . his wife . . . not dressed over fine yet she much have somthing decent . . . her gown, a plain English mantua silk manufactured at Spitalfields . . . Her under-petticoat, a piece of black calimanco made at Norwich – quilted at home if she be good housewife but the quilting of cotton from Manchester, or cotton wool from abroad . . . Her stockings from Tewkesbury, if ordinary–from Leicester if woven . . . Her muslin from the foreign trade; likewise her linen . . . Her wrapper . . . a piece of Irish linen printed at London . . . the furniture of their house . . . the hangings at Kidderminster, dyed in the country and painted or watered at London . . . Bedding, the curtains from Taunton, Exeter or from Norwich . . . the blankets from Whitney in Oxfordshire;

Queen Henrietta Maria and King Charles II in raised embroidery on a stump-work mirror frame, English, about 1660.

the sheets of good linen from Ireland. The rugs from Westmorland and Yorkshire.'

It is a conscious summary of British self-sufficiency, the strengths and few of the weaknesses of the British home and export textile trades.

The Independence Day celebration at Philadelphia in 1788 was a triumphant affirmation of the principles on which development of the textile trades within the period was based; technological innovation and the positive role of the state. Under banners inscribed 'May the Union Government protect the manufacturers of America' and 'May Government protect us' marched eighty weavers escorting a thirty-foot float on which was a wool carding machine, a spinning jenny with eighty threads, a lace (braid) loom, 'a man weaving jean with a fly shuttle' and Mr and Mrs Hewson together with their daughters, printing and pencilling cotton as hard as they could go. Homespun and colonial dependence was a memory and a new contender was entering the international textile scene.

Brocaded silk for the Palace of the Escorial, Madrid,
designed in 1788 by J-D Dugourd, and made at Lyons.

THREE

The Industrial Revolution 1780–1880

Rhiannon Williams

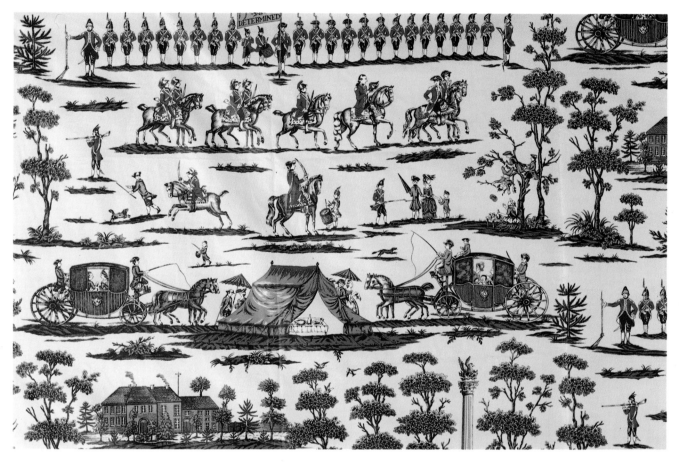

'The Irish Volunteers in Phoenix Park, Dublin', 1782,
a copper-plate print by T. Harpur of Leixlip.

THE YEARS from 1780 to 1880 were crucial for the shaping of the textile industries of the modern world. A century of technical innovation, and intensive and extensive production of printed and woven cloth would play a dynamic role in the Industrial Revolution. Production progressed rapidly from the home through the workshop to the factory and, as communications improved and manufacturers responded to demands from the new bourgeoisie, markets expanded at home and overseas, spreading fashionable taste across geographical and class boundaries. Production of cotton was an important stimulus to this expansion. Until the late eighteenth century cotton was an Eastern import of comparatively little importance in the Western textile market. Yet by the 1830s, in the United States, where it had only been grown since the beginning of the century as fibre and finished cloth, it accounted for a third of American exports. In the United Kingdom, which was dependent on cotton as a raw material, it accounted for half of imports. Easily washable, cheap and most cheerful of available textiles, its social importance was great and it helped to bring cleanliness and comfort to people as well as homes which had often known little of either.

Supply and demand for textile goods now operated on an international scale as regional manufacturers keyed into a network of cosmopolitan fashion. Illustrated periodicals such as Ackermann's *Repository of Arts, Literature, Commerce, Manufactures, Fashions and Politics* (1809–28) and illustrated books like Thomas Hope's *Household Furniture and Interior Decoration*

(1807), the bible of classical style, ensured that modes in furnishing and dress reached beyond the trend-setting countries of England and France to encompass the American colonies. Throughout the eighteenth century the American home was an arena for displays of imported cloth. It is ironical that as the quality of American goods improved they were sometimes given foreign import labels to make a sale.

New inventions

By the 1780s, inventions by Kay, Arkwright and Hargreaves had confirmed Britain's position in the forefront of the textile indus-

'L'Arbre des Indes' (Indian Tree), woodblock printed cotton
from Mulhouse, about 1790 and still in production today.

try. Although spinning and weaving had both become much swifter, there were significant problems: yarn quality was variable, spindle speed was inadequate, and weaving capacity lagged and held up production. England's new cotton industry was centred in Lancashire where the damp climate was sympathetic to cotton fibres, water-power was available and fuel was cheap. It was here that machines were successfully incorporated into the factory system. Production increased, and with it a heightened awareness of the accompanying social problems: lack of regulation of factories and workshops, and a new workforce which included a high proportion of women and children. One of the technical problems of the new industry, however, began to be solved when Samuel Crompton perfected his mule spinning frame in 1779, combining features of the spinning jenny and the spinning frame. Strong yarns could now be spun for warp and weft. Crucial, too, was the invention of the power loom, patents for which were taken out by Edmund Cartwright in 1785. It utilised a vertical warp and ran on steam. Watt's steam engine was introduced in 1783 and aroused the antagonism of handloom weavers who saw it as a threat to their livelihood. Their opposition came to a head in the so-called Luddite riots in 1812 and 1826. Nevertheless, steam power was accepted and improved upon, and, by the 1820s, steam-powered machines were able to weave fault-free cloth at high speed. By the 1840s, John Harrison of Blackburn was producing looms which were to be among the marvels of the 1851 exhibition. One man could now mind six looms, though the completely automatic loom invented by J.H. Northrop was not introduced from America until the end of the nineteenth century.

The textile industry in the United States began to expand when British colonial restrictions were removed at the time of Independence (1776). Mechanisation was to be an important factor in American industry because there was always a shortage of workers, wages were high and demand esca-

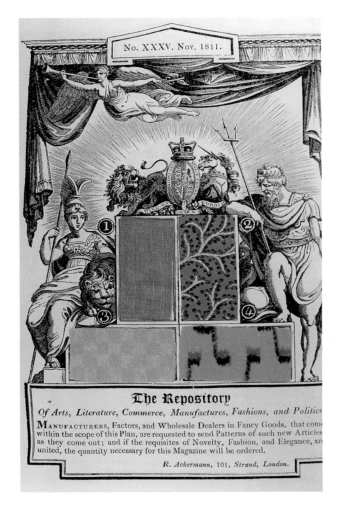

English fabrics as advertised for the popular market and export, from *Ackermann's Repository*, November 1811; 1 'lustre' (glazed wool); 2 printed cotton; 3 'Merino' (wool); 4 'cassimere' (wool).

lated rapidly. Cotton, a product of the West Indies, had adapted well to the climatic conditions of the southern states, though it was difficult to process until Eli Whitney invented his cotton gin in 1793. This involved a mechanical method of removing the seed pods from the raw fibres. Operated by horsepower, one gin could do work which had occupied fifty slaves. However, acquiring the necessary knowledge and technology for new and complex textile machines was not easy. Communication with Europe was difficult during the War of Independence, the Revolutionary and Napoleonic Wars and the War of 1811–14, and there was an embargo on trade with Britain between 1804 and 1819. Emigration of skilled workers and export of machinery was forbidden by Britain until 1842, as well as by France, America's new trading partner. This state of affairs took courage and ingenuity to overcome. The spinning jenny had been in use in America before the Revolution, but it was not until Samuel Slater, an Arkwright apprentice, who has been called the father of American cotton manufacture, emigrated secretly to America, disguised as a farm labourer, that in 1790 America acquired the Arkwright frame with its capacity for spinning the strong warp thread. With the assistance of Moses Brown, a Quaker merchant, he installed the first Arkwright mill at Pawtucket in Rhode Island.

The United States

Subsequent improvements by Americans Charles Danforth and John Thorpe, who in 1828 introduced the ring traveller, improved the fineness of thread and almost doubled the speed of spinning. The power loom was introduced to America by Boston merchant Frederick Cabot Lowell, who had studied textile machinery during a trip to England in 1810–12. Working with Paul Moody, an engineer of genius, he installed in 1814 the first spinning mill and power loom under one roof, the so-called 'Waltham system'. After a fire it moved from Waltham to the Merrimack, the nucleus around which the town of Lowell, cotton centre of America, was to cluster. The first spinning machines were manual or used horsepower but, later, water-power was extensively used and the textile industry began to congregate around the river valleys of the Eastern seaboard. Rockdale in Pennsylvania, a group of mill villages, has been studied as a microcosm of the Industrial Revolution in the United States. It was in Lowell that Samuel Batchelder and William Cromton introduced the first power looms for fancy fabrics. There was a slump in the United States textile industries when English manufacturers offloaded surplus fabrics after the Napoleonic Wars but the protective tariff of 1824 guaranteed the survival of these new industries together with the woollen industry, which had been founded in 1792 in Massachusetts by John and Arthur Scholfield, who had emigrated from Yorkshire. Cloth for uniforms in the war of 1812, as well as the nineteenth-century fashion for trousers rather than breeches, ensured its prosperity. By 1867, the American woollen industry had attained international status and had won a gold medal at the Paris International Exhibition. According to the United States Report, 'in style, taste and perfection of manufacture we excel the English and nearly approach the manufacture of France', as well as being 'cheaper than any similar fabric in Europe'.

Printed cottons

In the last decades of the eighteenth century, Britain's textile manufacture had begun to orientate itself towards the making of cotton rather than traditional woollen cloth, in fact, threatening the existence of woollen and worsted weavers whose technical capability lagged behind factory methods, and was not to improve until the mid-nineteenth century. However, the new cottons remained crude, plain woven and bleached with chlorine. The range was basic and included bed linen and tickings, and simple stripe as well as plain fustian, all adequate for surface printing but uninteresting in themselves. Patterned weaves were too complex for the early machine looms and there were no changes in finish until John Mercer introduced mercerisation in 1850. Nevertheless, such basic fabric was crucial to a market which craved novel printed patterns and a cheap reponse to fashion. For women's dresses, fashion prescribed simple countrified washable materials with small floral patterns or white muslins in the classical mode, though it was difficult for European weavers to emulate the fine fluid muslins directly imported from India. For formal occasions, silk was generally worn. Although patterns were smaller, silk was expensive and still woven on the cumbersome drawloom.

By the turn of the eighteenth century block prints were increasingly replaced by engraved copper prints, which had enlarged

Woodblock printed cotton, designed and printed by William Kilburn, about 1798.

image size but were usually monochrome. For the most elaborate colour work, wood blocks were still used, with metal strips and pins enhancing the precise carved impression. The finest examples are by William Kilburn, a London designer and printer, whose designs have been described as 'perhaps the nearest approach to nature in drawing'. Copper plate prints were ubiquitous throughout Europe and America, though more for furnishing than dress, except for the very popular souvenir handkerchiefs. London and later Lancashire were the British centres of production into the mid 1780s. In France, Oberkamp's *Toiles de Jouy* continued to attract a steady market, winning patronage from Louis XVI and then Napoleon I. Jouy stayed in operation until 1843 and continued to be the flagship for similar establishments in Paris, Rouen, Bordeaux, Marseilles and Provence. Mulhouse, profiting from its proximity to the printing centre at Basle, and to France and Germany, as well as the enterprise of its early founders, including the Koechlin family, had become an important centre. No longer restricted by protectionism of the silk interests, the printed cotton industry rapidly expanded, with important centres being set up in Holland, Germany and Switzerland as well as

Domestic scenes, copper-plate printed
cotton from Rouen, about 1825.

Britain and France. On the whole, America kept in step with European trends either by direct import or home production. French influence was particularly marked in the 1780s and 1790s. The alliance stimulated the vogue for French style. The Francophile tastes of Thomas Jefferson who had returned from France with eighty-six packing cases of goods, as well as James Monroe and John Quincy Adams confirmed it. Between 1816 and 1839, Joseph Bonaparte's house at Point Breeze, New Jersey, was a show case for French taste. Large-scale classical scenes became popular, as did striped formal designs and, by the 1820s, pillar prints. French influence was strengthened by emigrés who had settled on the Eastern seaboard and entered the textile trades.

In step with printing developments, industrialists began to address deficiencies in dye quality. Difficulties centred on non-fast, dull pigments which were restricted in colour. To a certain extent this resulted in fabrics that were standardised and tended to fade rapidly. Moreover, dyes that took easily on silk and wool were not suitable for cotton. New reliability was assured with the introduction of turkey red, a pigment tested in France by M. Papillion and brought to Glasgow in 1790. The dye used alum as a mordant applied to woven cloth rather than yarn and created a brilliant hue both on cotton and flax. The process was eagerly adopted, although the dyer John Wilson pointed out in his book *Light and Colour and What Colouring Matters are that Dye Cotton and Linen* (1786) that between twelve and thirteen separate stages were needed to attain full colour. Inevitably, turkey red sparked a vogue for monochrome cotton designs showing red on a bleached ground. However, it was not until synthetic dyes were developed in the mid-nineteenth century that a comprehensive range of fast colours was achieved.

Developments in printing

Full mechanisation of printing was attained in 1783 when Thomas Bell patented a roller or cylinder printing machine. Each metal roller carried an intaglio engraved plate capable of printing over a width of fabric a single colour in continuous repeat up to about 36 inches. Initially powered by water, then steam, cylinder printing reduced labour and increased output. In 1827, a Person in the Trade commented; 'Four minutes sufficed to print by machine a design that would take two people six hours to work on the same length of cotton by hand'. Initially, cylinder printing was used for copper plate-type monochrome pictorial prints, small all-

A copper-plate print, designed by Jean
Baptiste Huet for Jouy, about 1805–10.

over designs and, in combination with wood blocks, for polychrome florals. The Lapis pattern which juxtaposed red and blue and was popular for handkerchiefs illustrates the international character of nineteenth-century industry: invented in England, it was named by Hartman of Munster in 1808, and perfected by Daniel Koechlin Schouc of Mulhouse and James Thompson of Clith-eroe, Lancashire.

Additional colours were added either by wood block or pencilling. This continued into the 1830s when technical precision and improved printing inks allowed several colours to be printed 'wet on wet' in one design. When the cylinders themselves were engraved mechanically, the hand craftsman became peripheral as mill and die engraving and the pantograph came into operation in the first half of the nineteenth century.

Mass-produced materials such as these were exported worldwide from England, and French factories soon contributed their own versions. Available to all, cheap Lancashire cottons were later criticised for reducing price at the expense of quality both in colour and design. Nevertheless, this did little to reduce popular consumption of the latest patterns. American manufacturers continually battled against imports; foreign reproductions from books such as Audubon's *Birds of America* (1827–8) were in great demand.

Cylinder printing gained ground and was in use in Lowell by 1824, though basic production of 'slave cloth' and plain woven cotton predominated in rural if not town manufacture, and there were fashion-conscious printing establishments at Rhode Island, Boston and Philadelphia.

'Butterfly', block-printed cotton, English, about 1850.

Looms

Considerable progress had now been made in areas of yarn and printed cloth production. However, manufacture of woven patterned cloth still relied on the time-consuming and expensive drawloom technique. Elaborate figured silks were made in this way, but were too expensive to reach a wide fashion market. A significant advance

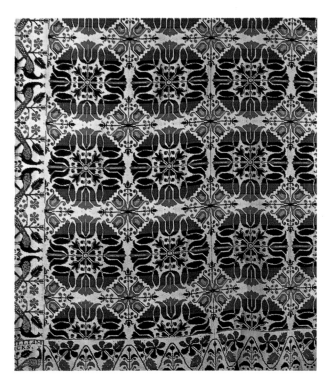

Jacquard beiderwand woven quilt; a double weave joined only at pattern edge, made by W. Hicks, Indiana, American about 1850.

was made in France when Joseph Marie Jacquard launched the loom which eventually bore his name. The Jacquard loom was in effect an automated version of the drawloom. Dual operation of a figure harness and punched card system allowed manipulation of a single warp thread without manual involvement. Thus, the drawboy became obsolete. Moreover, designs could be prepared separately on cards before coming to the weaver and could be changed quickly on the loom once weaving had begun. As a result, production was speeded up with reduced labour costs. Jacquard fabrics were first exhibited at the Paris Exhibition of 1801 and looms increased in number during the first few decades of the nineteenth century, initially in France but reaching England and the United States by the early 1820s. The Jacquard loom still had a number of difficulties to overcome before its impact was fully felt: the loom itself was costly, while card-cutters and designers required specific training. It was however eminently suitable for heavy floral patterns of the 1830s in which variety of design and colour were paramount. Jacquard production thrived at this time, taking on cotton, worsted and carpet manufacture. Designs with curved contours and figurative intricacy were easily attained, thus matching the taste for robust naturalism. A popular American speciality was double-cloth coverlets which were woven often with a commemorative theme including sections of text as well as the weaver's signature. From 1824, the Jacquard was supplemented by the dobby loom which worked with groups of warp threads lifted on a shaft system and was suited to small repetitive geometric designs.

Throughout the nineteenth century technical achievement and mechanisation were constantly blamed for general degradation of public taste in matters of art and design. Calls for rejection of industrially produced cloth and 'improved design' originated in Britain, at the time paradoxically dubbed 'The Workshop of the World'. Extensive retailing of cheap 'bad' cloth was com-

Furnishing silk by Prelle of Lyons, 1876,
cut and uncut velvet on a satin ground.
Made for Gillow, later Waring and
Gillow.

mented on by *The Journal of Design* in 1844: 'There are upwards of six thousand patterns for calico-printing registered annually, and this we estimate to be only a third of the number produced. In the spasmodic effort to obtain novelty all kinds of absurdities are committed. The manufacturer in 'solid' forms turns ornamental heads into tails and tails into heads and makes the most incongruous combination of parts.' Descriptions tell of dark floral brocades, velvets and worsteds, densely packed architectural prints and uncontrolled recycling of historical styles. Printing firms proliferated, particularly in Alsace which became renowned for its cheap colourful roller-printed fabrics. At the upper end of

the market, traditional silks were still in demand, but likely to come from Lyons as the importance of London diminished and unrestricted French imports operated after 1826. In Britain, attempts to improve taste were consolidated with the opening of Government Schools of Design in the 1830s. Encouraged by patrons such as Henry Cole (later Director of the South Kensington Museum), new standards were set in the hope that artists would work for industry rather than in isolation. The Royal College of Art and Royal School of Needlework formed part of this initiative. Similarly in France, the Societé Industrielle de Mulhouse was formed in 1832, together with a School of Design.

Berlin woolwork, about 1855.

Hooked rug, American, mid 19th century, made from wool and cotton thread on a linen ground.

Taste

Decline in taste not only occurred at an industrial level; inevitably it penetrated the home and the domestic needlecrafts of the leisured Victorian woman. Home-produced 'fancy-work' was wide-ranging, from canvas work and whitework to needlework pictures and appliqué, all of which were in vogue in the first half of the nineteenth century. Particular pleasure was given by Berlin wool-work, a crude form of canvas stitchery suited to the amateur. There was an influx of cheap ready-to-make patterns from the 1800s as Berlin publishers supplied Britain with designs akin to coloured engravings overprinted on grid grounds. Around 14,000 designs were available by 1840. Subjects included floral, sentimental religious, Arcadian, and copies of paintings, worked in harshly coloured wools. Such pieces now adorned the cluttered middle-class interior, decorating *prie-dieu* chairs, fire-screens and the occasional pair of slippers. Copious manuals were printed to assist ladies in their task, including the very popular *A Useful and Modern Work on Cheval and Pole Screens, Ottomans, Chairs and Settees, for Mounting Berlin Needlework* (1845) by Henry Wood.

Embroidery

The Gothic Revival was well underway in Britain and America by the 1840s and did much to encourage women to embroider for the church. Consequently, amateur ecclesiastical work was undertaken using basic techniques, especially appliqué. Only towards the middle of the century was this counteracted by professional embroiderers, guided by architects such as A.W. Pugin, G.E. Street and G.F. Bodley, who favoured a return to the gold and silk techniques of Opus Anglicanum. Ecclesiastical furnishing companies were established during the 1860s, for example, Watts and Co. in London, whose medieval-inspired designs opposed the highly ornate Catholic vestments arriving from the Continent.

Enthusiasm for domestic embroidery also

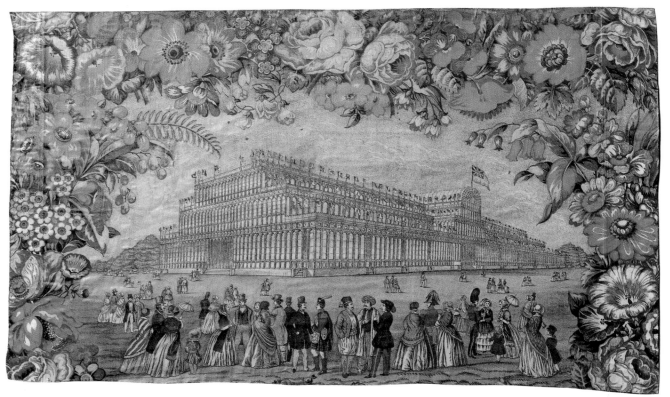

The Great Exhibition 1851, the buildings and the visitors. A roller-printed cotton,
manufactured in Manchester, 1851.

gripped America to parallel Victoriana in Britain. Berlin wool-work, whitework, beadwork, tatting and crochet were all practised and were made popular by publication of home journals. Both the popular *Godey's Lady's Book* and *Peterson's Magazine* carried patterns and advice. Traditional needlework samplers now received little attention. A number of methods and styles evolved which were peculiar to the United States; beaded articles made reference to North American Indian patterns. Particularly noteworthy are the American quilts though they

were also made in England and Europe as well. They were produced throughout the Victorian period, often made with appliqué motifs cut from chintzes and coloured wools. Patchwork predominated in the second half of the nineteenth century and several traditional schemes were named at this time, for example, 'Joseph's Coat' and 'Hens and Chickens'. However, quilting was mostly restricted to rural locations by the 1870s, and was considered quaint and passé by townsfolk.

The Great Exhibition 1851

One of the most important events for assessing developments in textile manufacture was staged in 1851 in London. The Great Exhibition was launched to promote art of all nations and free trade in industry and manufacture, and included exhibits from all over the world. Textile machinery and products were divided into various categories. Inventions included Pardoe, Hoormans and Pardoe's velvet pile carpeting-machine and Mackintosh's improved rubber cloth for waterproof garments. The American con-

Screen fans, embroidered with beads. English, about 1860.

tribution was considerable: Erastus Bigelow's innovative mechanical ingrain carpet loom was competed for by several British firms, and his mechanical Brussels carpet loom was bought by Crossleys of Halifax, Yorkshire.

The *Art Journal Illustrated Catalogue* commented that lace, fans and embroidery were superior on the Continent although rather ornate, and Persian carpets were applauded. England presented a 'Medieval Court' designed by A.W. Pugin, reinforcing the Gothic Revival in which heraldic prints and embroideries were displayed by Newton, Jones and Willis of Birmingham. Another feature was the range of fancy shawls, woven and printed, many in the Pine pattern now considered synonymous with Paisley. Deriving from Kashmir originals, they were made in many places, notably in Lyons as well as in Paisley, Norwich and

Vienna. It was to be a market which the United States fancy woollen industry would enter with considerable success by the 1860s. The most complex Paisley pattern might include hundreds of combinations of colours. English dominance in the mass production of basic articles, and the supremacy of French luxury textile production centred on Lyons were features of the 1851 and subsequent exhibitions. The most elaborate textiles were commissioned for the luxury couture fashions, a feature of the later nineteenth century. They have an extraordinary opulence and are subtle combinations of colour, pattern and texture.

As a whole the Great Exhibition was seen as a crisis in taste which led to a movement for reform. Textiles came under close scrutiny at consecutive international exhibitions, including the Paris World Exhibition of 1855 at which 'Dangon's Loom' (a version

Crazy quilt cover, silks re-embroidered with beads.
American, about 1885.

A 'Paisley pattern' Kashmir shawl,
made in India for the European market,
about 1860.

of the drawloom) was shown. The World's Fair in New York (1858), Exposition Universelle, Paris (1867) and Centennial Exposition of Philadelphia (1876) all served as new arenas for display and evaluation.

During the 1850s, standards of design began to shift. In order that pattern should be appropriate to the medium of textiles it was advised that flat, conventionalised motifs should be used in preference to three-dimensional drawing, and that imitation of other art forms should be avoided. Architects became increasingly involved with textile design; Owen Jones made extensive studies of ornament and his publication *The Grammar of Ornament* (1856) was especially influential though in less discriminating hands such a variety of available motifs could lead to bewildering confusion. Jones worked with Warners in the 1870s,

producing silk tissues that broke with traditions of High Victoriana. However, although suited to Jacquard and roller printing techniques, such fabrics remained in the minority, while home furnishings and dresses carried eighty per cent floral patterns.

Dyes

An important feature of the period was the replacement of natural by synthetic dyes. This was underway by the 1850s, largely as a result of the use of aniline dye stuffs, based on benzine oil which was extracted from coal tar and combined with acid to achieve colour. W.H. Perkin's mauve, later called 'mauveine', based on murexide, was considered the earliest man-made or synthetic dye. Significant developments were made in Germany whose dye industry, coupled with that of Basle in Switzerland, led Europe throughout the nineteenth century. It was here that experiments with aniline began in the 1830s. By the late 1850s a range of vibrant pigments had been produced; in 1858 magenta, or fuscine, a fierce purple pink, purple blues and greens were successfully created, able to saturate cloth in a single process. One particular dye, aniline black, was suited to cotton, and manufactured for calico printing in about 1860–63 by John Lightfoot. These dyes were easily applied to wool, but required a mordant for cotton. Deficient mordants weakened the strength of synthetic dyes in comparison to some natural alternatives, for example, indigo and madder. Consequently, many dye works continued with old recipes unless fashion required a certain shade. Colours were added to the European repertoire throughout the 1860s – Manchester brown and yellow and Congo blue by 1884, together with an indigo substitute from Germany. By the early 1880s, Germany had raised its output to cope with half Europe's dye production and tapped an expanding American market.

The first aniline dyes: samples of Perkins original Mauveine, 1856, and Alizarine.

Aniline did much to provoke design reformers, as this comment from one of the leading antagonists of aniline dyes, William Morris, illustrates: 'It must, I suppose, be considered a negative virtue in the new dyes that they are as fugitive as the older ones are stable'. Part of Morris's campaign during the 1870s involved a revival of natural dyeing as a move against contemporary industrialisation.

New machine techniques

Arguments associated with the craft versus machine debate were fuelled by widespread adoption of machines for laborious hand-sewing craft techniques. The sewing-machine for domestic and small-scale manufacture was introduced during the 1850s. This gave rise to needle trade sweat shops in England and America, in which semi-skilled and child labour were exploited for easy profit. Both they and the new garment factories used quantities of the cheap cloths as well as shoddy, mechanically recycled wool, introduced in 1814 and a cheap source of material for a growing mass market ready-to-wear industry. The dressmaker, coping with complex and voluminous High Victorian fashions, found the sewing-machine useful, but its most important application was for basic necessities, household furnishings and underwear. Thomas Saints, an English cabinet-maker had patented a prototype in 1790, but it was not until 1830 that sewing-machines were used commercially by the Frenchman Baptiste Thimonnier for military uniforms, though he was threatened by protests from the local tailors. The Americans Elias Howe and Walter Hunt devised alternative solutions for the perennial quest for a mechanical substitute for hand sewing. Elias Howe patented his lockstitch machine in 1841. But it was Isaac Merrit Singer, entrepreneur as well as inventor, who promoted the sewing-machine on the wider international market. The sewing-machine was practical and viable by 1851 but not easily available until the patent pool of 1856. The firm of Wheeler and Wilson almost equalled Singer in importance and

A pattern book of silk and wool woven variations on the
Kashmir shawl, about 1800–1820, probably French, Lyons.

A sample of machine embroidery by H. Holdsworth, Manchester, England, 1853.

the machine was generally available for home and industrial use.

Technically these machines were capable of a looped continuous stitch operated by a hand or treadle mechanism and they can be seen as the last stage in an ongoing move towards mechanisation of textile production, giving finished wearable and usable goods.

Machines that dealt specifically with embroidery are contemporary with these inventions. In 1854, José Heilmann of Mulhouse exhibited an embroidery machine at the French Industrial Exhibition which he had worked on since 1828. This allowed for 140 swing needles operating simultaneously on a shifting frame. A patent was secured the following year in England which permitted sole right of production to Henry Houldsworth, a silk manufacturer in Manchester. All-over, small-scale repeat patterns were embroidered for upholstery and waistcoat materials, while copious dress trimmings were mass-produced. Typical motifs are described in the *Journal of the Society of Arts* in 1852: 'Two needlefuls make one flower; three flowers make one repeat; twenty repeats make one border; four borders make one tablecloth decoration.' Machine embroidery was taken up throughout Britain and in Ireland; examples appeared at all International Exhibitions after 1851. Advanced machines came out in the last quarter of the nineteenth century, for example, the Rieter which worked on a shuttle system. There was great demand for white on white embroidery to satisfy the insatiable High Victorian taste for lingerie trimmings, or for plain black silk crepe, the latter produced for mourning dress.

Machine-made lace was also available from the third quarter of the nineteenth century. Attempts to make mesh by machine had been attempted by the machine-knitting industry in the 1760s, and by 1787 it was possible to make point net as well as hosiery on the warp knitting machine. The basis of the machine lace industry was John Heathcote's twist net machine patented in 1809, a good foundation for hand embroidery.

Lace, made on a Leaver's machine, probably in Nottingham, about 1850. This type of lace became very popular for curtains.

Patterned net was to become feasible with the introduction of the Pusher machine in 1812 and the Leaver's machine in 1813. By the mid-nineteenth century Nottingham, England was the world centre of the machine-made lace industry, and could make by machine close facsimiles of most types of hand-made lace.

The Arts and Crafts ethos

In all areas of textile manufacture, by the 1880s interests began to shift away from technical improvement and quantity production to accommodate an Arts and Crafts ethic. William Morris is credited with initiating this movement through the establishment of his firm Morris, Marshall, Faulkner and Co. in 1861 (changed to Morris and Co. in 1875). The firm was based in London and Oxfordshire and produced embroidery, printed and woven furnishing fabrics, tapestries and wallpapers, the majority of which were naturalistic or medieval in theme. Morris textiles sold to a limited market due to their high cost, but their influence was widespread. During the 1870s, a movement for Art Embroidery was inspired by Morris and the Design Schools which captured European and American interest. Morris promoted hand techniques and handcrafts as superior to machine-made articles; in this he stood against the worker being uninvolved with his product and the concern for profit of the textile industrialists. These industrial attitudes set the standard for textile design into the late Victorian period, when individual artists and craft groups joined Morris's cause: 'It is not this or that tangible steel and brass machine which we want to get rid of, but the great intangible machine of commercial tyranny, which oppresses the lives of all of us.' Through Morris, textiles became part of a social as well as industrial concern.

Tapestry designed by Gunta Stölzl, 1929, and made at the
Bauhaus studios.

FOUR

The artist's reaction
1880–1939

Kate Woodhead

Textile and interior design by Sonia Delaunay, gouache, 1925.

THE artistic reaction to the effects of industrial change on the textile industry was to look backwards and attempt to recreate the standards of design and working conditions which it was believed had prevailed in the past. Discontented murmurings about the standard of contemporary British design had been heard from the 1830s onwards, when it was felt that falling British exports were due in part to poor design and that this was the result of machine production. It was realised that division of labour and mechanisation had separated responsibility for the appearance of the product from the task of fabricating it, whereas, formerly, craftsmen had been responsible for both design and making. To reinstate the role of the craftsman was the main aim of all those concerned with improving standards of textile design and fabrication.

Select Committees were instituted by the Government in 1835, 1840 and 1849 to investigate falling standards of design and as a result Henry Cole was selected to organise Schools of Design which would educate artisans and eventually the general public on the link between aesthetics and techniques. Cole, originally from an obscure background, enjoyed a close friendship with Prince Albert. This beneficial alliance, combined with his prodigious energy, enabled him to achieve many of his ambitions. Before his death in 1882 he had reformed the Public Records Office, introduced the penny post and the Christmas card, formed Summerly's Art Manufactures, published

'Woodpecker', tapestry designed by William Morris, about 1885. The style recalls the verdure and mille fleurs tapestries of the 15th and early 16th centuries.

the influential *Journal of Design and Manufacture*, established over 200 Schools of Design, and was the moving force behind the Great Exhibition of 1851. The exhibition inaugurated a succession of universal and international expositions which astonished visitors by their size, grandeur and innovations; indeed they have been called the Disneylands of the nineteenth century. Cole, with the profits from the 1851 exhibition, instigated the building of a Museum of Ornamental Art at South Kensington and became the first Director of what is now the Victoria and Albert Museum. This pioneering example led to the formation of similar institutions in capital cities across Europe and America.

Cole and his fellow design reformers followed the precepts of the architect August Welby Northmore Pugin, who had written texts on the superior moral and aesthetic qualities of Gothic art. His writings and those of John Ruskin dominated the Gothic Revival movement and fostered the belief that the more moral society of the Middle Ages had resulted in finer art. Truth to nature, truth to materials and a just society were the significant criteria for the production of good art and design.

The philosophical and sociological thrust of Pugin's and Ruskin's argument was ignored by Cole, who had been appointed to improve design for commercial reasons, but in another disciple, William Morris, all these aspects merged and his reforming zeal encompassed art and society.

Morris & Co.

Perhaps following Pugin's example, Morris, when he married Jane Burden in 1860, wanted to build a Gothic house and to decorate it with suitable furniture and textiles. Philip Webb, a fellow architectural student, designed the Red House at Bexley Heath and much of the furniture; Edward Burne-Jones was responsible for the stained glass; the embroidered hangings were designed by Morris and executed by his wife and other family members. The involvement of many of his friends in the furnishing of his

'Cray', printed linen designed by
William Morris, 1884.

home led to the formation of Morris & Co., and again it was Ruskin's ideas which were influential. Ruskin thought the division of labour which separated thinkers and doers was bad for both parties and produced 'morbid thinkers and miserable workers'. A co-operative of artist-craftsmen was the ideal solution; Morris & Co. can be seen as the precursor of the later Arts and Crafts guilds.

Embroideries, worked by relatives and friends, were the first textiles produced by the firm and these formed part of their prize-winning exhibits in the Medieval Section of the 1862 International Exhibition held at South Kensington. Their success led to many commissions from churches for stained glass windows and ecclesiastical embroideries and for wall hangings, screens, etc. for private houses. Morris gained much of his inspiration for designs from the South Kensington Museum and he used many antique motifs and patterns in his designs for embroidery and for the printed and woven textiles which the firm began to produce from 1870.

Because of the invention of aniline dyes in 1856 and the rapid adoption of them by the textile industry, the old methods of dying using natural dyes had become almost obsolete. Morris and Thomas Wardle, a silk dyer from Leek, spent years trying to recover the old skills which the lack of raw materials made more difficult. However, Morris persisted and when the firm moved to Merton Abbey in 1881 most of the problems had been solved. The majority of textile patterns were produced between 1875 and 1885 and 'Cray', printed in 1884, is an example of the emphasis placed on the diagonal line in his late textile designs and Morris's talent for co-ordinating individual motifs into an harmonious whole. The richness and variety of colours, created by using 34 different blocks, made this one of the most expensive of Morris's printed textiles.

Schools of Needlework

Although printed and woven fabrics, carpets and tapestries expanded the firm's production of textiles, embroideries still formed a large part of the business and in 1885 this section was taken over by May Morris. The embroidery designs by the Morris family were appreciated by the Royal School of Needlework, founded in 1872, and the success of the school led to others being started. The Glasgow School of Art had a very influential needlework class run by Jessie R. Newbery, and it shared the stylistic features characteristic of the 'Glasgow style', made internationally famous by Charles Rennie Mackintosh. Ann Macbeth, who trained at the Royal College, moved to Glasgow in 1900, and she was responsible

for training teachers to encourage students to invent their own designs and to use more utilitarian materials instead of silk or satin; this made the art more egalitarian and loosened it from its upper- and middle-class origin (see illustration on this page). Paradoxically, the craft of embroidery was a significant aspect of the emancipation of women in the late nineteenth century. Middle-class single women were barred by social mores from many commercial activities but embroidery had always been seen as a feminine attribute. Through the Arts and Crafts Movement, women were able to progress beyond the simple needlepoint technique needed for the ubiquitous Berlin wool-work to find financial support as well as creative pleasure from re-creating the lost skills of English Opus Anglicanum, the fame of which was world renowned, and other embroidery techniques. Skill with a needle helped the cause of women even more directly when suffragettes created art needle-work banners for the mass rally and procession of the National Union of Women's Suffrage Societies on 13 June 1908. The beautifully worked banners celebrated the history of women and were described even by the anti-suffrage *Times* as 'the art exhibition of the year'.[1]

Corner of a linen curtain, designed and embroidered by Anne Macbeth, about 1900.

Banner of the Women's Freedom League, about 1909 and
inscribed 'Dare to be Free'. It was designed and
embroidered for the women's suffrage protest processions.

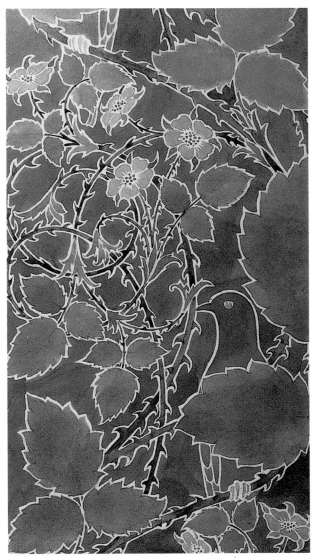

Textile design by C.F.A. Voysey, 1901, and woven into a
silk and wool double cloth by Alexander Morton and Co.

Formation of the Guilds

Morris's reforming fervour inspired other groups of designers to form guilds. The Century Guild was the first, in 1882, led by A.H. Mackmurdo, an architect who designed textiles which moved away from the designs of Morris towards the sinuous lines of Art Nouveau. C.F.A. Voysey, another architect and friend of Mackmurdo, though not a member of the guild, designed for all forms of decorative art and sold his textile designs to several manufacturers. The illustration on this page shows a typical Voysey design from the period 1900–1910 with its use of pastel colours, stylised foliage, and confronting birds.

The most important guild was the Art Workers' Guild (1884) whose members formed a pressure group to call for the reform of the Royal Academy, which had become increasingly undemocratic over the years and favoured painting above all other arts. In a spirit of rebellion, having had no success in changing the Academy's intransigent attitude, the Arts and Crafts Exhibition Society was created. The influence of this group was felt in Europe and America and it continued to raise the prestige of the craftsmen. Their ideals were disseminated by exhibitions and such publications as the magazine *The Studio*; it was said 'When English creations began to appear a cry of delight sounded throughout Europe. Its echo can be heard in every country'.[2] Continental workshops were formed, following the example of the Arts and Crafts Exhibition Society, and these were to foster the changes in design which introduced Modernism to the twentieth century.

'Floral Sea' textile design by Arthur
Silver for Silver Studio, 1894.

Liberty & Co.

The 1862 Exhibition which had presented
the products of Morris & Co. to the general
public also introduced decorative art from
Japan. In 1858, after centuries of cultural
isolation, Japan had signed a commercial
treaty with Britain and America. The
Japanese, along with other nationalities,
quickly discovered that the universal expositions were an ideal forum for cross-cultural
influences. Many of the 1862 Japanese
exhibits were bought by the merchants
Farmer & Rogers, who opened an oriental
warehouse next door to their Regent Street
premises; two young assistants, one named
Arthur Lasenby Liberty, were chosen to
look after the new establishment. Within a
year Liberty was manager, and during the
next ten years the oriental department became the most profitable section of the shop.
In 1885, after being refused a partnership,
Liberty decided to open his own establishment. At first only silks from the East were
sold, but it soon expanded. E.W. Godwin,
architect and designer and leader of the
aesthetic movement, helped in its promotion
and it quickly became successful. Eventually, Liberty was unable to buy sufficient
supplies to satisfy the demand he had
created, and he persuaded English textile
manufacturers to produce Eastern style 'art
fabrics'. He collaborated with the same
Thomas Wardle who worked with Morris to
produce what came to be called 'Liberty
colours'; delicate pastel shades as well as
soft pliant silk which enchanted customers
wearied by the harsh brightness of aniline
colours, and the heavy fashionable fabrics.

'Peacock Feather' design by Arthur Silver, exhibited 1887:
it later became almost a logo for Liberty's.

Printed velveteen, designed by Alphonse Mucha, 1899–1900, and printed by Strand and Co.

Arthur Silver in 1880, designed textiles for Liberty's until 1965. The 'Peacock Feather' design which has virtually become Liberty's corporate logo was designed by Arthur Silver and exhibited at the Manchester Royal Jubilee Exhibition in 1887. The peacock was to be the design motif of the aesthetic movement and in 1903 it was still being used by the Silver Studio, though the illustration opposite shows the flamboyant birds tamed and stylised.

European Response

Architects and designers gained prominence via the successful national exhibitions as nations vied with one another for prestige and expansion of their markets. The rising middle classes of Europe became increasingly interested in the home as an expression of the owner's individuality and many books and periodicals were published to inspire and advise. Continual revivals of former styles had led to a sterile historicist tradition and there was a great desire for a complete change. The English Arts and Crafts Movement was the catalyst for reform in opposition to the industrial product but their followers developed different stylistic characteristics. There were two distinct versions of the 'new style' and both were reflected in textile designs (see illustrations on this page). The first was made popular in France and Belgium by the architects Hector Guimard, Henri Van de Velde and Victor

Liberty's was to become world famous as an emporium of art furnishings, so much so that the art nouveau style in Italy was known as 'Stile Liberty' although another shop, the Galeries de l'Art Nouveau, opened by Samuel Bing in Paris in 1895, supplied the name most commonly used for the new style.

Talented textile designers associated with Liberty included Lindsay P. Butterfield, Walter Crane, C.F.A. Voysey and Christopher Dresser. The Silver Studio, formed by

'La Veille des Anges', hanging designed by Henri van de Velde and worked by the artist and his aunt, 1892–3.

Dress cotton roller print for Steiner and Co., 1906.

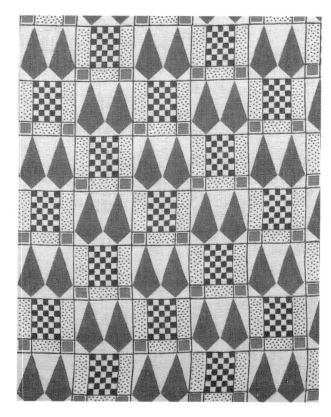

Art nouveau-style cotton, block print by the Wiener Werkstätte, about 1908.

Horta. They developed the organic curving line, so expressive of natural plant life, to heights of great beauty. The Paris Metro stations designed by Guimard still delight and confound the spectator with their sensuous, sinuous iron structures. Nevertheless, the style was relatively short-lived and reached its apogee in the 1900 Paris Exhibition.

The second version was closely associated with the geometrical lines of the Scottish architect C.R. Mackintosh. He influenced the artists of the Viennese Secession who, in 1897, under the leadership of the architect

'Waves', a Japanese-type design 1902, a roller print for export by F. Steiner and Co. of Germany.

'Consider the Lilies of the Field', curtain designed by Candace Wheeler. Mixed media, embroidered and painted, the design won a prize at the Society for Decorative Arts, 1879.

Otto Wagner, formed a splinter group from the Künstler Wiens (Vienna Society of Fine Artists). Josef Hoffman, Josef Maria Olbrich and Koloman Moser joined with others in building a new exhibition building, designed by Olbrich, and investing all the arts with the new style, again very linear but based on the square and the ovoid. They formed the craft studio, the Wiener Werkstätte, in 1903 and this continued in existence until 1939. The textile department produced a massive output, some 18,000 designs by over eighty artists, which included designs for fashions as well as home furnishings. Illustrated is one of the hand-printed fabrics which were a speciality of the workshop. The painter, Gustave Klimt, who was elected president of the Secession, designed caftan-like garments for the workshop. In many of his portraits of women they are clothed in magnificent textiles which completely dominate the paintings.

America and the Arts and Crafts Movement

The Royal School of Art Needlework spent £2,000 on their special pavilion at the 1876 Centennial Exposition in Philadelphia and the impact they made on the jurors and public alike justified the expense. Wall hangings, portières and curtains following the designs of William Morris, G.F. Bodley and Walter Crane were embroidered by the lady members of the school. They won the highest possible award, and their impact on American women instigated the revival of art needlework in America. A School of Design for Women had been started in 1844 by a prominent citizen of Philadelphia, Mrs King Peter, and this was followed by schools in Boston and New York.

Candace Wheeler was the most noted American textile designer of the period. She was a founder member of the New York Decorative Arts Society formed in 1877 and

Printed cotton designed by Atelier Martine about 1918.

in the exhibition of 1879 she was awarded first prize for the embroidered and painted portières shown on the previous page. In the same year she joined forces with Louis C. Tiffany and others in a collaborative venture under the name of Associated Artists, which worked in a similar way to Morris & Co. They were given several prestigious commissions, including the redecoration of the public rooms at the White House. In 1883, Tiffany started a separate decorating company under his own name and Wheeler continued with Associated Artists. Only women designers were employed and they designed textiles for many manufacturers, including Cheney Brothers of Connecticut. Having been inspired at the Philadelphia Exposition it seemed very fortuitous that Candace Wheeler should be involved with the Chicago World Fair in 1893; she was made Director of the Applied Arts exhibition in the Women's Pavilion, which portrayed the worldwide role of women as decorative artists.

Many arts and craft societies were founded in America during the last decade of the nineteenth century. Gustave Stickley, furniture designer, promoted the 'Mission' style of décor which followed many of the ideals of the English Arts and Crafts movement, though the textiles were on the whole much plainer. In October 1901, the first issue of Stickley's influential journal *Craftsman* was devoted to William Morris; articles on Ruskin, the Gothic Revival and medieval guilds followed. While openly acknowledging the British influence, Stickley was at pains to develop vernacular and democratic native sources. He was very interested in American Indian designs found in weaving and on baskets and pottery. He expressed the view that his furniture echoed the 'fundamental sturdiness and directness of the American point of view'.[3] Long neglected by the collector's market, Gustave Stickley furniture is now highly prized; the sideboard from his own house was sold in 1988 by the New York branch of Christie's for $363,000, the highest price paid for any Arts and Crafts furniture of any nationality.

Twentieth-Century Developments

The verve and vitality of the avant-garde fine art movements Post-Impressionism, Expressionism and Cubism, which sought inspiration from primitive and folk art, were paralleled by two workshops formed at the end of the first decade of the twentieth century: the Atelier Martine in Paris and the Omega Workshop in London. Textile design was an important part of their productions and had wide-ranging influence. The Parisian venture was started by the couturier Paul Poiret, who, inspired by a visit to the Wiener Werkstätte, decided to open his own decorative art workshop. Desiring a totally unconventional effect for his products, he employed teenage girls with no design training to decorate pottery, murals and painted furniture and to draw designs for wallpapers and textiles. He encouraged his young designers to use their imagination freely and the result was a charming naïvety. The increased brilliance of colours seen in the art of that period, especially that of the Fauve group of painters, and the emphasis given to colour in Bakst's designs for the Ballets Russes primed the artistically-inclined Parisian public for

Evening scarf in overprinted gold brocade, French, mid 1920s.

the gaiety and brightness which were features of Atelier Martine and its affinity with contemporary art was always stressed. In the 1912 Salon d'Automne, Poiret exhibited sketches, patterns, curtains and wall hangings, and rugs from the workshop were hung in the Galeries Barbazanges in rue Saint-Honoré, alongside work by Sonia Delaunay and Marie Laurençin.

It is probable that Roger Fry, the leader of the Omega Workshop, saw work of the Martine group when he arranged an exhibition of English paintings at the Galerie Barbazanges in 1912. Fry, an artist and a very influential art critic, had left his job as advisor to the Paintings Department of the Metropolitan Museum in New York and returned to London in 1910. He had mounted the first English exhibition of Post-Impressionist art the same year. The exhibition and his opinions were criticised by the press but he gathered around him young artists who had been excited by the exhibition, among them Vanessa Bell, Duncan Grant, Frederick Etchells, and Wyndham Lewis, who all became involved with Omega.

'Amenophis VI', printed linen by Roger Fry in the Cubist style, 1913.

Fry had several aims: to improve British taste in the decorative arts, to provide financial assistance to young artists by paying for part-time design work which would not interfere too much with their painting, and to widen the market for artistic products. The workshop opened in July 1913 at 33 Fitzroy Square, Soho, and although it had an active life for only six to seven years it produced work which continues to gain in stature and is now seen as the precursor of the Art Deco style. The illustration on this page shows a Cubist-inspired textile design by Fry.

1925 Paris International Exhibition

Paris planned an exposition of the decorative arts in 1908 to rival that held in Turin in 1902, but events, not least the First World War, meant that it was postponed until 1925. The *Exposition des Arts Décoratifs et Industriels* exhibited to the assembled nations the climatic flowering of the decorative arts which became known as Art Deco. The variety of textile displays at the Exposition was very comprehensive and displayed a rich and exciting eclecticism. Ideas were culled from the fine arts and folk art, and included decorative motifs from Persia, the South Sea Islands, Africa, the Orient and Egypt, as well as Central Europe. Following the discovery of King Tutankhamun's tomb in 1922, Egyptian motifs were very much in vogue, though by 1925 the style was beginning to wane.[4]

Mantle of printed velvet in Renaissance style and 'Delphos' dress of pleated silk, designed by Mariano Fortuny, about 1910.

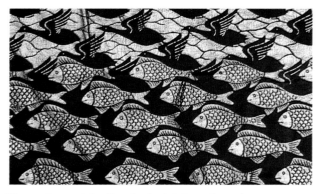

'Sky and water', batik print by M.C. Escher, about 1930.

One of the dominant textiles of the exposition was batik work. It was done on velvet, silk, and cotton, and was made up into shawls, handkerchiefs, umbrella covers, scarves, handbags, stockings and lampshades as well as wall-hangings and screens. Malayan batik-dyeing had been introduced to Europe by the Dutch in about 1905 and its novelty and exoticism appealed to most European countries. In France shawls and textiles in this technique were introduced to the fashionable world by Madame Paungon. Many of the designs were sophisticated, though still maintaining an ethnic vitality, as can be seen for example, in some of the batik work executed by the American designer Lydia Bush-Brown, who spent a year in Syria and incorporated ideas and influences gained from her travels in her work. Batik was popular in America and, in 1919, textile

'Fleurs et Musique', designed by Raoul Dufy, 1914–19.

'La Promenade au Bois de Boulogne', design by Raoul Dufy for printed silk, 1914–19.

designers Ruth Reeves, Martha Ryther and Marion Dorn produced it for an exhibition at Brooklyn Museum.

Printed textiles were an important feature of the Italian Pavilion where interesting attempts were made to blend old and new techniques. Maria Gallenga Monaci won the Grand Prix with her printed velvets, an innovatory fabric which featured largely at the Expo Deco. They were stencilled, the gold and silver patterns fixed with adhesive so that the textile was not bruised. She worked in the tradition of the Venice-based painter and designer Mariano Fortuny who exhibited in the Spanish Pavilion. An important textile technician as well as designer, he had first hand-blocked and stencilled his adaptations of classical, Renaissance and oriental patterns and then, in 1910, introduced a version of silk-screen printing which could be adapted to larger-scale production. Less appreciated were the colourful and ingenious textile designs of the Italian Futurists, which, according to the United Kingdom exhibition report, were considered old-fashioned and 'a matter of mirth among visitors'.

Wall-hangings, embroideries and tapestries formed a large section of the textile exhibits and were still an essential part of décor for the wealthy home. Poiret's Atelier Martine decorated three barges with four-teen wall-hangings designed and executed by Raoul Dufy, who had been involved with the Martine workshop from its inception. In 1912, Dufy had started to work for Bianchini-Ferier, the giant Lyons textile manufacturer, though he still designed for Poiret and others (see illustration). This was the period of the interior designer, and ensembliers such as Maurice Dufrèsne, Eileen Gray, and Emile-Jacques Rühlmann in France and Marion Dorn and Betty Joel in Britain designed textiles for the wall-coverings, drapery and upholstery which formed such an important and integral part of their interiors. Although the main emphasis at the exposition was on luxurious materials and expensive craftsmanship it also introduced the tenets of Modernism. These included the seminal concept that form should follow function, with no excess ornamentation, and that good design specifically for mechanical mass production would improve the quality of life for everyone. The new machine-based aesthetic challenged the traditional craft base and encouraged artists to look favourably on industry and to consider the advantages of machine technology and new materials. It was a concept with advantages at a time when there was already awareness that post-war shortages of money and materials might become factors of increasing importance.

Art, Industry and Modernism

The long-desired collaboration between artists and industry was a feature of the inter-war years but it varied in different countries. There was greater cohesion on the Continent, particularly in France, where designers were considered the equal of artists. Many artists designed for textiles: Sonia Delaunay and Raoul Dufy were prominent artist-designers, and Georges Braque, Henri Matisse, Georges Rouault, Fernand Léger and Picasso designed tapestry cartoons for Aubusson.[5] This not only enabled a wider public to enjoy and possess examples of art but, in years when finances were insecure, provided welcome extra income for artists.

The move towards a more egalitarian status for art and design was already in progress in the Soviet Union. Following the October Revolution, artists designed textiles which reflected their enthusiasm for the new society. Thematic or agitational designs such as 'Industrialisation', 'Pioneers', 'Construction', reflected the belief that textile designs could be invested with political and ideological significance. The hammer and sickle motif was seen at the 1925 Paris Exposition, as well as the geometric designs produced by the Cubist artists, Liubov Popova and Varvara Stepanova. Liudmila Mayakovskaya also exhibited her airbrushed velvets and silks which equalled the sumptuousness of many French and Italian fabrics and were obviously not destined for the proletariat.

The severity of modernist architecture created a foil for textiles and they provided welcome relief from austerity. Plainer colours and monochrome décors made textural qualities important. The new artificial silk, rayon, invented in the late nineteenth century was in general use by the 1920s, as well as unusual natural materials such as raffia and jute, which caused woven materials to become as popular as printed fabrics. Though the main thrust of the ideas behind the Deutscher Werkbund and the Bauhaus was the promotion of links between artists and industry, many of their products still maintained a craft element, particularly the weaving

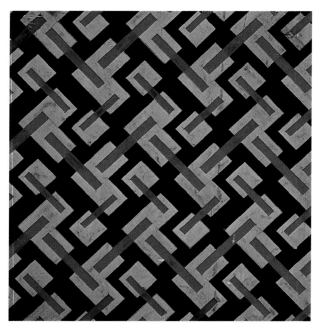

Constructivist design by Varvara Stepanova, 1917.

workshops. The illustration on page 72 shows a wall-hanging by Gunta Stölzl who was in charge of weaving at the Bauhaus from 1926 to 1931. Experiments with materials, such as cellophane additives, were aimed at improving physical properties such as light reflection and sound absorption. Following Hitler's closure of the Bauhaus, many of the tutors and pupils emigrated and disseminated their ideals abroad. Anni Albers went to America to teach; Margaret Leichner and Marianne Straub came to England where both were closely involved with industry.

England had already formed the DIA (Design & Industries Association) in 1915, in direct imitation of the Deutscher Werkbund, but although valiant efforts were made to raise the standard of mass-produced designs they had little effect. When, in 1916, the DIA decided that their second exhibition was to be of textiles in Manchester, they wrote to sixty manufacturers asking if they would like to submit designs: only three answered. It seems hardly surprising that the exports of textiles continued to fall. The designs produced by the majority of manufacturers were based on safe traditional patterns and the impact of modernism on the mass market was minimal.

86

However, some textile manufacturers had continued the practice of employing artists on a freelance basis and some artist-designers worked independently and set up small printing workshops. Of these, the most successful were Edinburgh Weavers who used designs by, among others, Ben Nicholson and Barbara Hepworth for their woven fabrics. Allan Walton, a designer and manufacturer, commissioned work by Duncan Grant and Vanessa Bell. Walton used different methods of printing, including screen printing which was gaining in popularity for 'art textiles', to produce outstanding textiles. The artist Paul Nash collaborated with Tom Heron of Cresta Silks in an attempt to raise the standards of British textile design, emphasising the need for modern textiles to complement contemporary architecture.[6] Nash, although primarily a painter, was very interested in design; he wrote articles, broadcast, and, in 1932, his treatise on interior design *Room and Book* was published. He was critical of most textile manufacturers. He thought they were unmindful of the need for new designs and relied on superficial changes to the old traditional styles to maintain their market, which was rapidly diminishing due to competition from America and Europe. He was supportive of what he described as 'Another industry of a different sort, one of longer standing and, from a purist standpoint, of a more thorough character. This represents a group of artists, all of them women, who design and engrave their own blocks and dye and print the materials themselves.'[7]

One such artist, trained at the Slade, was Elspeth Anne Little and when she planned to open a small shop in London to sell textiles, Nash designed the shop signboard and letterhead and chose the name, 'Modern Textiles'. Although the shop-showroom only existed for two years, with textile printing continuing at home, it was an important venture. It was one of the first small shops which exhibited and sold top-quality craftwork. The interwar years had seen a great revival of crafts, both amateur and professional, in Britain. Top-quality work by such artist-craftswomen as Enid Marx, Phyllis Barron, Dorothy Larcher, Joyce Clifford, Gwen Pike, Nancy Nicholson, Frances Woollard, and the weavers Ethel Mairet, Ruth Beales, Dorothy Kemp and Elizabeth Peacock, offered very attractive alternatives to mass-produced fabrics. The pioneering use of vegetable dyes, lino and woodcut blocks for hand printing, and fine hand-woven linen, were complemented by the revival of embroidery and lace-making skills. Craft guilds, fairs and national and international exhibitions promoted the crafts, and more shops opened to provide a forum for craftworkers and their small but increasingly discriminating public. Among

'Musical Felix', nursery print based on cartoon character Felix the Cat, by British Calico Printers, 1924.

'Stars and Stripes', design for printed crêpe de chine by Helen Wills Moody for the Stehli Silk Corporation, 1927.

the designers who attracted attention at this time were Barron & Larcher, who exhibited at the 1925 Paris Deco Expo and became fashionable when they were commissioned to print all the curtaining and upholstery for the Duke of Westminster's yacht, *The Flying Cloud*.

The most successful craft shop, the Little Gallery in London, was opened in 1929 by Muriel Rose. Exhibitions of craftwork, where makers and market could meet, were a feature of the Little Gallery. Although not a craftswoman herself, Muriel Rose was an enthusiastic promoter of quality crafts and continued to be so after wartime difficulties had forced the closure of the gallery in 1939. She selected an exhibition of British handicrafts and toured America and Canada with it during the war years. The exhibition opened in 1942 at the Metropolitan Museum, New York and was very well received.

In the 1930s, the Little Gallery was also the main outlet for the quilting work done by the miners' wives of Northumberland and Wales. During the depression, encouraged by the Rural Industries Bureau, the older women formed schools to teach young wives the traditional patterns and methods of quilting. Many of the fine silk and cotton quilts featured in today's interior design schemes are from these years. Quilted dressing-gowns and bed-jackets were very popular; they were commissioned and made to measure for royalty and other members of the Little Gallery's high-class clientèle.

If artist-designed and craft-based textiles were the response in Britain to unadventurous mass-produced fabrics, the situation was different in America. Although in 1925 the United States had declined to exhibit in Paris, fearing that they had nothing modern to contribute, many of their indigenous designs, based on 'primitive' objects in American museums, included patterns with stepped or jagged edges and geometric motifs that were similar to the styles of Art Deco. Investment in the textile industry at the beginning of the twentieth century had resulted in the United States dominating world production of textiles, and being less reliant on traditional designs meant that they were more receptive to modern designs. Moreover, the 'machine aesthetic' seemed to

'Festival', cotton printed for Tootal, 1938.

Floral design for printed silk dress fabric by Ducharne, 1937.

'Fun and games', British Calico Printers, 1936.

coincide with the vigour of American industrial expansion.

Many manufacturers and consumers were still conservative but companies such as Cheney Brothers and The Stehli Silk Corporation employed artists to illustrate contemporary features of the American way of life. The 'machine age' was represented in fabrics by designers who photographed mundane items, sometimes enlarging the image by photocopying and using the results as the basis of the design. One such design was 'Mothballs and Sugar' by Edward Steichen; 'Aspirin' by R. Green was another, when massed tablets formed the simple motif. Modern toile designs, pictorial elements with overlapping or juxtaposed planes, were seen at their wittiest in the United States during the 1930s. 'Manhattan' by Ruth Reeves showed a complex picture of city life, 'Thrills' by Dwight Taylor was based on a wooden roller coaster, 'April' by Clayton Knight was a brightly coloured design of umbrellas and rainbows, and 'Stadium', a crêpe de chine printed dress fabric by René Clark. Both France and Britain produced similar designs. Raoul Dufy was particularly good but the British were not as imaginative, though 'Fun & Games' (illustrated), a rayon crêpe by Calico Printers

Association, imitated the leisure and fun element seen in the American designs.

Unfortunately, gaiety and optimism as components of design are fragile and all too ephemeral. Another world war and 'utility' measures restricted the artistic input of designers and the uneasy alliance between art and industry, never very widespread, was just another casualty.

Floral design for rayon crêpe dress fabric by British Calico Printers, 1935.

'Punk' mixed media hanging designed by Candace Bahout, 1981, an example of her interest in personal self-expression. In the early 1980s Punks began to exemplify anti-establishment modes of dress and behaviour.

FIVE

A world industry today

Dierdre Campion

An interior by Marimecko of Finland, 1990, designed by Fugimo Ishimoto. An example of their use of bold colours and abstract shapes.

THE change from economy to affluence and from a deprived to the consumer society – the story of the last fifty years – has brought many radical changes in the field of textiles, where style makes beauty of necessity. After the Second World War, developments and techniques which had been halted through wartime restriction were re-investigated. Wartime shortages and the special needs of the military had led to many adaptations of fibres and fabrics, and, with peace and the lifting of restrictions, industry was able to expand and experiment with its new-found knowledge. It was a period of change in the direction of design and its link with the product, as well as restructuring in the industry. The growth of multi-national companies was to strengthen the development of the textile industries of the East, to which technology could be exported and where labour was still cheap. Textiles were to become a challenging art medium while there was to be an unprecedented revival of

91

craft textiles. Recently the industry has seen the introduction of the computer into the realms both of textile design and production and the effects of this are only now beginning to be appreciated.

Man-made and synthetic fibres

Since 1940 the world production of natural and man-made (including synthetic) fibres has increased dramatically. Man-made fibres, as distinct from those occurring naturally, is a term which relates both to regenerated fibres from natural sources which are chemically altered, and to synthetic fibres, which are derived solely from chemicals. Their development has been very striking and the demarcation between them is becoming less clearly defined due to improvements in the finishing processes.

There was much pre-war experimentation with man-made fibres, including various methods of making viscose and acetate, more familiarly known as rayon and art silk. Both were made from regenerated cellulose and invented in the late nineteenth century. Well-established, they continued to be produced throughout the 1960s when they were overtaken by synthetic fibres. Synthetics had by then overcome most of their early disadvantages, such as poor draping, yellowing and dirt attraction. Their advantages as marketed in the 1960s included drip-dry qualities, a minimum ironing requirement and the capacity to be pre-shrunk and to retain permanent pleating. Nylon was the first synthetic fibre. It was discovered in the mid-1930s by the American Du Pont De Nemours Company and exhibited at the New York World's Fair in 1939, but it was only spasmodically available to the general public during the war. Further research into polyesters led to the invention of Teryline which became known as Dacron in the United States.

Vinyls were another wartime development. They were exploited to fill the need for water-proofed materials and rubber substitutes. By 1950 these could be printed and embossed, and early uses tended to be for shower curtaining and kitchen table-cloths.

Printed rayon, early 1950s, for David Whitehead.

They were later introduced as plastic sheeting for furniture and in a lighter weight for curtains and monofilaments for weaving.

Another non-woven fabric with upholstery applications was knitting or jersey. Its application to free-form furniture was a post-war development which contributed in part to the demise of woven fabric for this purpose. Problems which occurred in the production of patterns which could stretch without distortion, allied to the belief that the loose-cover market was limited and conservative in its tastes, prompted Heals to ask art colleges to examine possibilities. The American designer and manufacturer Jack Lenor Larsen was by 1969 exploiting the two-way stretch properties and was creating designs of great panache. Stretch-cover chairs have now, however, become a mass market cliché.

New technology

Technology has to be developed to keep pace with new fibres and also new dyestuffs. Traditionally the industry tended to devote its time to improving conventional textile looms rather than developing radically new forms of machinery. Some of the significant textile machines of the twentieth century had been developed by engineering firms not normally associated with textiles. Competition for the market, high wages and increased costs have reversed this situation. Spindles have had to be re-designed for faster spinning, with a rotor spinning method developed in Czechoslovakia in 1967 proving the most successful. Many developments have focused on the traditional shuttle-type loom, with improved methods of automatically replenishing the weft such as those found in the Dornier Rapier loom and the Sulzar machine.

Screen-printing and its mechanical derivatives have made a significant contribution to the textile printing industry but it is the hand-screen method which has changed the character of textile design throughout the world. Introduced in the 1920s and 1930s, it was developed to find a quick cheap method of printing new designs for viscose and acetate rayons. In the 1930s the first Sundour screen-printed range of furnishing fabrics was produced. The companies in the United Kingdom which became known for innovative designs and quality fabrics were Edinburgh Weavers, Allan Walton Textiles, Heals and Ascher. Hand screen-printing contributed to a radical change in design styles. It was the only method by means of which experimentally drawn patterns could be executed on cloth. Colourings could easily be changed and the relatively low cost of making screens was an added advantage. Alastair Morton at Edinburgh Weavers created for the 'Britain Can Make It' Exhibition in 1946 a series of fabrics which he called 'Unit Prints'. These designs showed the immense versatility of simple elements, such as horizontal and vertical stripes and straight or wavy lines. Motifs such as stars, flower-heads, polka dots, or large and small rings were also employed: each element was based on the same module so that combinations of one, two or more screens could be used together.

In the 1950s screen-printing began to be mechanised with the Bursar machine and the Zimmer model, which were both flat-bed printers. The rotary screen-printing principle was developed in 1954. It was now possible to respond swiftly to fashion changes and achieve more economic production. In the early 1960s transfer printing was introduced. This method of patterning synthetic fabrics has become very important to the knitting industry.

Although technology and development in new yarns and machinery extended the resources of the designers there were still considerable limitations. Many of the synthetic yarns were dyed as they were manufactured, while textured synthetics were not available until the mid-1960s. Throughout and after the war supplies of yarn and grey cloth had been scarce and there were strict limitations of fabrics to tightly drawn utility specifications, including standardisation of colours and officially acceptable designs. This left little room for individual creativity or high-quality ranges, although in 1943 Enid Marx was appointed to design small-scale four-colour weaves for use with the Board of Trade's utility furniture.

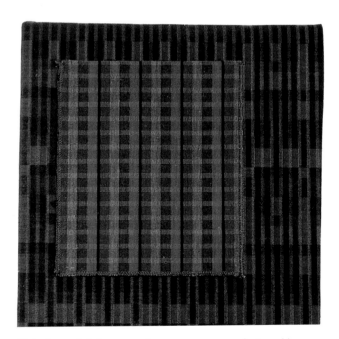

Upholstery fabric, cut and uncut moquette, designed by Marianne Straub for London Transport, 1967.

The role of designers

The war had also prompted many British manufacturers to operate smaller-scale studios and to rely on freelance designers. This practice was to be continued in the post-war period by such firms as Heals Fabrics, David Whitehead, Edinburgh Weavers and Cavendish Textiles. Jane Edgar, Dorothy Martin, Lucienne Day and Margaret Leicher were among those providing the designs that they used.

The textile industry in the United States looked to its designers for a move away from the tired and traditional styles which had been in use during the war years. There was a reaction against over-ornate patterning; instead the avante-garde used colour sparingly or allowed the texture of the fabric to remain as a design element. Among those associated with this change were Angelo Texta, Ben Rose and Knoll Associates.

'Kontiki', printed cotton, Liberty's, 1958.

Weaves were simple, relying on innovation with the use of new fibres and work on their weaving potential by Marianne Strengell, Dorothy Liebes and Anni Albers had great influence on the industry. Handweaving was a significant feature in the case of designers such as Liebes and Ed Rossbach, who created richly-textured fabrics for individual clients. Techniques using the power loom were developed so that fabrics could be woven mechanically to produce a hand-loomed look, and among the fibres utilised were natural fibres, nylon, rayon, viscose, jute and metallic lurex.

The importance of design and the designer in the aftermath of the war was recognised internationally for its valuable export potential. National attitudes to the textile industry were being consolidated in Europe where much of it had suffered as a consequence of the war. Italy was becoming conscious of the potential of the luxurious interior styling for which it would become internationally known. The French produced a mixture of traditional and modern designs, hoping to regain their pre-war predominance in the luxury and fashion market. The Germans were to make interesting use of the new textile machines installed as part of the Marshall plan for post-war reconstruction, and Stuttgarten Gardinenfabrik were re-

'Allegro' by M O'Connell and 'Calyx', 1951, designed by Lucienne Day for Heals of London. 'Calyx' won a gold medal at the Milan Triennale in 1951. Screen printed linens.

Designs based on the crystal structures of insulin, by the Festival Pattern Group, 1951.

sponsible for innovative designs in furnishing fabrics.

In the United Kingdom, always conscious of the importance of its textile industries, but aware even before the war of the challenge of cheap textiles from the East, textile design was promoted by various organisations such as the Society of Industrial Artists and Designers, the Council of Industrial

'Apples', printed cotton, 1952, designed by Stig Lindberg for Nordiska of Sweden.

Designers and the Cotton Board. Their aim was to revitalise Britain's greatest traditional export and to educate the public to recognise and appreciate the design element. The status of the designer was fostered and promoted while knowledge of modern technology and its products was spread by a number of exhibitions such as 'Britain Can Make It' (1946) and the 'Festival of Britain' (1951). The 1946 exhibition attempted to show British potential for a rapid change from war to peacetime production as well as its high standard of design. In the 1940s other bodies had organised exhibitions of fabrics and furniture in home settings to stimulate the public's awareness of the available range and its potential in the home. The Council for Encouragement of Music and Arts, for example, had organised 'Design in the Home' in 1943 and 1945.

In the United States, the Museum of Modern Art in New York launched a public education programme centred around the 'Good Design' exhibitions inaugurated by Edgar Kaufmann Jr. in 1940. 'Textiles USA' in 1946 at the Museum of Modern Art continued public education in textile design and its potential.

Scandinavian influence, a very important international inspiration, was promoted by touring exhibitions such as 'Design in Scandinavia' (1954–57). It was swift to move to the 'upper-middle' section of the international market where a taste for natural homespun weaves and shaggy colourful rugs in the Ryas style developed to complement

'Sutherland Rose', 1940, designed by Graham Sutherland for Helios Ltd.

the fashionable pale wood furniture. Astrid Sampes innovative policies in her role as head of the textile design studio of the Nordiska Kampaniet in Stockholm were influential throughout this period, as too was the work of Stig Lindberg who contributed to an internationalism which was evolving in many European and American firms.

By the end of the 1950s, mass production at the cheaper end of the fabric market had been taken over by the Near and Far East, though quality fabrics continued to be produced in the West. Britain, for instance,

A wool furnishing fabric by Marianne Straub for Warner and Sons, 1951.

specialised in textiles which proclaimed good design and technical excellence rather than attempting to compete on price. In contrast with the defined national styles emanating from European companies, Britain's diversity was apparent. There were vigorous flower drawings such as Graham Sutherland's 'Sutherland Rose', and a new vogue for line drawings of domestic objects contained within a square or rectangular form, such as those designed by Jane Edgar and the naturalistic line drawings of Jacqueline Groag. Scientific diagrams were adapted by some leading manufacturers for the decoration of products such as dress and furnishing fabrics and floor coverings. Among the well-known exponents of this style were Marianne Straub with designs such as 'Surrey' and 'Helmsley', Lucienne Day with 'Calyx', and Alex Hunter with 'Harwell'. The Festival of Britain in 1951 had set the trend for abstract design as well as confirming the prevailing mode for representational pattern.

By the 1950s, the range of printed patterns in the United States was very varied. Some were inspired by primitive art, defying the conformism of the age; freely drawn and assymetric, they were either completely abstract or highly stylised figures or objects. The modernists preferred small-scale geometric designs such as those by Alexander Girard for Herman Millar Co. These patterns were intended to accent rather than conflict with the architecture of the room. There was also a vogue for splashier patterns complementing sparse modernist interiors. The average American consumer continued to prefer conventional designs. There were floral patterns available, although they were less fashionable than the abstract and primitive. However, the suave and stylised florals of Jack Lenor Larsen and Leslie Tillet provided a compromise. Woven fabrics were highly textured, demonstrating the prevailing influence of the Bauhaus and Scandinavia.

In Britain, new firms joined those already established, such as Tibor Ltd, Conran Fabrics and a rejuvenated Liberty's. The

'The twentieth century turns to romance', pastiche of Victorian styles as featured for the US market by *House and Garden* in 1940.

influence of design directors in many companies was strong and stimulating. There was an encouraging new influx of talent as the colleges of the 1950s and 1960s began to develop their textile courses. Among their graduates were Althea McNish, who worked for Liberty's, Colleen Farr, Pat Albeck, Howard Carter and Shirley Craven, who worked for Hull Traders.

Publications by the Society of Industrial Artists and Designers from 1947 to 1964

show the interaction of designers and artists in the production of printed and woven textiles. They include the work of designers of the calibre of Lucienne Day, Thomas Bradley for Allan Walton textiles, Alistair Morton for Morton Sundour Fabrics, Hans Tisdall, Marianne Mahler, Marianne Straub, Graham Sutherland, Margaret F Leicher and Enid Marx. British firms had also begun to commission textile designs from established artists; Edinburgh Weavers under Alistair Morton from Elizabeth Frink, William Scott, Humphrey Spender, Victor Vasarely, Ben Nicholson and Leon Zak. Ascher's, which specialised in fashion fabrics, approached Matisse, Henry Moore and Felix Topolsky, as well as bringing out out a range of artist-designed scarves which became art objects in their own right and included work by Henry Moore, Ben Nicholson, Barbara Hepworth and Miro. In the United States, Herman Miller and Laverne collaborated with Alexander Calder and Yves Tanguy. Artist designers also contributed to the quality and couture textiles in France and Switzerland.

'Calla Lilies' designed by Stanley Coventry, 1940, for Stroheim and Romain. It is an example of the fashion for tropical motifs.

The 1960s

The expanding economy in the 1960s and an increasing number of young consumers, the product of the post-war baby boom, stimulated a dramatic design change. There was a period of exuberant eclecticism, enthusiasm for the ephemeral and sheer zaniness. Fabrics reflected the varying moods and themes, among which space programmes and scientific adventures, culminating in the first American Moon landing, were to inspire an enthusiasm for space-age motifs. Contemporary art was very influential, and designs by Victor Vasarely and Barbara Brown were typical of a brief vogue for Op-art designs in the middle of the decade. Silk-screen printing and photographic techniques facilitated the influence of pop artists such as Roy Lichtenstein and Andy Warhol. Even the abstracts of Piet Mondrian were transmuted into mini-dresses by Yves Saint Laurent. In the latter half of the 1960s, there was a feeling of nostalgia, in strong contrast to the optimism and excitement so evident in the early 1960s. This was focused stylistically on Art Nouveau, Art Deco and Victoriana, usually carried out in large-scale repeats. Many of the Art Nouveau designs were in bright, vivid and often lurid colours, termed psychedelic and associated with hallucinatory visions and the drug cult. Patterns with large flattened and boldly stylised flowers

'Bye bye Blackbird', polished cotton, 1969, Sanderson and Co.

were popular with the mass market, symptomatic of flower power, and the most famous graphic symbol of the 1960s was perhaps the Mary Quant floral logo. Elsewhere, large and bold geometric designs were given a stylistic lead by Marimekko in Finland.

New materials were brought into the fabric range. Non-woven and paper yardage typical of the affluent throwaway society was an inspiration to some designers. PVC (polyvinyl chloride), with its combination of flexibility and strength and its ability to take printed patterns well, was also popular. It made an exciting fashion fabric, promoting a short-lived vogue for see-through dresses, and was in tune with the space age theme. Marjatta Metsovarra of Helsinki used plastic film and wire for handweaves. In the United States, Ben Rose examined fibre glass for its reaction to dye and pigment and Jack Lenor Larsen developed warp prints of heat-set plastic film. Dorothy Liebes continued her exploration of unusual fabric combinations with DuPont.

The oil crisis of the early 1970s, combined with a reduction in the level of economic growth, had a devastating effect on the synthetic fibre market, especially in Britain. The higher cost of plastics and oil-based synthetics led to a greater emphasis on natural fibres and woven upholstery fabrics. This

'Floppy Poppy', printed cotton designed by D and D Collard for Sandersons, 1967. Pink, orange and psychodelic flower shapes were features of 1960s' fabric design.

'Love Comic', printed cotton designed by Leon Rosenblat, 1974.

was in line with the 1960s preference for an alternative natural lifestyle and a subsistence economy. The very successful Habitat shop opened by Terence Conran in 1964 promoted the Scandinavian 'natural' look. The simple folksy style and the cottons with a hand-print look of Laura Ashley were another aspect of the natural fabric movement. Also important was her stress on formal and floral Victorian revival patterns. A growing craft revival promoted individual hand-made products and a preference for homespun which continued until the late 1970s.

New firms and old

Revivalism in textile design is still a mainstay of the industry. Many major design houses rely on archives built up over the years: among them Colefax & Fowler, Osborne & Little, Warners, and Sandersons. Brunschwig & Fils and Scalamandre have important archives in the United States. Courtaulds also have a large collection of design documents. Such documents can be reproduced but are usually modified in colour and detail according to the prevailing fashion. Painterly sources are also an influence and it is marked in the work of both Collier Campbell and the Designers Guild. Architecture and ancient history are the

source for Timney Fowler's black and white classical prints.

Small design-led businesses were producing the more innovative and interesting textiles outside the mainstream of fabric production. The Cloth were a group of four designers who worked with textiles but also involved themselves in illustration, graphic work and interior design. It was a radical and energetic style. Nigel Atkinson specialises in inventing new textures and print methods and Georgina Van Etzdorf produces free expressive printed textiles. There is a new collaboration in the 1980s between the architect as well as the artist and textile designer: Michael Graves, Robert Venturi and David Hockney have designed textiles and carpets for the office and home.

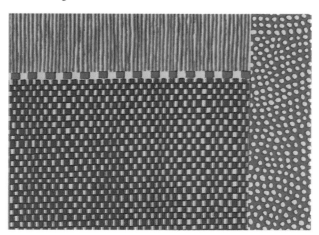

'Ma', printed cotton designed by Katsujo Wakisaka for Wacoal interior fabrics, 1977.

A blend of traditional design and contemporary technology is to be found internationally. In Japan, an ageless aesthetic together with new computer age technology have produced textiles devoid of nostalgic representation. They look at nature in terms of·light and shade. Hiroshi Awatsuji and Fujiwo Ishimoto are leaders in the field of surface design, while Junchi Arai creates effects with pattern and tactile qualities. It is mathematical and scientific, using fibres and yarns which he knows will disappear during finishing. The Milan-based Memphis group designing fabrics, carpets and plastic laminates owes much to the work of George Sowden and Nathalie DuPasquier. Working individually and together, their hallmark is brightly coloured anonymous decoration with graphic patterns. Graphic designs have also become elements in their textile repeats, and Javier Mariscal of Spain has translated such iconographic ideas and emblems with a unique freehand quality.

The rise of the designer as a 'folk' hero has been occurring since the 1950s as exhibitions have promoted their work both as individuals and part of a group. The manufacturers of textiles have assisted public awareness by conscious marketing, involving the use of names as a selling factor to add cachet. Initially this was introduced to counteract the mass-produced blur of the product and the customer's generalised perception. Designer ranges in co-ordinating fabrics extending to bed linen and towels have become fashionable. Firms such as Laura Ashley and Designers Guild, started by Patricia Guild, were established on the strength of an idea and a name. Introducing the element of fashionability encouraged demand but allowed aesthetic ideas to become an expendable commodity. The media has also played its part in the style-conscious decades. There is an acceptance of fashion and design as important dynamics in the consumer revolution.

Many firms in Britain and America are experimenting with computers to control looms and other machinery. Some systems also aid the designer; patterns can be drawn directly on to screen or scanned; multiple variations of colourways and repeats are simple; designs can be combined; elements isolated and developed in co-ordination or new patterns produced altogether. It is also possible to superimpose a design on to an image of a garment or a room. The designer Annick Top has used data processing in preparing printed textile panels as well as cartoons for tapestries and carpets.

Laura Ashley and Courtaulds are among the growing number of companies committed to computerisation. With the machinery becoming more sophisticated and fabrics from Japan powerfully innovative many firms will undoubtedly invest in the equipment. It may bring an end to familiar working practices but whether it will threaten the skilled designer and artisan is an open question. It is now included in the syllabus of art and design colleges, many of which work closely with manufacturers, examining the potential of systems and ensuring a new generation of computer literate designers.

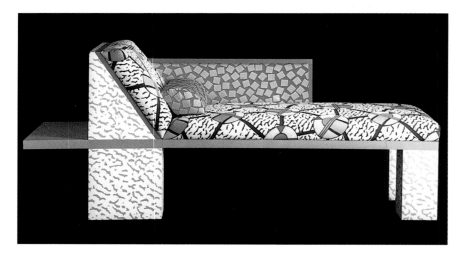

'Royal' divan, designed by Nathalie du Pasquier for Memphis, 1983, made in plasticised print and 'Cercio' printed cotton by Rainbow production.

'Hommage to Gunta Stölzl', A close adaptation of a classic Bauhaus design by Collier Campbell in 1967 subsequently printed on various fabrics: silk, cotton, and wool.

The craft revival

The craft revival began in earnest after the Second World War. There was more leisure time and creative hobbies were pursued. Wartime restrictions on fabrics had stressed 'Make do and Mend', encouraging patchwork and appliqué, and designs of the period tend to be illustrative. With the end of wartime restrictions and the development of new engineering technology in the 1950s, manufacturers of sewing, embroidery and knitting machines began to focus on the domestic market. By the end of the 1950s, embroidery was again established as wall decoration with emphasis on appliqué and mixed media. Abstract motifs were popular as well as birds and flowers. In the early 1960s new materials such as metal thread and plastic fabrics were introduced, encouraging mixed techniques and larger hangings. The range of materials had expanded by the late 1960s to include found objects such as stones, shells, wood and cardboard. Moderately sized wall hangings incorporating mixed media, dyeing and screen-printing became geometric and abstract. Soft sculpture was important by the end of the decade and 3-dimensional forms were to influence the 2-dimensional work in padding and quilting in the 1970s. Machine embroidery and multi-media have been important since the late 1970s and, while embroidery has retained a link with the traditional craft, it has also become a means of expression as an art form.

Two traditional types of embroidery were revived in the post-war period. Ecclesiastical embroidery was stimulated by the post-war Church revival, reorganisation and rebuilding programmes, and this continued into the late 1960s. Beryl Dean's work at St George's Chapel, Windsor is noteworthy; traditional in concept and modern in technique and design. Embroidery also regained its importance in fashion design and haute couture. In the 1950s couturiers such as Balenciaga and Dior made much use of it, their designs being made up by long-established Paris embroidery houses such as Rebé and Lesage. Their work, and that of earlier couturiers, has been adapted into revivalist romantic couture of the 1980s, though, for reasons of price, much of it is now done in the Far East.

'Dark Presence', tapestry in wool and sisal by Myriam Gilby, 1984.

A number of groups and societies have been active in raising the standards of embroidery in the United Kingdom, including the Embroiderer's Guild, the Royal School of Needlework, the Centre for Embroidery, Fashion and Textile Studies and the 62 Group, founded in 1962. The Crafts Council includes embroidery in its more generalised brief. Britain is one of the few countries where embroidery may be studied as a specialist subject.

Cross-fertilisation in the visual arts and particularly the entry of young artists into embroidery has, since the 1970s, produced much exciting and innovative work. Michael Brennan-Wood is a leader in the more robust style, and Stephanie Tuckwell and Catherine Virgils use hand-made paper as an integral part of their creations. Large life-size constructions in fabric are the speciality of Catherine Riley and Polly Hope. Sally Freshwater has experimented with spatial concepts and Verina Warren, Kate Wells, and Audrey Walker with landscapes, subtle blends of colour and texture

'Revelation' altar frontal, mixed media embroidery by Polly Hope, 1986.

hand- and machine-work.

Pauline Burbridge's speciality is patchwork, which together with quilting has enjoyed a revival on both sides of the Atlantic and of which there have been many exhibitions. In the United States, the tradition was still alive and the older techniques were re-examined and reproduced and had added to them hand-made paper work, felt and basketry. Surface design and embroidery have become linked in the United States, and dyes, photographic images, xeroxes and other transfer processes have become incorporated. American soft sculpture tends to be more whimsical and eccentric than in England, diversifying into food, animals and figures which are often amazingly lifelike.

Knitting

Until the last two decades, knitting has been seen as a conventional feminine skill, more utilitarian than artistic. As a craft it regained popularity in the 1970s, when traditional designs and patterns were re-explored. This created a rich repertoire of ideas and led to

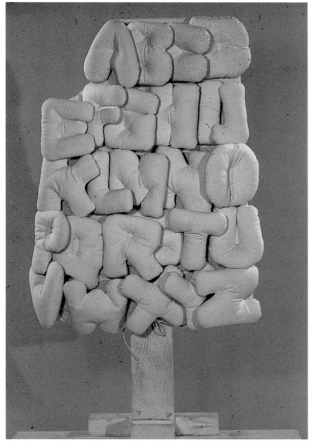

Alphabet 'Good Humour', 1969, cloth study by Claus Oldenburg, a sculptor's exploration of the tactile and dimensional potential of textiles.

Hangings designed by Beryl Dean, 1974, for St George's Chapel, Windsor. The panels depict incidents in the Life of the Virgin. There is an interesting variety of techniques, including appliqué.

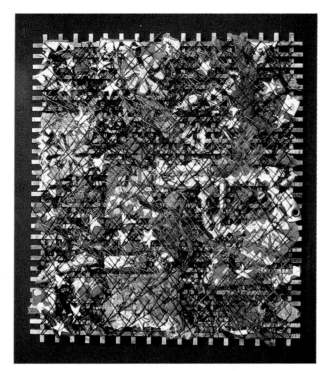

'Reba-o-o-o' by Michael Brennand Wood, 1979. It is in mixed media, an organised combination of layers and textures which include wood, fabric, thread and plastic.

many new interpretations in colour, texture and design. Fashion collaborated, and an increasing number of designers began to use it in their collections. They gave it a new image compatible with the sporty informal look. Pictorial patterning was an important feature from the early 1980s and new attachments for home-knitting machines made them easy for amateurs to adapt. Hand-knitters created new and interesting textures and shapes with sculptural effects. Readily available yarns such as angora, cotton, mohair, silk, linen and handspun wool have developed an awareness of surface texture, while among the more avant-garde knitters plastics, rubber, nylon, transparent mono-filaments and computer wires have been utilised to great effect. The breaking down of the high-fashion knitting mystique was to a large extent the work of American Kaffe Fassett, whose rich colour and textural palette and simple no-nonsense techniques aided the emergence of a new popular interest. Machine-knitting has inspired many designers to experiment with lighter-weight yarns, transparent and man-made fibres as well as natural fibres such as wool, silk and chenille. The associated art of crochet has considerable appeal for the

'Ribbon shawl', knitted, designed by Kaffe Fassett, 1988.

'Butterfly', machine embroidery by S. Lewis, about 1980.

'Man in Glory and Peace' from the tapestry Le Chant du Monde, designed about 1950 by Jean Lurçat.

artistic-craftsperson. Work by Dina Knapp and Sharron Hedges in Julie: Artisans' Gallery, New York, is coloured textural sculpture skilfully adapted to clothing the human form.

Tapestry weaving

Areas outside mainstream textiles have also undergone changes since the war. Attempts to reform and revitalise tapestry weaving in the Gobelins and Aubusson establishments had begun before the Second World War and modifications in the traditional practices allowed the potential of the medium to

re-assert itself. The state-owned Gobelins factory had recognised that changes were essential if the tapestry of tradition was to survive, and the painter Jean Lurçat had become involved in the radicalisation of the firm by the late 1930s. His work within the company led to a revolution in tapestry weaving. Graham Sutherland's design for Coventry Cathedral woven at Aubusson was the largest tapestry made since the war. However, the powerful imagery of the seated Saviour could not disguise its technical limitations; initially it sagged. In the United Kingdom, Dovecote Studios, under their director Archie Brennan, emphasised a close, informed working relationship between painter and weaver. Among the Dovecote products have been tapestries designed by Eduardo Paolozzi and Tom Phillips. Henry Moore's drawings have been translated into tapestry form by the West Dean studio in Chichester.

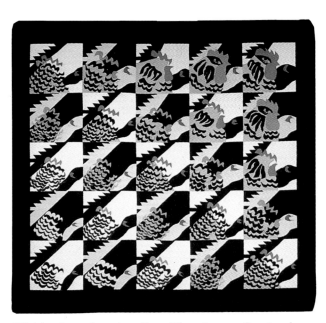

'Chicken', patchwork quilt wall hanging, appliqué and machine pieced by Pauline Burbidge, 1987.

A furnishing fabric in cut and uncut
moquette, 1980s, by Jack Lenor Larsen.

New frontiers

It has been in the studios of individual artists
and craftspeople that the greatest changes
have occurred. An international movement,
a compulsion to break down traditional
beliefs and practices, has begun. Textiles
have been reduced to their most basic form
of fibre and filament, and non-traditional
materials are being used in both conventional and innovatory production. The Eastern
block, particularly Poland and Hungary,
began to question traditional techniques earlier than the West, mainly because of their
lack of traditional materials. They explored
alternatives, village handspun wool, sisal,
hemp, rope, cotton and paper twine. The
materials dictated forms other than a flat
woven surface and moved into three dimensions. The interpretation of the medium
beyond its limits was encouraged by artists
such as Magdalena Abakanowicz, Jolanta
Owidzka, Barbara Falkowska and Wojiech
Sadley from Poland, Romanians Ritz and
Peter Jacobi and Jogoda Buic from Yugoslavia. The first international exhibition of
tapestry took place in 1962. The Biennale
International de la Tapisserie held in
Lausanne under the presidency of Jean Lurçat was to become an international forum
for the medium. The original intention was
to mark the revival of the ancient form of
tapestry, but a number of works set out to
make a different statement, principally those
by Abakanowicz, Sadley and Owidzka.
'Woven Forms', 1963, at the Museum of
Contemporary Crafts in New York, showed
American artists such as Sheila Hicks, Do-
rian Zachai and Clare Zeisler working in a
similar way to the Europeans. These exhibi-

'Permutation', interlace, a construction
of knitted wool tubes, 1972, by Anne Sutton.

'Backs', burlap and glue, soft sculptures by Magdalena Abakanowicz, 1976–82.

tions and 'Deliberate Entanglements' at UCLA Galleries in 1971 contributed to a growing awareness of fibre as a means of artistic expression. In Britain, as a reaction to the large-scale size stipulated at Lausanne (an area of five square metres), the British Crafts Council with the aid of Ann Sutton conceived the idea of an alternative show. The 'First International Exhibition of Miniature Textiles' was held in 1974. It consisted of the work of an invited panel, but the show provoked such interest that open selection became the format for the next three exhibitions. Among the United Kingdom group Tadek Beutlic exhibited at the Lausanne Biennale in 1967 and 1969 and at 'Deliberate Entanglements' in 1971. At the Triennale in Lodz, Poland, Archie Brennan, Maureen Hode, Fiona Mathison and Ann Sutton exhibited. These artists, and a designer of the calibre of Peter Collingwood whose work has a wide general appeal, have broadened the sphere of textiles in Britain, allowing the craft-based textiles to merge with textiles as an art. Others have included the tapestry weaving of Marta Rogoyska and Joanna Buxton, the woven cloths and panels of Mary Restieaux and the felt creations of Annie Sherbourne. This trend is also marked in Australia, where textile craft and design has become increasingly important in recent years, as an extension of investment

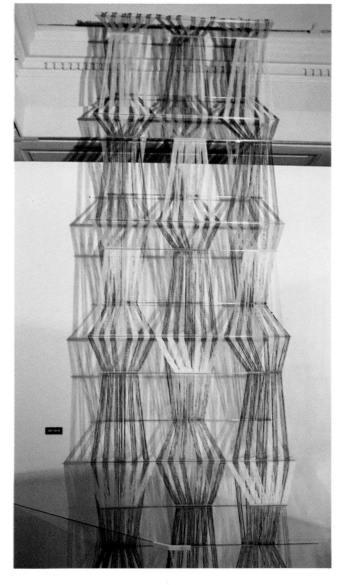

'Macrogauze', wall hanging by Peter Collingwood, 1973, made from linen cords and thin steel rods.

'The Bird Catcher' designed by Jean Picart Le Doux in 1946.

Valley Curtain, Grand Hogback, Rifle, Colorado, 1970–72, created and constructed by Christo. An artist's manipulation of textiles as a large-scale flexible medium.

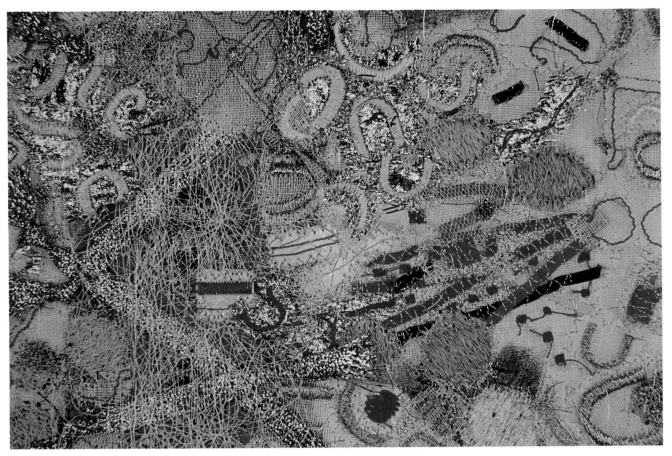

'I went to the British Museum to Look at the Mummies', detail of a machine embroidery, 1982, by Christine Risley.

in the wool trades. The Powerhouse in Sydney has provided a sympathetic environment for designers and is the focus for fixed and touring exhibitions.

With so many types of textiles and techniques of production it is difficult to envisage what the next century will bring. New types of fibres are continually being explored and developed. Natural products are again enjoying a renaissance in their own right and in combination with synthetics. Methods of production are now governed by technology of space-age complexity. Techniques and forms cross-fertilise and habitually cross traditional boundaries. More than ever in an age of mass communication it is an international industry. Designers' work is syndicated and firms are multinational. Fabric production has moved East and to compensate, as it were, their design repetoire is becoming Westernised. The possible contribution of Eastern Europe has yet to be fully assessed.

Design which has become synonymous with style in the last decade will continue to be important. The cachet of the designer label is a convention of prestige marketing, and licensing a cornerstone of the very profitable fashion industry, as well as prompting the growth of a number of independent firms which create styles of great individuality. Fabric design will no doubt be as eclectic as before but the computer will ease the designer's control of an infinite number of variables.

There is an interraction between the designer, the artist and the craftsworker. Each added talent and experience extends the boundaries of the media and adds new and interesting forms, surface texture and colours. Fibre Art, the synthesis, has to be recognised as a phenomenon of our times, when textiles are regarded as compatible with art and its present-day potential.

PART TWO
A Collector's Guide

Carpet, knotted pile, mid 16th century, from Cuenca,
Spain.

SIX

Carpets

William Robinson

A carpet either of knotted pile or tapestry woven, and probably of English make, covers
the table around which sit 'The Somerset House Conference', discussing peace between
England and Spain; anonymous painting, 1604.

CARPETS are among the convention-al furnishings of most Western homes, but their origins are firmly rooted in the Orient, where the early technical sources and the early design motifs are to be found. Genuinely old carpets are rare collector's pieces; their designs and patterns survive and are adapted to the technology of the modern mass-produced carpet industry.

Their precise birthplace is, as yet, undisco-vered, but the earliest known examples, from the Pazyryck burial of a Scythian prince in the Altai mountains of Siberia, dated scientifically to around the fifth cen-tury BC, demonstrate a technique that is already well developed. No other example is known from the period between this and examples from Egypt that use a different technique dating from around the sixth cen-tury AD. The gap is partially filled by Greek and Roman textual references, but by no surviving examples.

The continuous history of oriental carpets

starts in the thirteenth century and by the fifteenth century oriental carpets begin to be depicted in paintings of the period by European artists. Almost invariably of Anatolian origin, they are shown in use on the floor and in other situations within Western European interiors. They were luxury items not easy to obtain and there is an account of Cardinal Wolsey who in 1518 demanded one hundred Damascus carpets from Venetian traders in exchange for relaxing import controls on Candian wines to England. Eventually he received sixty carpets, but the difficulties which the traders had in obtaining them fully bears witness to their rarity. In the later sixteenth century the responsibility for importing oriental carpets into England passed first to the Turkey Company and in 1601 to the East India Company, making direct Eastern imports cheaper and more easily obtainable.

The other geographical area from which early carpets were imported was Spain, colonised by the Moors and in close touch with the Muslim world. The craft continued after the Moors were driven out in the late fifteenth century.

Early Spanish carpets are characterised by the so-called Spanish knot, which is attached to alternating single warp threads, giving a marked diagonal emphasis to pile and pattern. The Ghiordes or Turkish knot which is passed over double warp threads was not introduced in Spain until the seventeenth century. In this later period designs were European and eclectic but earlier examples are strongly influenced by the East, featuring geometric designs and *kufic* inscriptions. There are also heraldic carpets, long and narrow with armorial devices.

Texts are of help in determining the details of the early trade. Eleanor of Castile, who married the future Edward I of England in 1255, brought in her dowry a number of tapestries and carpets with which she decorated her palace apartments in London, and mention is made of *tapis sarassinois* captured from the Moors by the French Louis IX in the fourteenth century.

Throughout the medieval period the number of carpets imported into Western Europe was extremely small and had little real impact on how people furnished. They were only available to a minute proportion of the population, even of the wealthy classes. The situation was thus ripe for the creation of local industries.

England was the first country to create a local tradition that vied with the foreign imports. While inventories of the great houses of the sixteenth century occasionally mention *Turkie carpitts*, they also begin to include *Turkie Worke* – which imitated the pile characteristic of carpets possibly with needlework – and there is a single reference to carpets of *Kidderminster stuffe*. We shall see later that this refers to carpets of a slightly different technique, thus explaining its mention as a separate type.

Many of the earliest English carpets were direct copies of the Turkish originals, with hardly any deviation in design. Three attri-

English carpet, 1585. Made from knotted pile, it has the arms of Sir Edward Montague worked in the borders. The date and the initials of the weaver also appear.

Savonnerie carpet, knotted pile, 1670–83. Possibly designed by Le Brun for La Grande Galerie du Louvre. The *fleurs de lys* of France are central between the landscape vignettes.

butes, however, clearly distinguish them from their prototypes. Firstly, the technique is different. Flax was usually employed as warp, occasionally with silk, rather than the wool of the Turkish foundations. The knots were also less tightly compressed than in the Turkish originals, making the design more drawn out. The second is the inclusion of armorials in the English borders, together with the frequent use of a brief inscription and/or date. The colour scheme also differs.

At the same time, a number of carpets were made using new designs. Most display a repeating pattern, as do the Turkish imports, but the floral origins of the motifs are much more obvious. Scrolling tendrils terminating in stylised flowerheads or bunches of fruit replace the arabesques of the Orient. In some examples, the field is almost entirely filled with dense floral sprays, often including recognisable flowers. However, most of these also include the armorial bearings of the patron, often occupying pride of place in the centre of the field. Many are also dated, and the combination of dates and precise armorial bearings makes the chronology of these early English carpets a relatively easy subject.

Carpets at this time were by no means all for use on the floor. Inventories mention *foote carpettes* as a separate category. Others were placed on tables, in windows (presumably on the seats), on stools, as cushion covers, and even to cover cupboards. Many of these uses had already been filled by embroidered furnishings, so it is not surprising that slightly later there was a reciprocal development of needlework floor carpets closely related in design to the pile examples.

Other countries made pile rugs but most of these ventures took the form of cottage industries. Thick, shaggy examples made for warmth and called *ryas* were made in Scandinavia, particularly in Finland. They are mentioned by the twelfth century, used as floor and bed coverings, and possibly inspired by the animal skins they replaced. In Spain similar dual-purpose rugs were made in Alpujarra. They had an unusual weave with looped weft pile and long decorative fringes. Early examples have initials and dates, later ones have variants of oriental motifs. In Italy the centre for pile carpets was Abruzzi. All these products were, however, from small centres and not for use in grand houses. They were usually typified by a coarse weave and limited palette,

Savonnerie carpet, knotted pile, first quarter 18th century, probably designed for Versailles.
The *fleurs de lys* of France can be seen in the centre.

having little influence on future development of carpet industries in the countries
concerned, but were to be of great interest to
artist designers in the twentieth century.

In the first half of the seventeenth century,
a French innovation was to affect the subsequent history of carpets throughout the
Western world. It started in 1601 with the
protection through tariffs of the native industry and the inauguration by Henri IV of a
consultative committee to encourage and
establish indigenous trades and professions.
One of the areas of concern to the commis-
sioners was the carpet industry which had
been the province of non-French craftsmen.
In 1604 Jean Fortier of Melun suggested the
manufacture of carpets 'tapis de Turquie'.
But though as in England the earliest products were near direct copies of carpets from
the Orient, this did not continue for long.

The innovation of the French was the employment of an artist as designer.

From the reign of Louis XIII the aesthetic
was the same as all the other furnishings of
the royal houses. The royal workshops were
first established at the Louvre and by 1627
also on the site of an old soap factory on the
outskirts of Paris, thus giving them the name
'La Savonnerie'. These two workshops were
initiated by Pierre Dupont and Simon Lourdet. From the start there was a determination to produce carpets of superb technical
quality using the best materials and a finely
knotted weave. They were made on vertical
looms with linen warp and woollen pile, the
knots formed over a rod and cut to an even
pile, though the pattern's edge was sometimes bevelled. The venture was given a
royal charter in 1663, under the guidance of
Louis XIV's finance minister, Colbert. So

long as royal patronage was forthcoming carpets were woven of a quality and size hitherto unthinkable in Western Europe. Throughout its long and continuing history, the fortunes of this manufactury have fluctuated with those of the French crown, or, subsequently, state. The story is thus one of great extremes of prosperity, as under Louis XIV and Napoleon I, alternating with periods when it has nearly had to close, as during the French Revolution.

The workers at the Savonnerie, initially charity children from a hospice on the site, had to undergo a long and arduous apprenticeship. Becoming a fully qualified weaver required eight years' training, a period during which each stage of development was strictly laid down in the regulations. It is through these rules that the quality of the products was maintained.

The carpets were exclusively for the use of the court or state; private commissions were not allowed. Designers were appointed by the crown and were often well-known artists, such as Charles Le Brun, *Premier peintre du roi*, who inaugurated the classical-style decoration at the palaces of the Louvre, Tuileries and Versailles. The weavers themselves had no hand in the design process. Thus it was, as in the Ottoman court a century before, that the designs for all the royal household's interiors were produced by a school of design, ensuring that all the various artefacts harmonised. Le Brun, whose best-known work in this context is the Grande Galerie des Glaces at Versailles, was succeeded in 1667 by Belin de Fontenay, then by his son, who introduced lighter floral forms, and in 1749 by Pierre Jose Perrot.

Products of the Savonnerie workshop thus closely reflect the taste of the period. Those dating from the reign of Louis XIV are typified by heavy scrolling acanthus leaves on a dark ground. Pictorial cartouches are frequently included depicting the Virtues or similar emblematic figures. During the reign of Louis XV the rococo style was fashionable with its flurry of flowing leaves and floral swags. Restraint was introduced under Louis XVI together with the more classical style which culminated with Percier and Fontaine, the architects of the Empire style for Napoleon. Another artist, La Hamayade de Saint-Ange, continued through to the 1840s adapting his designs during the period. The floral and leafy motifs of these various styles often incorporate symbols of royalty such as the entwined letter 'L' and the fleur-de-lys, superseded by the Roman 'N' and bees of Napoleon. The turbulent years at the end of the eighteenth

French carpet made at Aubusson,
mid 18th century.

and start of the nineteenth centuries, though often resulting in poor fortunes for the factory, kept a few weavers busy unpicking the symbols of the last ruler and replacing them with those of the current monarch.

With the tight royal control exercised over the Savonnerie workshops, it was only natural that a similar, though slightly downmarket, competitor should be created. There was already a local tradition of weaving in the town of Aubusson in the Creuse valley near Limoges and, in 1665, only two years after La Savonnerie, it received its royal charter. This was, however, followed by a series of setbacks that meant that, for all practical purposes, the start of carpet-weaving at Aubusson dates from 1743 when the workshops were re-founded, to cope with renewed competition from Turkey.

From the start, two completely different types of carpet were woven at Aubusson. The first was a pile carpet, similar in style to the products of Savonnerie, but inferior in the quality of weaving and materials. The second, which has given Aubusson its fame, is a flat-woven carpet using the tapestry technique, worked on horizontal low-warp looms. This is obviously quicker and easier to weave, resulting in a cheaper, if less

hard-wearing, product. So-called '*pile velouté*' carpets were produced from 1746.

The principles under which the workshops were established were similar to those at Savonnerie, with designs created by resident artists to be converted into carpets by the weavers. They also tend to follow the court design traditions. On occasions, the weavers used designs which had originally been created for the Savonnerie workshops but often simplified and placing a greater reliance on repeating patterns. Their market was the nobility and the better-off merchant classes who, even in times of prosperity, were glad to have Aubusson carpets at prices that vastly undercut those of Savonnerie.

Although by the late nineteenth century, the centre had much diminished, the great majority of surviving Aubusson carpets were made in the nineteenth and early twentieth centuries. One factor that makes precise dating difficult is that, while there was a definite development of styles over the years, the earlier cartoons were never discarded and were often used decades or even centuries after they were first created. The same occurred, although to a lesser extent, at Savonnerie. Since the techniques remained the same, and different conditions of use

English carpet, knotted pile, made at Exeter in factory of Peter Passavant, with woven inscription 'Exon 1757'. The central motif, the dog in the basket, is a very English touch.

English carpet, knotted pile, made at Axminster, about 1820.

render dating by condition unsatisfactory, it is only by slight differences in the colour tones that dating can be established.

Other minor workshops were set up in France, often as a by-product of a tapestry manufactory. Beauvais and Gobelins itself produced a number of carpets. At the moment much work needs to be done to enable the products of the various centres to be distinguished one from the other.

By 1750 the manufacture of pile carpets in England appears to have completely died. The initiative had passed to cheaper 'foote cloths', reversible double weaves and patterned flat weaves whose makers had received royal charters in 1701, 1706 and 1725, and which were made at Kidderminster, Wilton, Mortlake and Norwich as well as at Kilmarnock in Scotland. The range widened when in 1730 Lord Pembroke smuggled in French weavers and began to make loop pile on horizontal treadle looms at Wilton. It was called 'Tournai' or 'Brussels' after the town in which it was said to

have originated in 1710.

Due to the strict working conditions in the French workshops, it is not surprising that two workers decided to set up independently. Since the regulations ensured that this could not be done in France, they crossed the Channel to England in 1750. Having secured the help of Pierre Norbert or 'Peter Parisot', a French emigré, they obtained the favour of the Duke of Cumberland in May 1751, and their first carpet was produced as a gift for the Princess of Wales. The two men, however, were greedy and were discharged, and Peter Parisot moved the workshop to Fulham where by 1753 he was employing 100 men and many apprentices. Thus began a new period of carpet weaving in England.

However, the carpets were expensive and, by 1775, this original factory had already fallen on hard times. In the meantime the industry had attracted many patrons, together with the offer in 1756 of an annual prize by the Royal Society of Arts. In the next three years, three competitors came through to win, each from a different factory. These are the main workshops to flourish in the later eighteenth century.

Louis Passavant, a Swiss from Basle who had bought the Fulham workshop and taken it to Exeter was the first. Little remains of his work; only two signed carpets are known, while a third, now in the United States, is attributed to his workshop. Although the designs obviously derive from the French, there are small details, such as the dog seated on a cushion in the centre of one, that confirm their English origin. He seems to have ceased trading by 1760.

The second was that of Thomas Moore, who operated from Chiswell Street in Moorfields, London, and who founded a more long-lived establishment. This was principally due to his collaboration with the famous architect, Robert Adam, who worked on a large number of houses for the aristocracy. Adam designed carpets often to mirror the painted and moulded plaster motifs on the ceiling. As with the furniture of the period, the carpets are considerably more restrained in decorative detail than their French counterparts, and the motifs classical in inspiration. This workshop seems, however, to have executed few commissions after 1780, and was sold by 1795.

The third to commence trading, Thomas Whitty of Axminster, founded the greatest of all the workshops and was succeeded by his son and grandson. He had had the idea of making pile carpets for some time, but it was only after a visit to the Fulham factory that he saw how their construction could be achieved. His first carpet was begun in 1755. The *tours de force* of Axminster were the carpets made for the Royal Pavilion at Brighton. That for the music room, the largest of its kind ever made, was 61 × 40 feet and weighed 1,700 lbs. The factory closed due to financial pressures in 1835, transferring its activities and looms to the establishment at Wilton. They produced some of the very best carpets woven in this country, almost entirely unsigned, but characterised by restrained designs and well-chosen, subtle colours.

All these ventures were in the manufacture of pile carpets. A few needlepoint and tapestry-woven carpets were made. However, the latter were usually by-products of tapestry workshops, while the former were principally one-off designs for great houses, frequently supervised by the lady of the house herself.

Other European countries also started to manufacture carpets, but few created products that rivalled the English or French in quality.

Portugal already had a tradition of making good quality but coarse needlework carpets in Arraiolos, a town that is still engaged in the same craft. The early examples of these often have an armorial bearing in the centre, surrounded by scrolling leaves. Later influences from France and Spain, encouraging a more floral style, subsequently adapted at the end of the last century to accommodate some of the Art Nouveau ideas, can be seen in the products. Current production shows a combination of the floral and oriental styles.

Spain followed French styles more closely. In a factory set up in Madrid under royal patronage in the late eighteenth century, carpets were woven following the French Aubusson and Savonnerie designs. Due, however, to the comparative coarseness of the weave and poorer quality of wool, the designs tend not to be as finely worked. This is compensated for by the strength of colour; usually brighter and bolder than their models, an attribute more suited to the stronger sunlight prevalent there. Many are also signed and dated. As in Portugal, this is a tradition that is still continuing today.

Other countries in Western and Central Europe also established workshops, which copied the French styles approximately, but in a coarser weave. Germany and Austria set up factories in the mid-nineteenth century, while the earlier centre of Deventer in Holland was re-established at about the same time. Most products from the workshops are well-woven but with a limited and uninspiring choice of colours.

The knotted pile carpet made by Thomas Moore of London echoes the main features of the
moulded ceiling in the Library at Chatsworth House.

Although few examples survive from Eastern Europe, some of those that do are of extremely high quality. Some reflect the influence of France, while others bear witness to the proximity of the Ottoman Empire. In the eighteenth century, a workshop at Lwow in Poland achieved prominence, using Western European designs, but employing a technique that owed more to the East. Russian carpets are also known. These, however, are entirely French in influence, being made in tapestry technique or embroidered in *gros point* as a response to the prohibitive cost of imports. Many of those worked in *gros point* bear the names of the noble ladies who sponsored them, while the tapestry woven examples were created in the royal St Petersburg tapestry factory. Both are typified by an abundance of various flowers, either on a black ground (also encountered in England), or in bright colours set off by a pastel background.

In Colonial America, the cottage industries of New England produced comparatively small amounts of the various types of basic flat-woven carpets known variously as English, Scottish, Kidderminster, Kilmarnock, Ingrain, Venetian, spotted or mottled. Rag rugs were also made at home. Foreign imports were the main source for quality floor coverings.

One extremely rare example of knotted pile carpet, now in the Smithsonian in Washington, was made by William Peter Sprague of Philadelphia in 1791. He is advertised as making Axminster, ingrain or carpets 'in the Turkey manner'. An account of it is to be found in the *Gazette of the United States*, of 22 June 1791. Intended for the Senate Chamber in Congress Hall, Philadelphia, it included 'centrally a device representing the crest and armorial achievements pertaining to the United States'. Apart from a central eagle and the devices of the States, the motifs are directly taken from carpets made at Aubusson, and indeed, earlier this century it was thought to have been made there. Only the joined strips show that it was woven on the narrow looms of Mr Sprague.

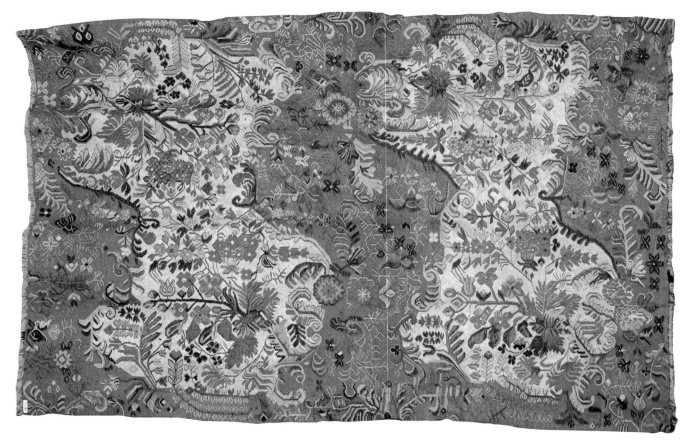

Tapestry woven carpet from Poland, inscribed 'Dobzrnskle', mid 19th century.

North American hooked wool rug, third quarter 19th century, probably made at home
from a commercially produced stencilled design.

Rag rugs begin to survive in increasing quantities from the nineteenth century, especially in the United States, though they must have been in use throughout the civilised world. They were made from plaited or woven strips of re-used materials. Some were also knitted and later crochetted. Shirred rugs in which rags were couched on the surface were fashionable from 1825 to 1860 when they began to be superseded by hooked rugs. Also popular were yarn-sewn rugs embroidered in thick wool. All were made on burlap or even flour sack foundations. Some designs were home productions but others were commercially derived, either as metal stencils such as those sold by Edward Sands Frost of Maine, a tin peddlar, or stamped, of which many were produced by Chamber and Leland of Lowell, Massachussets. The bold naïve designs have great appeal. In the twentieth century domestic crafted rugs have become a flourishing cottage industry. Many kits also have become available through the mail-order firms leading to increased uniformity of design but popularising a traditional craft.

The nineteenth century saw enormous advances in the uses of machines, some of which were applied to the manufacture of loom-woven carpets. The first important development appeared in 1801, when Joseph Jacquard invented and patented his loom. Until then, the pattern in a carpet was created by the selective raising by hand of the warp threads. The Jacquard loom could pre-ordain, on a series of punched cards, an infinite variety of warps to be raised by machine, and thus any pattern.

It was not long before loom-woven carpets were increasing in popularity. In 1807, before the Jacquard loom was introduced, there were 1,000 carpet looms at Kidderminster, while in 1838 the figure was 2,020. By 1820 the Jacquard loom was in use for carpets in Philadelphia. Early in the nineteenth century it was entirely acceptable to furnish a house with loom-woven carpets. In Germany, at the same time, the designer Biedermeier, when he applied himself to the problem of carpeting, invariably used machine-made examples. After all, they fulfilled the same basic function as hand-knotted pile carpeting, and were available at a fraction of the cost.

In the United States, there was stress on developing a home industry, especially after the interruption in supplies during the revolutionary wars of the early nineteenth century and the 25 per cent tax on imports

Above: A closely fitted and probably machine-woven Kidderminster carpet completes the bedroom furnishings of the 'old house' at Balmoral, Scotland, Queen Victoria's country house. The carpeting also covers the foot stool. A watercolour of 1855.

Flat weave carpet, in the Art Nouveau style, late 19th– early 20th century, probably made by Alexander Morton and Co.

124

in 1824. Lowell became an important centre and Erastus Bigelow was brought in by Frederick Cabot and Alexander Wright. In 1841, he made the first successful power loom capable of making ingrain carpets on which production began in 1846. After his loom was shown at the 1851 Exhibition, his invention was taken up worldwide. The British firm, Crossleys of Halifax, Yorkshire also purchased his invention for the mechanical weaving of Brussels-type carpeting. Alleged by some to be of even greater significance was the mechanisation of hand knotting to pattern in 1867.

Although the hand-made carpet centres suffered from competition, the middle of the nineteenth century saw a revival of interest in hand-made rather than mass production, an aspect of the Arts and Crafts movement. Although John Ruskin and William Morris are the names most closely associated with

this, A.W. Pugin was an earlier advocate of many of the ideas. They tied in with the return to Gothic architecture and Christian morality, although one of his criticisms was of the unnecessary blossoming of Gothic minutiae over every available surface. Among his designs preserved in the Victoria and Albert Museum are a number for carpets, very few of which have, unfortunately, survived.

William Morris is probably the best-known European carpet designer of the last century. Early designs were for loom-woven carpets, but later, in line with his principles, he established a small hand-weaving loom at Hammersmith, in West London. His main source of inspiration was the Orient. As he stated in a lecture, 'To us pattern designers, Persia has become a holy land, for there in the process of time our art was perfected'. His aesthetic ideas were taken up and

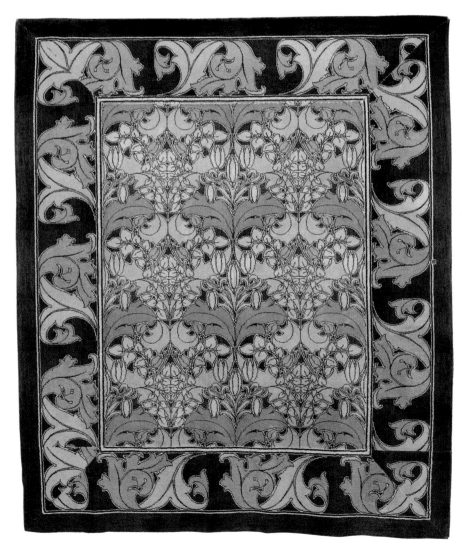

Machine-woven carpet, designed by C.F.A. Voysey in 1896 for Tomkinson and Adams.

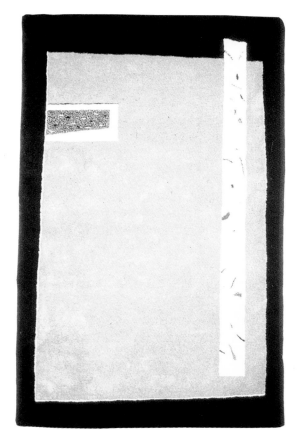

Hand tufted rug in wool and nylon
designed by Helen Yardley, 1985.

Flowers and stems, detail of a hand tufted
rug designed by Jennie Moncur, 1988.

developed by the exponents of the Art Nouveau style.

Among others, C.R. Mackintosh, Walter Crane, Archibald Knox, and, above all, C.F.A. Voysey all produced designs for carpets, many realisations of which survive.

In the twentieth century there was a continuation of the idea of the carpet draughted by well-known designers often as part of a total interior decoration scheme. The 1920s, in particular, saw an upsurge in the popularity of this art-form. Some designers, such as Marion Dorn and Marian Pepler, designed for well-established manufacturers such as Wilton; Jean Lurçat did similarly at Aubusson. Others worked with machine-weaving companies, some of which set up specialist offshoots. A third option has been provided by the cheap labour available in developing countries. Both Turkey and India have

Knotted pile rug, designed by Marion Dorn, 1929, for Wilton.

Knotted pile rug designed by Charles Le Plaie, Belgium, about 1928.

produced rugs and carpets to new designs sent out to them from Europe.

Between the wars, modernist rugs were made by a variety of different manufacturing techniques many of very novel design. Since the war, however, the taste in carpets has become conservative. The main European manufacturers put most of their energies into traditional patterning, making copies of earlier carpets, or examples approximating to earlier styles. Designs by Da Silva Bruhns and Jean Lurçat for the French workshops in the middle years of this century, though using the ideas in a new way, are based on earlier motifs and forms. As in the middle of the nineteenth century, very few new ideas are being produced. A few modern artists have worked in this medium, but their production concentrates on the textural capabilities, creating fabrics that are not suitable (or intended) for use on the floor and which merge with decorative wall hangings or drapes. For the traditional pile carpet, the centre of manufacture has again returned to the East.

Knotted pile rug, designed by Ivan da Silva Bruhns, about 1932.

Detail from a crewel-work curtain.
English, early 18th century.

SEVEN

Embroidery

Lucy Ginsburg

'The industrious mother', about 1720. Engraved after
Watteau.

THE ADORNMENT of cloth with decorative stitchery links the needlecrafts with the history of the fine
and decorative arts. Highly evocative of the lifestyles of the past, embroidery
reflects social and artistic trends, as well as
religious and political affiliations and priori-
ties. To the craftsperson it is an irreplacable
inspiration. Contemporary work exploits its
potential, and although it can be portrayed
as a demure and self-effacing craft, its basic
techniques are sufficiently adaptable for it to
explore the multidimensional aesthetics of
today. Above all it is a very personal artefact
with an intimacy of appeal which makes it
among the most popular items for individuals and museums to collect.

Until the last century it was hardly
affected by technological change in tools or
materials, and designs were adapted swiftly
and widely and are helpful in dating historic
pieces. As in all the applied arts there can be
problems of identification as well as in
distinguishing reproductions and restora-

The Clare Chasuble, Opus Anglicanum, embroidered in silk and couched gold thread, English, 1272–94, associated with Margaret de Clare and Edmund Plantaganet, Earl of Cornwall.

early period, metal thread – silver, gold or silver gilt – was available in several forms, as wire or strip or purl (tightly coiled), or wrapped around a silk core. It was most economically and effectively used when couched on the surface, or given a more uninterrupted flow with the technique of underside couching. There were often additional jewel embellishments. Opus Anglicanum (English work) was a prestige product with a wide international demand. The design repertoire was akin to that found in other applied arts of the period, with the subjects enclosed in formal cartouches, and the ground variegated with floral and animal motifs. Embroidered purses illustrate its adaptation on a smaller sometimes secular scale. An amusing distinguishing feature of English work are many-winged archangels mounted on 'monocycles'.

The quality and prestige of Opus Anglicanum began to wane during the fourteenth century and was supplanted by Continental work, from Italy and Flanders. There are records of the cooperation of secular artists in the design, and the technique of needle-painting then reaches the heights of realism. The sumptuous quality is enhanced by *Or Nué* or shaded goldwork. The mid-fifteenth-century Golden Fleece Vestments represent the *tour de force* of this embroidery. They are unusual in being a complete set in original, unaltered condition. The custom of re-making ecclesiastical vestments, and changes in ecclesiastical practice, has frag-

The Crucifixion, detail from an altar frontal, Opus Anglicanum in split stitch and couched goldwork, English, 14th century.

tions. Actual forgeries are, however, usually too labour-intensive to be profitable, especially when it is only in recent years that prices have approached those of other applied arts. Nevertheless, there have been instances of the reworking of dates and reusing of old material. The collectors' best guide is the wide range of authentic and documented material to be found in public collections throughout the world.

There are references to embroidery from classical times but the earliest extant European embroideries date from the ninth century and are ecclesiastical. Pieces like the chasuble of the Saints Harlindis and Relindis, now in the Cathedral Church of Maeseryck in Belgium, and the vestments of St Cuthbert in Durham Cathedral, both probably professionally made in convent or secular workshop, illustrate technical competence in the use of polychrome silks and gold thread on a canvas ground. From an

Cope with orphrey applied with biblical scenes. There are archangels and lilies embroidered and applied to the body of the cope. Flemish or English, late 15th–early 16th century.

mented and dispersed much embroidery of this type, which can now often be only appreciated as detached fragments, reapplied orphreys or restyled vestments.

The secular work which survives is only a fraction of what was produced. The Bayeux Tapestry, vivid and dramatic, embroidered in wool involving laid and couched work on a canvas ground, is unique in its survival not in its creation, and narrative large-scale embroideries vied with tapestries as room decorations. In the Marienkirchen Convent, Austria, is a fourteenth-century wool Klosterstich embroidery of 'The Legend of Tristan and Isolde', and, in the Victoria and Albert Museum, an equally lively German appliqué version. By the fifteenth century, the canvas work techniques of gobelin, cross and tent stitch, which were to develop into *gros* and *petit point*, were practised and understood.

There was also a tradition of whitework,

Detail of an orphrey, Swedish or German, 15th century, embroidered in split stitch and couched gold thread. The abrupt shading lines suggest it may not have been experienced professional work.

Opus Teutonicum, mainly white silk embroidery on linen. Swiss, about 1300.

The Crucifixion, a needlepainted version, of Tintoretto's painting, about 1609, probably
designed by his son and from the inscription given by his daughters to the church where
the painter was buried. His portrait is bottom left.

Panel in *punta rosa*, the background
embroidered in cross stitch. Italian,
second half of 16th century.

'Elizabeth I' about 1599. Her petticoat is embroidered
with flowers and animals, as much decorative as
emblematic, and her gown and gloves with gold and jewels.
The petticoat may have been worked by Elizabeth Countess
of Shrewsbury, as a gift to the Queen.

which exploited the techniques of open and
drawn threadwork, the origin of lace, and
also a form of smocking. Although associated with Germany and Switzerland and
generally termed Opus Teutonicum, it was
probably practised throughout Europe and
many examples are Italian. It was ecclesiastically relevant for festivals of mourning and
purification and had wide secular application for clothing and household linen.

Examples of embroidery become much
more abundant from the sixteenth century
onwards. Much of it is domestic and fairly
small scale, and a high proportion is the
work of amateurs, though their skills equal
that of their professional medieval predecessors. There is a great unity of theme and
motif, the contribution of the new printing
and engraving industries which from the
early sixteenth century were able and willing
to produce a steady stream of books of
designs for the embroiderer, amateur and
professional. The linear stitches, double running or Holbein stitch, and back stitch,
adapted easily to copying engraved outlines,
while speckling conveyed the stipple technique of the engraver. In the early sixteenth-century monochrome embroidery, often

'The fancie of the fowler', embroidered canvas hanging from Hardwicke Hall. Possibly embroidered by Elizabeth Countess of Shrewsbury, about 1570.

black in Mooresque designs, geometric or interlace patterns, or formal floral and leaf motifs sometimes called Spanish work, were popular and were associated in England with the influence of Catherine of Aragon, first wife of Henry VIII, and examples were published in the book by Thomas Geminius in 1548. Design becomes much more figurative in the reign of Queen Elizabeth and the magnificent embroidery on her dresses can, with the aid of emblem books, be read as symbols as well as appreciated for its liveliness, colour, ingenuity and technique. Her wardrobe lists include many examples of embroidery, obviously a valued adjunct to dress. The style was long lasting, and many of the caps, coifs and jackets as well as covers and pillowcases have been dated to the early seventeenth century from their analogy with pattern books such as those by John Schoorleyker (1631) and Thomas Trevelyan (1620), in any case based on earlier works. In England, its characteristics are charming, formalised yet naturalistic, flowers, butterflies and animals arranged in interlace patterns of coiling stems. Many are in multicoloured silks enriched with metallic thread and spangles. The stitches are varied, adding extra relief to the patterns with detached buttonhole, stem, plait, braid, chain, long and short, Romanian and speckling stitches, and French knots.

Canvas work was not neglected, and was employed for the more prestigious and large-scale furnishings. Some pieces, like the large table carpets and the embroidered

'Lady Dorothy Cary' by William Larkin, 1614, wears an embroidered jacket with flowers and birds enclosed in scrolls, typically English in style; her skirt has a 'grotesque' style border as well as floral sprays, possibly 'slips', and her gown is edged with gold. The cap, collar and cuffs are trimmed with Flemish bobbin lace.

Sampler inscribed 'jane bostocke 1598 alice lee was borne the 23 of november being tuesday in the afternoone 1596'. It is embroidered in silks, metal thread and pearls, in a variety of stitches, including satin, back, Holbein, cable, and the patterns include interlace, animals from design books and the alphabet.

'Ahasuerus', detail from a stump-work picture of Esther and Ahasuerus, about 1660. It has a striking three-dimensional effect.

hangings, were professional work and made in one. Another popular method was, for instance, employed by the two most famous needlewomen of the age, Mary Queen of Scots and Elizabeth Countess of Shrewsbury (or Bess of Hardwick as she is known), the practice of embroidering small motifs – emblematic, floral or animal – based on engravings, in the form of small tent stitch canvas pieces or panels, which were intended as 'slips' to be attached to plain materials.

Most contemporary motifs and stitches are to be found on the samplers of which the earliest known dates from 1598, and is by Jane Bostocke. The word derives from 'exemplar', and they are both exercise and sketchbook for the embroiderer, enabling her to store, try out and practise needlecraft techniques. Early examples often have 'spot' or scattered motifs, but by the beginning of the seventeenth century these tend to be organised into bands of motifs as well as inscriptions or alphabets or numbers: essential housewifely aids for the marking of linen. The genre was to continue through the next three hundred years, but samplers lose their functions as 'try-out pieces' for new techniques and colours, tending to become stereotyped, with a limited number of stitches, conventional pictures and pious verses: schoolroom exercises rather than creative needlecraft.

There are national variations; German samplers owe much to Johan Sibmacher's *Neues Modelbuch*, Nuremburg (1598), worked in cross stitch with religious motifs, the Crucifixion and the Agnus Dei; Dutch samplers have elaborate alphabets, human figures, gable houses, windmills and ships; Spanish samplers have the entire surface covered. Predictably early American colonial samplers follow the indigenous national styles of their embroideresses. The earliest example in the English style is by Leora Standish, about 1629. Open-work samplers explore whitework techniques and merge with needlepoint lace. Darning samplers, mainly eighteenth and early nineteenth century, raise a domestic necessity to an art form.

The type of seventeenth-century embroidery quintessentially and charmingly British is stumpwork, allegedly so-called because it was 'worked on the stump' (stamp), and the designs based on popular contemporary prints. It is mainly three-dimensional, small figures, Kings, Queens, or bible stories anachronistically enacted in contemporary clothing, worked in brilliant silks, and couched purl thread over a padded foundation, usually of cream satin, with additional details worked in detached button-hole stitch, darned silk pile, beads and metal strip. The effect is sometimes enhanced with carved wooden or ivory faces and hands. The workmanship is superb, the lack of scale charmingly naive. It is often found on trinket boxes, as pictures, or on mirror frames. Accompanying documentation suggests that it was often juvenile work, a graduation piece after a sampler, and professionally drawn and mounted. The vogue was limited from the mid-1650s to the

1670s, and the most noticable analogies are medieval raised work and fine costume accessories such as gloves and purses of the early seventeenth century, which had an international vogue.

On a larger scale is crewel work, made from slackly plied worsted yarn either single or multicoloured, worked on a heavyweight linen or mixture foundation, and used extensively for bed furnishing. The designs are outlined in stem and double back, cable and chain stitch and the fillings in satin, buttonhole, rope coral stitch and French knot give an almost lace-like effect. American examples tend to be worked more lightly, with

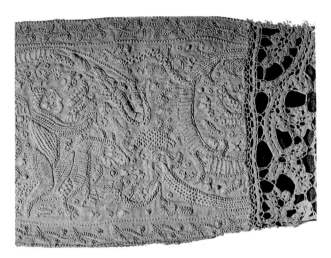

Detail from an altar frontal embroidered with linen, trimmed with bobbin lace. Spanish, early 17th century.

smaller-scale motifs, time and material saved with the use of Romanian stitch which gave a solid colour effect but wasted little wool on the reverse. The designs are a blend of Eastern motifs, deriving from the popular Indian palampores which were first imported in the early seventeenth century, and the luxuriant foliage of the sixteenth century verdure tapestries. Even though designs in America as in Britain may be professional, there is a greater reliance here on home-woven linen cloth and home-dyed yarns, especiallly in the more remote areas away from the sophistication of the towns of the Eastern seaboard. The indigo blue used in colonial America, where this type of embroidery was very popular, was a tradition revived between 1895 and 1914 by Mss

An unfinished waistcoat with the embroidered panels as yet uncut. The pocket flaps and button covers can be seen in the centre. French, about 1760.

Whiting and Miller at Deerfield, Massachusetts. The embroidery from their workshop marked with D and a spinning wheel reproduced these and other traditional forms, also devising modern designs, though it used flax instead of wool and Russian linen instead of homespun.

In the later seventeenth century, international high style was predominantly French and Louis XIV's palace of Versailles set new standards of decor and design. The professional practice of embroiderers is set out in Charles de Saint Aubin's *L'Art du Brodeur* (1770). The only new form of embroidery that he mentions is tambour work, introduced from the Middle East and ultimately an Indian technique, a chain stitch quickly worked with a hook on a circular frame, and in France known as *Point de Beauvais*. It was widely used for muslin whitework, which, in keeping with the later eighteenth century preference for simplicity, began to replace lace, as well as the refined and subtle virtuosity of Dresden whitework with its monochrome play with contrasting textures. Tambour work was to remain popular right up until the end of the eighteenth century, with the vogue for classically draped muslins.

Silk embroidery was a feature on both men's suits and particularly waistcoats, and women's dresses, as well as vestments and large-scale furnishings. At its best it was the work of professionals, either purchased embroidered in the piece, '*en disposition*', or made to order. It was very expensive, since it was labour-intensive and used high-priced silks and metal threads. Mrs Delany, herself a notable embroideress, has left vivid eyewitness descriptions of dresses at the court of George II: in 1740 she writes of a dress 'white satin embroidered, the bottom of the petticoat brown with hills covered with all sorts of weeds . . . an old stump of a tree . . . broken and ragged and worked in brown chenille and around which were twined nasturtiums, ivy, honeysuckle, periwinckles, convulvulus and all sorts of twining flowers'. Such embroidery was needle-painting at its best, mainly in long and short stitch, often with the additional embellishment of couched gold work in which gold and silver thread in many textures was used to great effect. There were skilled embroiderers in London and most of the main cities, but Lyons remained a centre especially for ready-made work for the next two centuries. Silk embroidery was becoming very popular as silks became more widely available as well as cheaper, imported through the China and the India trade. Satin stitch and Chinese Pekin stitch naturalised as French knot stitch were other imports from the East. Among the new materials were very fine beads, used for small-scale

Detail of a whitework waistcoast, English or German (Dresden) embroidery, 1730–40.

An embroidered picture, American, mid 18th century, probably worked by a boarding school girl, and the design derived from a French print.

French beadwork, often pictorial (called *sablé* (sand)) and very popular in the last quarter of the century for costume accessories such as shoes and pictures: there is an interesting series based on the balloon ascents of the 1770s and 1780s.

Canvas work continued to be made, and many amateurs worked coverings for chairs and sofas, as well as firescreens and pictures. Usually of wool, they sometimes have fine detail added in silk. Many are floral or pictorial, following conventional decorative trends, Baroque, Rococco, Chinoiserie or Neoclassical and always somewhat static and genteel – the idyllic moment of reverie. Such work was a feature of urban Colonial America as well as Europe, and in addition to many provenance pieces of embroidered upholstered furniture, the skill of young American girls can be appreciated from the silk embroideries such as the Fishing Lady pictures made at a school in Boston in about 1748. Only distinctively American motifs, such as red wing blackbirds and steeple bush topping the hillocks, distinguish the urban American from the English product. The schools founded by the Moravian brethren in Philadelphia from 1749 also helped to foster silk embroidery, and among the specialities for which they became known are embroidered portraits and memorial pictures. There were also many examples of flamestitch embroidery, possibly even more popular in America than in England. A counted thread technique, it covered large

A tent stitch picture, embroidered in wool on canvas. The somewhat inexpert draughtsmanship suggests an amateur hand. English, second quarter of 18th century.

Quilt in 'Broderie Perse' with applied motifs from a printed cotton on a quilted ground, American, about 1800.

areas easily, quickly and to colourful and dramatic effect. On the whole, a feature of much Colonial American embroidery is the economy of means and materials used in a lively, fresh decorative way. Professional embroiderers were in short supply and the amateurs in a new society were making good use of the more accessible and effective techniques of the old.

An interesting aspect of Colonial Amer-

Quilt with a pieced Mariner's Compass design and an applied pattern border. American, about 1840.

ican embroidery is the inclusion of other European styles. Swiss Mennonites and the Amish of Pennsylvania produced embroideries inspired by Fraktur paintings, traditional elongated Gothic script birth and marriage certificates. Dowry pieces included ornamental show towels decorated with counted thread and drawn work, and samplers draw their motifs from the Tree of Life, pairs of birds, star and flower forms, and the Imperial double-headed eagle from Central Europe.

But the needlecrafts most closely associated with America are those of patchwork and quilting. They were techniques which from their utility had been known across the world from early times, but it was to be in America that they reached their heights of decorative achievement. They are still a lively craft today, considered as celebrations of mutual help and cooperation which are regarded as a feature of pioneering colonial days. Quilting was probably revived in Europe as a decorative needlecraft under the influence of the coverlets imported from India and Persia from the seventeenth century, which with yellow silk embroidery and quilting on a white ground resemble the Eastern originals very closely. It was used

Woollen piecework appliqué, German, dated 1776. It illustrates the cosmopolitan nature of patchwork.

for warm bed coverings and dress accessories such as waistcoat jackets and petticoats. Underlying any decorative design were the regular rows of stitching, straight or vermicular, to keep together the face, interlining, often of wool or cotton wool, and reverse, which might be glazed wool or calimanco. The additional patterns are ingenious combinations of simple geometric forms arranged as feathers, scrolls or flowers, and are often enhanced, especially in French or Italian examples, with Trapunto or stuffed work, corded quilting with an interesting three-dimensional effect. In Europe, such work was often bought ready-made from workshops, but, of course, in early America this was rarely possible.

Patchwork was often combined with quilting, an obviously commonsense and thrifty way of recycling materials for cheerful home furnishings and warm bedcovers, but examples only begin to survive from the eighteenth century, coinciding with the beginning of the new mass market in cheap and cheerful fabrics. A feature of the copper plate printing industry was the making of quilt centre pieces suggesting that their making, especially in the nineteenth century, had become a hobby. Pieces transcend the merely utilitarian and are often signed and dated, commemorating some important personal or community event. The Baltimore Album appliqué quilts, closely linked to patchwork, are unparalleled in design and skilful execution. The patchwork pattern shapes, basically simple, are arranged ingeniously and given often amusing or evocative local names. A very popular pattern, Log Cabin, made from strips arranged to form a square enclosure, is said to represent the hearth and the homestead. The Amish quilting tradition still lives, retaining deep borders and large-scale geometric designs, though materials now diverge from the plain fabrics and dark colours of the nineteenth century.

In Britain, the skills remained cottage crafts, and were only revived in the 1930s with the encouragement of the Rural Industries Bureau. An imaginative and socially conscious entrepreneur like Dorothy Black saw the advantage of a home craft industry in adding to family income in time of slump. Local traditions live on in Wales and Durham and a quilt designer could become a local celebrity and prized asset to the craft and the community.

There was a variety of bed coverings, especially in North America, a response to the extreme climate and multiplicity of national heritages. In addition to stitched quilts, there was woven double-cloth simulated quilting, sometimes locally made but a speciality of Manchester and also known as

Marseilles or Marcella quilts. Others were embroidered with fluffy candlewick, popular in the nineteenth century as naïve easily-made versions of the Trapunto-type corded quilting. The bed rugs, rare and unique to New England, decorated with pile embroidery on a homespun or linen ground in a floral formal or Tree of Life design, have analogies with seventeenth-century Turkey work, an imitation of pile carpets, as well as with other folk rugs which combine the roles of bed and floor covering.

By the beginning of the nineteenth century, the spread of education as well as industrialisation was beginning to effect the needlecrafts even in the most remote places. Sewing was stressed as a basic skill for every girl not merely those of the middle classes. It was the key to thrifty household management, as well as employment outside the home, paid if never overgenerously. The early elementary schools included simple skills as part of the formal curriculum; cross-stitch lettered samplers, knitting, plain dressmaking, patching and darning. The middle-class girl turned increasingly to fancy work to pass her steadily lengthening span of leisure, and to demonstrate fashionably non-utilitarian gentility. Popular were map samplers, ready printed to teach geography and sewing simultaneously; embroidered pictures with classical themes to suggest culture; aerophane floral embroidery, ribbon and bead work to make pretty gifts or accessories. Hairwork embroidery, sometimes with a deceased's hair, reinforced family kinship and demonstrated suitable sentiment. The increasing number of ladies' journals which always contained instructions and patterns did much to encourage the vogue for different types of fancywork.

Skill was much admired and the needle-painted pictures by Mary Linwood, copies from well-known paintings with specially dyed yarns and stitches angled to copy brushstrokes, were at the height of their vogue in the early nineteenth century, and very popular public exhibits.

The demand for finely-worked muslin accessories increased steadily in the late

Quilt in log cabin patchwork, made from narrow joined strips, American, 1888.

A man's agricultural smock, mid 19th century, from Sussex.

eighteenth century. In Britain it was met by the development of a new cottage industry for muslin whitework. It was started by Luigi Ruffini, an Italian, in Edinburgh, who in 1782 obtained official support for a new craft which would provide profitable employment for women and children, that of tambour work. It was a new outlet for the Glasgow fine muslin manufacture, and Mrs Jamieson, the wife of a manufacturer, extended its range when, in 1825, she introduced French whitework embroidery. The craft was also extended to Ireland. The Flowerers, as they were called, made quantities of whitework for home and export, caps, collars, and baby clothes, especially the fine and intricate triangular panels used to trim the fronts of baby robes. It was outwork, and the women embroidered designs, sometimes block printed, in an exquisitely worked satin stitch with very fine and intricate needlepoint fillings and French knots. There was steady competition from France and Switzerland but not until the middle of the nineteenth century was whitework embroidery really threatened by

A firescreen in 'plushwork' and canvas work, American, about 1860.

Portière (curtain) designed by Henry Dearle and
embroidered by Morris and Co. about 1910.

Chairseat designed by Alan Walton, about 1938.

the new machine embroidery, which could not manage either scalloping or openwork. The larger-scale Broderie Anglaise and Richelieu work, bolder in design and simpler in technique, made by amateurs and professionals and much used for underclothes and household linen, became very popular in the middle of the century.

An offshoot of whitework was smocking, an old technique of controlling pleated fullness, but in England, by the mid-nineteenth century, the speciality of a cottage industry for the making and decoration of 'best' overalls for rural workers. By the late nineteenth century it was adopted by the avant-garde embroiderer and adopted to reform dress and children's clothing.

Fancy work, and the provision of patterns threads and accessories, was becoming an industry, and by the mid-nineteenth century huge quantities of designs were printed – floral, fanciful and representational. Some even copied popular paintings such as Landseer's *Stag at Bay* and portraits of the British Royal family or famous statesmen. Drawing, drafting and pouncing and tracing patterns and choice of colours became problems of the past with the introduction of the coloured pattern on squared paper, such as the Berlin publishers were producing from the beginning of the century, though iron-on transfers were not introduced until 1874.

Canvases for this Berlin woolwork were evenly woven in squares and soft easy-to-use wools, produced in multitudes of lurid colours. For the conventional amateur, embroidery could become an obsessional sewing-by-numbers exercise, its aim some garish inessential.

The products ran completely counter to the dictum of William Morris, the prophet of the British artistic revival, so significant in the latter part of the nineteenth century: 'have nothing in your houses that you do not believe to be useful or think to be beautiful'. His disciples attempted to supplant it by allegedly aesthetic embroidery, more muted in colour and inspired by medieval and seventeenth-century designs. William Morris had taught himself to embroider and with his wife Jane made curtains and covers for his first home, the Red House at Bexleyheath. These, as Jane Morris described them, were 'worked in bright colours in a simple rough way – the work went quickly'. Embroidery designs became interchangable with those of Morris's other artefacts, such as wallpapers and tapestries, and were included among the productions of the firm of Morris Marshall Faulkner and Co. winning a prize at the 1861 International Exhibition. By the 1880s some of the finest pieces were being made by Mrs Catherine Halliday, a professional embroideress and his life-long

Waistcoat embroidered for the couturier Schiaparelli's 'Circus' collection in 1938 by Maison Lesage, Paris.

friend. May Morris, William Morris's daughter, supervised and designed many of the embroideries after the 1880s. Some were finished in the firm's workshops, others sent out as 'kits', ready-traced and started, with both the ground and the yarns, thin silk twist or twisted floss or crewels, specially dyed at the Merton Abbey workshop. The stitches most often used were outline, a loose stem stitch and darning stitch. This type of embroidery was equally important in the United States, and the Pomona, designed by Burne-Jones, originally intended as a tapestry and adapted to embroidery, was a great success at the World's Columbian Exposition at Chicago in 1893.

By the end of the nineteenth century, embroidery had been accepted into the art world and that of the fashionable interior decorator. The creations of the devotees of Art Needlework in the 1870s and 1880s and the Glasgow School were appreciated and adapted by the average amateur needle-woman, as were those of Leek embroidery worked on as printed silk ground, Kells embroidery, inspired by Celtic designs and using a polished flax thread, and Anglo-Indian, worked on silk. At its most basic, the needlework of the period exhibits a simplicity of technique, and is heavily dependent on simple satin stitch for smooth filled blocks of colour, stem stitch outlines and appliqué fixed with blanket stitch, and herringbone often worked on silk in muted colours. As influenced by the Glasgow School, it reflected the elongated sinuous lines of Art Nouveau, a new floral repertoire deriving from the Japanese and an interesting attitude to lettering and inscription as an integral part of the design. Very important, in the words of Jessie Newbery, the pioneering teacher and inspiration of the Glasgow School was 'a special aim to construct beautifully shaped spaces'. She also felt that fine workmanship and techniques were aesthetic means and not an end in themselves.

The Royal School of Needlework, founded in 1872 with the aim of 'restoring Ornamental needlework . . . to the high place it once held among the decorative arts', was very successful in raising its prestige and standard of technique. It had great success at the Philadelphia exhibition in 1876, and art needlework was as much a feature of the American as the British home. The designs of Candace Thurber Wheeler, one of the founders of the first Decorative Arts Society and of Associated Artists, were well known on both sides of the Atlantic. Perhaps in response to American patronage, which was artistically discriminating as well as generous, her pieces have a fresh beauty as well as grandeur, reflecting elements of both William Morris and more modish Art Nouveau and Japanese style. She was also technically innovative. Her needleworked tapestries were perhaps in the tradition of William Morris, though the technique simu-

The Jesse James quilted hanging by Edward Larson, American, 1982.

lated that of the original with more fidelity, but her large-scale curtains, such as those appliquéd with roses for Lilly Langtry, and her colleague Louis Comfort Tiffany's curtains for the Madison Square Theatre, looked forward to twentieth-century embroidery and the scope of mixed media.

Underlying the development of twentieth-century embroidery is the liberation of the craft from its traditions. As Lewis F. Day wrote in *Art in Needlework Design* (1900) 'the charm of tradition has snapped and now conscious design must be eclectic . . . one must study old work . . . and then do one's own, one's own way'. The craft had also lost its sole utilitarian connection with the introduction of the embroidery machine by the 1840s and the sewing-machine by the middle of the nineteenth century. The Cornely machine, introduced at the beginning of the twentieth century, made varied individual embroidery pieces and beadwork perfectly feasible. Embroidery by machine had been taught at art school from the 1880s. Embroidery was now a 'hobby', a leisure art and a creative pastime. At one level, in the words of twentieth-century embroiderer Catherine Christopher, it was 'a personal statement . . . enabling a woman to impress her creative abilities on her surroundings and personal belongings'. Its potential was, however, great, for it offered 'textures and colours that would not be possible in any other medium'. It is testimony to its versatility that it remains a craft which gives pleasure to many, a challenge to existing textile techniques, and a contribution to other art forms.

145

146

Man's tunic handknitted in moss stitch in damask pattern
and embroidered in gilt thread. A Norwegian import,
17th century.

EIGHT

Knitting

Irene Turnau

The Virgin knits in the Buxtehude Madonna by Master Bertram of Minden, late 14th century.
She is making a seamless shirt, knitting it in the round on four needles. The shirt was
sometimes included among the symbols of the passion of Jesus.

KNITTING is the branch of textiles which most closely connects production with consumption, since it is a technique used for producing ready-made clothing. Its origins lie in the need for close-fitting and elasticated covering for the body, in particular the head, hands and feet. It first developed in the Mediterranean countries and later in Central and particularly Northern Europe. Knitting may be defined as a textile technique involving the formation of elastic rows of stitches made from a thread of unlimited length, using two or more needles or, more recently, a machine.

Although its history is long and its products many, comparatively few survive, though fortunately sufficient to illustrate the items of highest quality, and provide an inspiration for today's craftspeople as well as a challenge to the collector. Much was for a popular market and, like other clothing in widespread demand, it tended to have been worn to ultimate destruction.

147

Woollen sock, Coptic, 5th–6th century. The characteristic twisted loops show it was made in single needle or 'nail binding' technique. The divided toe facilitated the wearing of toe-thong sandals.

The oldest relics from the history of knitting are socks and other small items of Coptic origin dating from the first centuries AD which survived because of the arid conditions of their original inhumation. However, some of these relics were made by the 'knotless netting' technique, sometimes termed 'Nålbindning' or single needle knitting, using one needle and the fingers of the other hand. The difference between knotless netting and knitting is well characterised by the Finnish country proverb: 'he who wears knitted mittens has an unskilled wife', – that is to say, knotless netting requires a great deal more skill and is thus more highly regarded than knitting. The older technique produced objects of greater strength, compactness, smoothness and durability. In Scandinavian countries both techniques are still in use, but the knotless netting technique tends to be linked more with home production for domestic use. Growing demand for elasticated garments gave rise to the first improvement in production, and knitting, which can use a much longer single thread than knotless netting, began to dominate.

The first products defined as knitted were small in size and usually of one colour. Later objects, mainly of Arabic production, such as cotton stockings, cushions or pieces of fine patterned knitting, have survived in larger fragments, and are generally made from multicoloured yarn. Among the items most frequently found, which date from the early Middle Ages, are Bishops' liturgical gloves. These were knitted from silk, linen, or, less frequently, wool, and are preserved in many Catholic countries. In Northern Europe, knitting developed in the form of gloves, caps and shawls, and many relics have been found in archaeological excavations in Poland and Latvia.

The first technical development in hand knitting involved the introduction of four or five needles, instead of two. Early liturgical gloves suggest knowledge of this technique, which facilitated more complicated shaping. The first indisputable iconographic representations date from as late as the fourteenth century. Four representations of the Virgin Mary from this time show her knitting children's dresses. There is some evidence to suggest that the technique using four or five needles can be connected with the first Parisian knitters' guild, which dates back to 1268, although it cannot yet be confirmed.

Other knitters' guilds appeared in Doornick (Tournai) in the Southern Netherlands in 1429 and in Barcelona in 1496. Guilds of English cappers and hosiers also existed in the fourteenth century. In the late Middle Ages the number of preserved knitted articles – mainly headwear, but also gloves and

Bishop's ceremonial gloves, handknitted in silk and gold thread with IHS on the backs, 16th century and probably Spanish. Such gloves were a part of a Bishop's regalia and emblems of purity.

Jacob's dream, the central motif on a handknitted wool carpet, Alsace, dated 1781.
It was probably a craftsman's masterpiece, a test for guild entry.

stockings – increases considerably in excavated materials from England, France and Germany, and there are also finds from Spain and Italy.

The increasing demand for knitted products, already observable in the fourteenth and fifteenth centuries, and the parallel improvements in technique stimulated the development of the hand-knitting industry in the early sixteenth century. The best-known source of production is the guild organisation, as it is much better documented than rural, home or convent production. The dates of statutes usually indicate the registration of several guild workshops in the towns. Hand knitting adapted easily to the 'putting out' system. As a relatively easy technique it did not require expensive tools, but was time-consuming. The main centres of hand-knitting were Naples, Milan, Genoa and Mantua, Barcelona and Toledo, many places in England and later in Scotland, Champagne, Languedoc, Normandy and Central France, Switzerland, the Netherlands, Austria, Bohemia, Silesia, Poland, the Baltic countries and the large centre in Jutland in Denmark. Guild production during the seventeenth century spread throughout Europe except for the Balkans.

The hand-knitting technique always adopted a vertical arrangement of stitches. The needles, which had to be approximately as thick as the yarn, were usually made of metal, although occasionally also bone or wooden implements would be used for knitting coarser fabrics. An additional implement, 'the knitting stock', facilitated the time-consuming work of a hand-knitter in many European countries. This is a stick of wood, metal or bone with a fork or eyelet, which supported one of the needles in a fixed position, thus relieving one of the

Man's cap, handknitted and felted wool, English, mid 16th century. In Tudor England, knitted caps were legally obligatory wear for middle-class and working men from 1571–1594.

hands of the knitter. It was either fastened to the belt or held under the arm. This implement appears in many countries such as France, the British Isles, Spain, Portugal, the Netherlands, Germany, Italy, Greece, Yugoslavia and Scandinavia. It is connected not only with the work of journeymen in workshops, but more especially with the work of itinerant knitters, shepherds or women supervising household chores for whom freedom of one hand was particularly important. Except for Southern Germany, in the area adjoining Alsace, there is no evidence of this tool in Central and Eastern Europe, which may indicate a smaller diffusion of hand-knitting for sale.

Guild hand-knitting in Europe involved mainly woollen fabrics, but also cotton, silk and linen yarn. In the assortment of items produced, the patterned knitted carpets made from the late sixteenth to the end of eighteenth century were technically the most

complex products and classed as a guild masterpiece. Production was concentrated in the territory within the German-speaking world, and was common in Alsace, Silesia, Bohemia, Slovakia, Austria and some princedoms of Southern Germany. Their production was the most important and most complicated of all the tasks that a future master craftsman had to accomplish. An exemption could be obtained but was costly, and in one known case the candidate had to knit a pair of trousers instead. It is interesting to note that they were the only non-clothing products of the industry. In their manufacture, up to twenty different colours of wool were used, and the largest are about three metres long and two metres wide. It is difficult to ascertain exactly how they were made. It is possible that they were simply stocking stitch on two needles without any additional tools. However, this would prove difficult even if the two needles were each two metres long, since the objects were large and heavy and the yarn very thick. Perhaps three or four needles were used only to hold the stitches since it was a flat piece of work. Once again this is difficult to prove, because the method of keeping the stitches on several needles and supporting the piece on a large table does not show in the final product.

A large carpet would take several months to make, sometimes even six months or a year. Some were heavily fulled and in some cases were raised with a teasel and possibly fulled again. Finally, any uneven surface was cut level. For very complicated designs a type of plan similar to modern graph paper was used. Altogether 29 knitted masterpieces can be found in world museums.

Fulling would obliterate the errors of over-hasty knitting of the woollen fabrics, smooth out the faults in thick coarse yarn, and give the products a suitable thickness while simultaneously reducing their dimensions. The felted surface of knitwear gave protection against stitches running and it was then possible to shear lightly the loose threads without the risk of weakening the durability of the product. The knitters' small

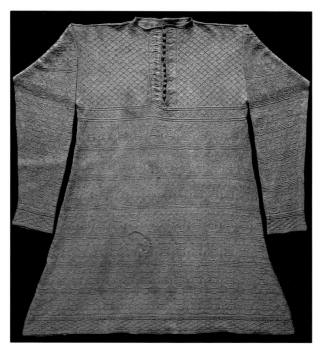

Undershirt or waistcoat, said to have been worn by Charles I at his execution in 1648, silk, handknitted in a damask pattern in moss stitch at a tension of 8½ stitches to the centimetre.

fulling mill performed similar tasks to the clothier's fullery. It was a fairly large trough and in its furrowed bottom woollen knit-wear would be kneaded while hot water mixed with fuller's clay or, later, soap was poured over it. After fulling, woollen garments such as stockings, gloves, caps or hats were dried on wooden forms giving them the required shape, and then ironed.

The best examples of Arabian-type knitting from the thirteenth century, such as the knitted woollen pillow covers found in the Spanish monastery of Las Huelgas near Burgos in Spain, were decorated with geometric patterns and with stylised birds. The European guilds' silk-patterned knitting is represented mainly by waistcoats dating from the sixteenth and seventeenth centuries. There are some scores of these to be found in various European museums, with the most plentiful collection, consisting of eleven nightshirts, existing in Norway. Some of these fabrics, used both by men and women, were knitted in one colour and then embroidered, but the majority were made with patterned knitting in different coloured silk thread. In the literature dealing with them it is suggested that they originated from Italy,

but this assumption is not confirmed by any of the objects preserved in Italian museums or contemporary sources. The earliest jackets from the sixteenth century are to be found in museums in Catalonia, Germany and Lyons. The shirts from Norway mentioned above were imported because they were made by professional craftsmen and the knitters' guilds had never existed in Norway. Coloured, and sometimes patterned, knitted fabrics largely came from the main centres of European silk-knitting production such as Italy, Catalonia or later England. Nevertheless, the determination of their true origin requires thorough investigation preceded by archival research and technological analysis of all the numerous relics preserved in museums. On the basis of my own comparative investigation it can only be said that it was a production meant for quite a large market. Patterned waistcoats in relation to similar garments sewn from patterned silk materials served a function similar to that of knitted carpets in relation to the more expensive figurative tapestries. Hand-knitting made use of much cheaper implements than patterned weaving and its products from poorer quality silk or coloured wool replaced the more expensive woven patterned articles.

A particularly interesting example of a patterned unicoloured knitted article is a petticoat from white wool which the Victoria and Albert Museum has dated at the turn of the seventeenth and eighteenth centuries and attributed to Dutch provenance. Apart from knitted carpets, and the most painstakingly executed waistcoats, it is an example of a beautifully patterned knitted article on which the most diverse types of animals, birds and plants are represented.

The guilds' mass production consisted of the carpets, cushion coverings and other small items for furnishing interiors, but mainly of clothing. From the early Middle Ages, different types of head-wear were one of their basic products. The name for the craftsmen registered in Paris in 1268 ('bonnetier') derives from 'bonnet', the article they produced. In countries with a warm climate they constituted above all a comfortable head covering, worn under a helmet, while in Northern Europe a close-fitting warm cap from well-fulled wool was an essential item of clothing. On the basis of items in museums, pictorial representations and descriptions of costume, four types of head coverings can be distinguished: a hood, usually fastened under the chin, which could be worn under other headwear such as helmet or mitre, berets of different shapes, brimmed hats and night-caps.

Knitted garments were more widely produced and used among the population than is indicated in current literature on the subject. Patterned waistcoats can be considered the highest achievement of hand-knitting. Paintings show the Madonna busy knitting dresses for small children. Although men's dress from the eighteenth century, being large items, indicate machine execution, handknit masterworks specified by many guild statutes were a woollen shirt together with trousers, berets and socks. Warm woollen garments were very useful in Central European climates. In Norway and Denmark, woollen shirts were also imported, being cheaper and popular with working men.

Knitted hand-coverings existed from early times and can be divided into four types:

gloves with five fingers, gloves made up of three parts, covering the fingers in a group of two without the thumb, gloves with one finger, and mittens with which four fingers were either fully or partly covered with a flap while the thumb was partly uncovered. Already in the sixteenth century, knitted five-fingered gloves are mentioned among the basic products of numerous knitters' guilds. The woollen gloves with one finger or made of three parts, used by workers in cold climates, were easily made at home.

Sometimes the history of knitting is linked with the history of the stocking. This is not quite correct because knitted leg covering came into use later than headwear and gloves. Guild statutes show the changes in type of hand-made stockings which from the beginning of the seventeenth century become the main items of production. At first, only woollen stockings and socks are distinguished, later silk stockings with gussets are added and these were expensive and much prized. There are references to knitted silk stockings in the wardrobe of Henry VIII and there is an oft repeated story, credible if not completely contemporary, that Queen Elizabeth on being given a pair of knitted silk stockings in about 1560 declared ' . . . I like silk stockings so well, because they are

A framework knitter's workshop from Diderot's *Encyclopedie des Sciences*, 1763.
The knitting frame can be seen on the left, near the window for the best light. The woman winds silk from hank to bobbin and there is a spinning wheel centre for wool or cotton.

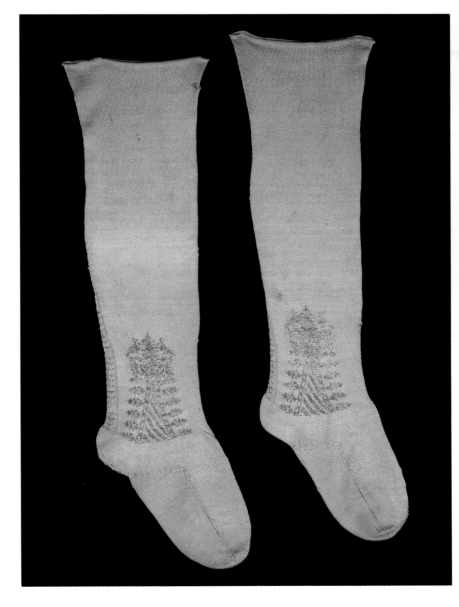

A Dutch lady at her toilette, about 1640, painted by Jan Steen (1626–1679). By the 17th century, stockings could be knitted both by hand or machine. Just below the lady's knees can be seen the ridges left by her garters. At the time a scene of this kind would have had salacious overtones.

Ladies' silk and metal-thread stockings, handknitted, possibly English, early 17th century.

so pleasant, fine and delicate, that henceforth I will wear no more cloth stockings'. The best seem to have been imported into England from Spain. The fashions of the late sixteenth and early seventeenth centuries, for women a slightly shorter skirt and shoes with raised soles, and for men, short padded breeches, made decorative stockings accessories of extreme importance.

Less common were linen stockings, drawers, leggings and trousers. In the peasant knitting of Slovakia, the woollen stockings were sometimes shaped over the calf with special wooden moulds, and heavily fulled. Also, in many European countries and in the Caucasus, a kind of woollen shoe with a heavily-fulled sole and upturned toe was particularly widespread.

Dress accessories were also made from knitwear. The belts and elasticated sashes, used with secular and particularly military attire for instance in Russia and Hungary have often survived. Less frequently used were garters and braces, though they may be found in English and French eighteenth-century relics, and in French cottage knitting of the nineteenth century. There are also aprons, narrow belts or girdles, pockets worn under ladies' dresses and finally ladies' handbags of various shapes and sizes, which were particularly characteristic of the nineteenth century. Peasant dress also included knitted bodices, knee and wrist warmers and knickers for women. Handbags, purses and pillow-covers from the seventeenth century are preserved, for instance, in the Victoria and Albert Museum. There are also numerous knitted panels for domestic

furnishing. These small, usually hand-made, relics testify to the wide diffusion of this technique in the seventeenth and eighteenth centuries. We can conclude that this branch of the textile industry was particularly linked with actual fashion requirements. The slow development of knitting in Russia, Poland, Slovakia, Hungary, Moldavia, Walachia and the Balkan countries was due to the national male costume not requiring stockings. The spread of Western European dress in the eighteenth century certainly increased demand for knitted garments.

Hand knitting was known early in the United States: stockings and other knitted garments were very useful in the harsh conditions in which the first settlers lived, and the technique was known to English, Dutch and German settlers. The local Assemblies encouraged production. The Virginia assembly in 1662 offered a premium of 10lbs of tobacco for every dozen pairs of wool or worsted stockings. Prices were high reaching half a crown (twenty five pence) a pair by 1698. An important centre of their production was Germantown in Pennsylvania.

The demand for knitted goods was such that in the late sixteenth century it was mechanised. The knitting frame, invented in 1589 by William Lee, from Calverton, Nottinghamshire, was the most perfect machine of this period and its complexity aroused the admiration of contemporaries. It was probably the most sophisticated textile machine in common use in Western civilisation in the seventeenth century. It was in use in London by 1599 and by 1612, he and his workers emigrated to Rouen in France and opened a manufactury there. By 1655, the craft was established and the London Society of Framework knitters was recognised as a Corporation. The fasted speed achieved in hand knitting was about 100 stitches per minute, the first of Lee's machines made 500–600 stitches per minute, and later it was possible to knit 1000–1500 stitches, though speeds were seldom consistent even after the frame had become fully established in the late seventeenth century.

In the seventeenth century, the handmade items were considered far superior and were more expensive than the early machine products. It has been suggested that it was the potential of Lee's knitting frame in making goods for the quality market which attracted his aristocratic patrons, for he is first recorded as a maker of silk stockings. His lack of success in obtaining a profitable patent for his invention from the Queen may have been because the government were aware that if it were used to make the staple of a large and flourishing home and export trade, woollen stockings for average daily wear, full-time hand knitters would lose their livelihood, and the women who knitted part-time, an essential supplement to the family income from agriculture. But even by the early nineteenth century its main application was for flat knitwear, which had to be stitched up, while as early as the fourteenth century the use of five needles had made the execution of more complicated types of garment possible.

The diffusion of the knitting frame took a different form in France and England than

Richard Sackville, 3rd Earl of Dorset, 1613, painted by William Larkin (fl. 1620–30), and detail (*opposite*). The knitted stockings with their elaborate embroidered patterns were a high fashion feature.

in other European countries. In England, owing to the weak guild system, hand-knitters did not put up organised opposition against the introduction of the machine, and later, from the second half of the seventeenth century, the powerful organisation of Framework Knitters defended the interests of this group of producers. Much was made in small workshops especially in the counties of Leicester, Derby and Northamptonshire.

Machine-knitting in France initially enjoyed strong state support; nevertheless, production was concentrated in regions far away from handknitting centres. In other European countries the introduction of knit-ting frames was usually connected with the formation of centralised areas of manufacture and a large home or export demand. The knitting machine was a costly and complicated tool, requiring specially trained metal-workers for its assembly and maintenance. Supervision of the whole process of making flat fabrics and finishing them required trained specialists and, consequently, the importation of foreign experts. Owing to these costs, machine-knitting was generally developed in manufactures subsidised by the state, magnates, entrepreneurs or joint stock companies.

In the seventeenth century, frame-knitting

spread throughout the British Isles, France and Italy. At the end of the century, knitting machines were known in Spain, Switzerland, the Southern Netherlands, Erlangen, Thuringia, Saxony and Prussia also in Copenhagen. In the borderland of Saxony and Bohemia, the first types of wooden frames were already prohibited in the early eighteenth century because they were used for the production of coarse woollen stockings, a staple of the home-knitting industry, a profession essential to the general welfare. The best Saxon machine differed from Lee's model in the construction of the wooden part transmitting the drive from the treadles to the working part. Instead of the single wheel of the English machine, the Saxon one had two wooden wheels on the sides. The

spread of the knitting frame in Europe made it possible to use some variations on the original frame, such as that patented by the Swedish inventor Christopher Polhem in 1749 although it was never introduced into Swedish manufacturing processes.

In the eighteenth century, the number of manufacture's using the knitting frames spread through different German countries, Slovakia, Austria, Hungary, Poland and Russia. In the Balkan Peninsula national dress did not require the use of hosiery.

Under the influence of English hosiery the first knitting frames began to be used in North America and later in the United States of America in the eighteenth century. But the introduction was hindered by the protectionism of the English. Like other forms of textile machinery, their export was forbidden under heavy fine. Nevertheless, according to the American *Weekly Mercury* they were in use by 1723: it is possible that they were imported by German immigrants. Bounties from the State governments encouraged the new industry. Selective sheep breeding made long staple yarn more easily available. They were not an unqualified success, because the machines were delicate and often out of order for lack of needles and spare parts. Also the tradition of hand knitting was strong in isolated communities.

The structural transformations of knitting machines which took place in the second half of the eighteenth century were connected with the changing demands of fashion in clothing, and particularly in patterned stockings. These transformations took place first in England, leaders of fashion in this respect, and then were gradually introduced to other European countries. The English engineer Jedediah Strutt built a machine for making knitwear with a ribbed surface which was patented in 1758. Technical discoveries leading to the transformation of the simple knitting frame in the years 1760–1798 prepared the ground for the invention of the rotary knitting machine. It was only with the invention of this machine that the production of tubular hosiery was made possible, because the

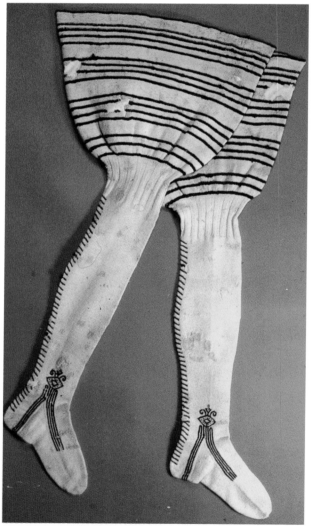

Boothose, handknitted in wool, English, mid 17th century. The wide cuffs would protect against dirt and rubbing from wide-topped riding boots.

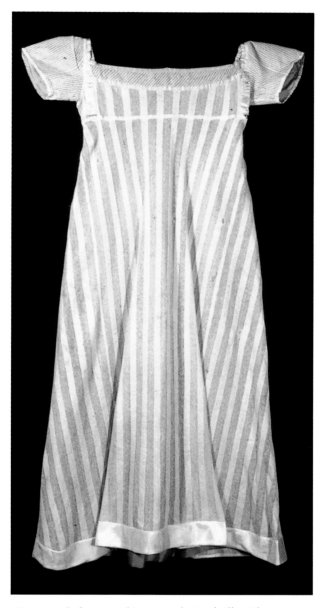

Dress made from machine warp knitted silk with a modified lace pattern. English, about 1815–20.

Man's cap, handknitted in wool and worn with regional dress. Norwegian, 19th century.

Shawl, fine wool handknitted in a lace-like open-work pattern. A contemporary example of a traditional Shetland craft.

needles in it were arranged radially forming a closed circle. This gave wider possibilities for fashioning cheaper knitted garments.

In the nineteenth century, the technical revolution, encouraging more innovative and complex machines for factory and workshop, coexisted with the domestic and peasant knitting industry. In the United States, Timothy Bailey of Albany applied mechanical power to a Lee-type stocking frame, as did Egbert Egberts at Cohoes, New York, allegedly the first to do so, as early as 1831. It was in England that the problem of automatically widening and narrowing fabric was solved. Arthur Paget of Luke Barton and William Cotton, both from

Scottish Landscape, coat, 1981,
designed by Kaffe Fassett for Aberdeen
Art Gallery, handknitted in mixed yarns.

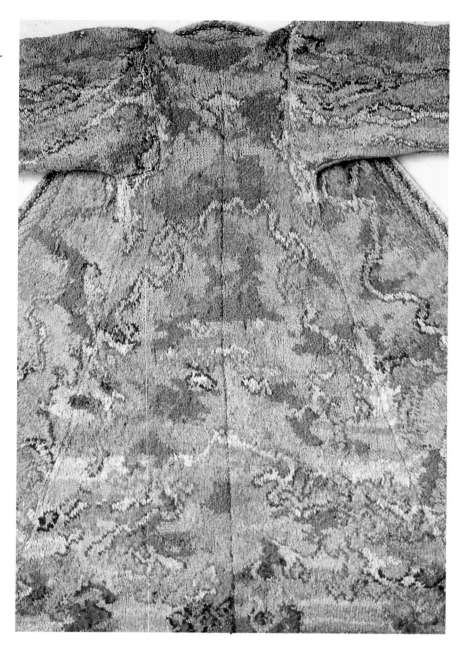

the English Midland counties, also contributed while the use of the wide frame meant that, by the late 1860s, several garments could be made and shaped at one time on the same loom. England was acknowledged to have been the world leader in the production of hosiery but American production expanded in proportion, though catering more for a home than an export market. The rotary machine could produce 144 million loops a minute, which was a hundred times faster than Lee's silk frame of 1599.

The mass production of fully-fashioned and seamless garments in the late nineteenth and twentieth century was dangerously competitive to traditionally woven and sewn clothing. As fashions changed, ladies and

children began to wear jumpers, cardigans, and, later knitted skirts, dresses, coats and nightwear. Men needed more fitted underwear under their more close-fitting suits and it has been suggested that official issue underwear in the American Civil War gave the soldiers new standards of warmth and comfort which they were loath to lose when peace came. Knitwear has had an almost continuous rise in public favour, and the popularity of sports has encouraged the fashion for flexible, easy-fitting and absorbent garments.

Together with large-scale machine production, domestic and popular knitting continues to exist in our late twentieth-century world. The home knitting machine, intro-

Half Yellow Moons, sweater designed by Yoshimi Kihara, handknitted in hand-dyed wool and mohair yarns, 1985.

duced in the 1860s, is now a commonplace, with computer control giving it amazing design potential. Popular knitting patterns from different nations, such as sweaters from Guernsey, Jersey and Aran or figured knitting from Scandinavia and the Baltic countries have become very popular.

The potential hand knitting has for multi-dimensional free form, as well as the wide variety of textures, yarns and colours on which it can draw, have been a great stimulus to the artist craftsman knitter. Originally a development of the crafts revival of the 1960s, it has stimulated many notable modern designers of whom one of the best known is Kaffe Fassett. In the 1970s and 1980s the results may be seen in the popular market and there is a constant interchange between hand and machine patterns.

In the local markets of European countries such as Poland, Bulgaria and Spain, and also in Africa, the Near East and Peru it is possible to see peasants sitting with baskets full of handmade knitted stockings, socks, caps, gloves or pullovers. These are produced for local needs but sometimes the peasants are also involved in making goods for export. This manner of offering knitted fabrics produced domestically for sale in local markets is a very old one, and we see that hand knitting, with its tradition reaching back as far as the Middle Ages, continues to exist in modern life.

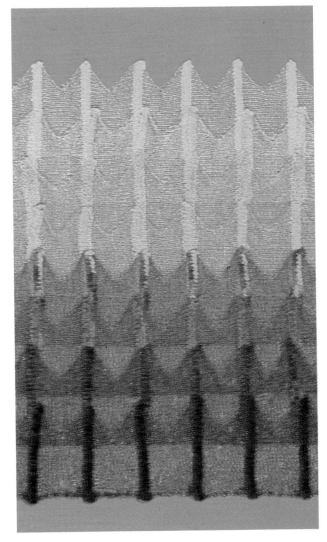

Machine-knit sample designed by Paula Rieu and made on a Jones knitting machine, 1974.

Franz Stephan von Lotheringen, later Francis I of Austria,
in formal court dress about 1740 by M. Mytens. This
portrait illustrates lace in all its varieties; his cravat and
sleeve ruffles are made from French needle lace and the
gold trimmings are made from gold bobbin lace.

NINE

Lace

Patricia Frost

Bobbin lace-making in a cottage at Asnières, France, about 1840, a painting by P. Soyer:
lace-making was outwork, comparatively ill-paid for the skill involved but a useful
supplement to low agricultural wages.

MOST people's interest in lace was probably first aroused by and can be traced back to finding in the attic a small tin trunk of lace wrapped in blue tissue paper, which had been there for as long as anyone could remember. This chapter is designed to provide assistance as the hypothetical layers in the tin trunk are unpacked. It is not therefore intended strictly as a chronological history – indeed, since the top layers in the trunk consist of the most recent items, this treatment is in reverse chronological order – but as a 'commonsense guide'. It starts with the items that are most likely to be found, and ends with those that everyone would very much like to discover.

Before the unpacking commences, it might be helpful to get acquainted with fashion and furnishing trends of the past. Even more useful than books at this stage would be a short tour of the nearest art gallery, or the National Portrait Gallery in London, paying particular attention to the

Brussels needle-lace shawl exhibited at the World's
Colombian Exhibition, Chicago 1893.

lace furnishings and accessories depicted in the paintings. You will also find it useful to buy a magnifying glass so that you can study the structure of lace and determine the way that it was made. However, by the end of your quest you will probably have decided that the best insight into the subject and key to appreciation would be a course on how to make lace.

In the trunk, the top layer, which may account for up to 90 per cent of the lace, will probably consist of highly decorative pieces such as embroidered net stoles, pretty chemical lace collars, cuffs and shirt-waist or blouse fronts dating from the late nineteenth and early part of the twentieth century. It is clear from the great quantity of surviving pieces that an important industry had arisen to supply these accessories during this period. The bulk of this demand was met by machine laces. These are not without charm, but a machine-made lace does not have the same texture or dramatic impact in close up as a handmade lace. Although not prominent after the Second World War, machine laces enjoyed a revival in the 1950s, being used to great effect by couturiers such as Balenciaga and Dior. As far as the trunk is concerned, the most common pieces are likely to be stoles or long shawls of machine net, usually worked with baskets of flowers, either in chain stitch, that is to say, tambour stitch, or with patterns darned into the

meshes of the net, that is to say of needlerun net. A considerable amount of this particular lace was produced in Ireland and is known as Limerick lace.

Alongside these white lace stoles it is quite likely that there will be found black lace shawls, typically 60 inches square, or triangular. They are finely worked, but are usually machine-made, only the outline of the stitches being run through by hand.[1] They date from the 1860s onwards. The feel in the hand is of a sturdy fabric, with a certain amount of stiffness in handling. Most are made from cotton, although some are made from silk (like those of Maltese lace). Generally speaking, these very useable laces can be acquired for very small sums at the present time and their value has certainly not kept in line with inflation.

The majority of recognisable collars that are likely to be discovered are of chemical lace, which has a three-dimensional quality which is easily mistaken for a handmade lace. It was made by machine-embroidering silk, and then dissolving away the silk ground, leaving a fuzzy outline to motifs — this is a particular characteristic which handmade laces do not have. Introduced as a very economical technique in the 1880s, it has been used to good effect ever since.

Of the handmade laces you might find, probably one of the most widely available and prettiest is Brussels lace which in its most usual form has bobbin lace flowers and foliage applied and lightly stitched to a machine-made net ground. If your lace is examined from the other side, it can be observed that the net continues untouched beneath the flowers. Wedding veils in this technique are particularly attractive, most of those surviving dating from the late nineteenth century. Brides are becoming much more interested in 'old' lace now, which means, of course, that once used, the lace becomes a family heirloom and thus disappears into a trunk such as the one we are imagining, for considerable periods of time. However, there are still a good number available at affordable prices.

Another attractive nineteenth-century Brussels lace, this time a needlelace, is *Point de Gaze*, a nineteenth-century descendant of fine eighteenth-century laces. It is widely collected, especially in Belgium, where enterprising lace-dealers have managed to cut up almost the entire native stock and sell it to tourists in the form of lockets and brooches. Both bobbin and needle laces share a common floral vocabulary, being mainly composed of fat roses against leaves with characteristic raised veining. Occasionally, shawls are to be found, such as that shown at the Chicago Exhibition in 1893, among the many collars, cuffs and flounces.

The Brussels lace industry had been established well before the nineteenth century. In the seventeenth century, lace purchases had already become affairs of state. Even as early as 1662, the British Parliament was forced to pass an Act forbidding the import of lace from Brussels because too much money was leaving the country to finance the British taste for fine collars and trimmings. Canny English lace-dealers first tried to lure Brussels lace-makers to Britain, without success. They then resorted to large-scale smuggling operations, calling the illicit imports *Point d'Angleterre*, after the country of consumption, not origin. Examples of seventeenth-century Brussels lace are relatively rare, many consisting of vermicellular lace composed of endless knots, occasionally with cherubs and other figures.[2]

Daisies and harebells, a corner of a Brussels lace collar, about 1860. The motifs are embroidered on a machine net ground.

Silk bobbin lace from Malta, about 1860. The Maltese cross and wheatear motifs are typical, and the Prince of Wales feathers suggest that it is a commemorative or presentation piece, perhaps for the wedding of the Prince of Wales in 1862.

Bobbin lace lappet, Brussels, mid 18th century. Ladies' formal caps were trimmed with a pair of these trimmings. The rounded end was characteristic of the period.

As we progress deeper into the trunk, let us consider eighteenth-century laces of which we will probably find examples together with those of earlier centuries (thankfully, the ladies of the late nineteenth and early twentieth centuries were often avid lace collectors). The general appearance and feel of eighteenth-century lace is of a filmy fabric very much like fine muslin or lawn. At the beginning of the century, it had very little net ground and was composed almost entirely of floral and other motifs, the proportions being reversed as the century progressed. Much of the lace which survives is in the form of lappets, the relics of the fashionable formal headdresses. Every well- and formally-dressed woman had to be seen wearing a 'head' comprising a cap

back, frill and lappets.[3] Many examples of these survive and regularly appear on the market. Lappets would hang from a cap on either side of the head, framing the face. They vary in length but are generally around 20 inches long. They remained an important accessory from 1690 to 1789, costing as much as jewels and treated with similar care. They obey certain stylistic trends and so can be fairly accurately dated: in the 1690s lappets are very narrow and their ends tend to be squared, by 1710 they widen slightly and have more toile, remaining square-ended. In the 1720s the lace is cloth-like and dense, whereas in the 1730s lappets for the first time have scalloped edges and often Chinoiserie designs, reflecting popular taste. In the 1740s lappets have rounded ends and more net ground. By the 1760s they have small trailing toile flowers against mesh grounds similar in motif and movement to contemporary woven silk designs. The lappets of the 1780s have almost straight sides. Exceptional are those of the 1770s designed for the French court. The towering headdresses of this decade demanded lappets at least five feet long.

Another important eighteenth-century lace accessory quite unfamiliar to us today is the sleeve ruffle. Early eighteenth-century ladies ruffles are slender and shaped, tapering from a deeper central motif. In the 1720s double ruffles became popular and in the 1730s they were shaped, often attached to muslin upper ruffles. The weeping ruffle, consisting of three layers, was introduced in the 1750s. After the 1770s, men's ruffles usually single and unshaped went out of fashion. At the same time, women's preference for more simple dress fabrics such as the new printed cottons and muslins, made elaborate lace accessories inappropriate and unfashionable.

Lappets, ruffles and cap backs of both bobbin and needle lace originated from a number of centres of lace-making in the eighteenth century. The honours are shared between Flanders, Italy, France and Dresden.[4] As can be seen, stylistically they are rather similar but they do vary consider-

A cap back made from Mechlin bobbin lace, mid 18th century.

ably in technique. The Mechlin cap back shows the characteristic unspun coarse flax thread outlining the motifs. This is known as the cordonnet. Technically, this lace developed from straight or flat-edged laces such as Valenciennes and stylistically owes much to the French. The first mention of this lace by name in English records is thought to be in the inventories of the wardrobe of Queen Anne. Contemporary accounts call it 'the queen of lace' and 'the finest lace of all'.[5] It was well-established in the seventeenth century but was dying out by 1834 when only 8 workshops remained. The high point of production was probably reached in the first decades of the eighteenth century. Flanders traditionally produced the very finest flax thread, having the moist climate necessary to spin the fragile fibres. Mechlin lace has a very cool feel to the touch, almost slipping through the fingers. By the beginning of the nineteenth century, handspinning was becoming rare, and laces became thicker and less filmy. Patterns involved repeated spot motifs, usually small flowers.

Valenciennes has a similar historical span. A characteristic of this bobbin lace is that the motifs are outlined by small pin holes. As it is all made in one operation on the pillow, large numbers of pins are needed, making it necessary to remove the lace from the pillow after every 8 inches. These technical peculiarities meant that, for example, Lille lace-makers could produce twice as much lace per day as a Valenciennes worker (3–5 ells against 1.5 ells). A pair of men's ruffles employing Valenciennes lace might take 10 months to produce, based on a 15-hour working day.

The high point of Valenciennes lace was probably reached in the 1720s when over 3,000 lace-makers were employed in the area, although seventeenth-century Valenciennes lace survives in small quantities. Valenciennes lace is mainly used to trim fine linen (it is too flimsy to be used as church lace). Hence the pieces that remain are usually in narrow lengths or lappets. It was no less grand for all that, being patronised by the wealthy aristocracy. Mme du Barry is said to have commissioned various *Tours de Gorge* (or neck frills) and lappets. After the French Revolution in 1789, the lace virtually disappeared, but was successfully revived later, both as a handmade lace and in its machine imitations.

The Brussels bobbin lace lappet shows the characteristic ridge-like cordonnet, part of the fabric of the lace, not a single gimp thread as in Mechlin laces. As can be seen, Brussels lace ground follows the outline of the flowers, whereas, for example, Flemish

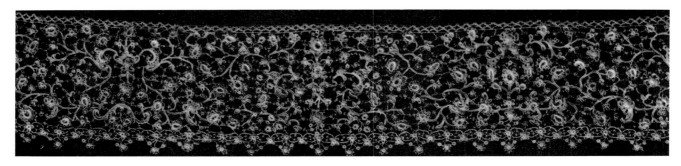

Needle lace from Venice, mid to late 17th century. From top to bottom: point de neige; flat needle lace; gros point.

lace, which is worked all at one time, has a ground that travels from side to side, regardless of the pattern, usually parallel to the sides of the lace. This is a direct result of the industry achieving specialisation at an early stage. Mrs Calderwood travelled through Holland and Belgium in 1756 and noted that the lace-makers divided the stages of lace-making between specialist workers — one would make the flowers, another would make the ground, and still others would work the raised hearts to the flowers. As the ground cannot be worked of a piece with the flowers, it therefore follows their outlines.

An important chapter in the history of lace is concerned with the twin centres of Alençon and Argentan. These cities produced fine needle laces from the seventeenth century onwards, and the history of these two centres is particularly well docu-

mented.[6] This is due to the fact that the lace-making industry was established by Colbert, Louis XIV's brilliant finance minister, as a means of stopping the flight of capital from France, predominantly to Italy, to buy lace. The deficit became so debilitating that Colbert authorised huge investment in Normandy, possibly because there was already a passement or lace and braid industry in the Duchy of Alençon which had been given to Catherine de Medici, a great lace patron, by Charles IX. In 1665, a Royal Ordinance founded the manufacture of *Points de France* with an exclusive privilege to supply the Court. On 17 November 1667, a fresh prohibition against the selling or wearing of Venetian *passementrie* or indeed any other foreign lace was enacted. Further interdicts were issued on 17 March 1668 against wearing foreign laces which should have been the livelihood of a number of persons in the Kingdom. In 1670, R Montague remarked: 'They are so set in this country upon maintaining their own manufactures that only two days ago there was publicly burnt by the hangman a hundred thousand crowns worth of *point de Venise*, Flanders lace and other commodities that are forbid'.[7] The French took the matter very seriously indeed. For the ten years of the monopoly, French courtiers wore only French laces.

Initially, this industry was very good at

Brussels bobbin lace cravat, early 18th century, possibly made for Louis XIV, and worked
with his monogram, the sun, his attribute, order of the St Esprit, mythological figures
surmounted by the rooster of France and war trophies.

copying Italian designs.[8] The monopoly ran out in 1675, after which merchants became exclusive owners of their designs, and the lacemakers paid a fee if they wished to sell their work through another merchant. The high degree of Royal patronage led to the most important artists of the day such as Jacques Bailly and François Bonnemer designing lace patterns. These laces are known as *Points de France* and are characterised by a *reseau* of hexagonal *brides* worked with *picots*. Usually, it was worked with raised work but it was also occasionally completely flat. One can make one generalisation about this lace – it was always a high-quality *dramatic* lace, spanning the late seventeenth and early eighteenth centuries.

After this time, Alençon and Argentan gained the ascendancy and became more and more distinct from one another. Alençon retained its *reseau rosace*, while Argentan developed its hexagonal mesh, each side of which is worked with buttonhole stitches. A further variant is Argentella, with hexagonal meshes containing further hexagons, much like spider's webs. Alençon often has a horsehair stiffening for the *picots*, which meant that it was more often used in winter when the humidity swelled and stiffened the horsehair. Again, after the Revolution and the banning of ruffles in 1794, production fell dramatically. Alençon continued to be produced well into the nineteenth century.

We must take a brief look at early English laces while we are sifting through these layers in the imaginary trunk. Seventeenth-century English bobbin laces match their European contemporaries in skill and design. There are some English specialities, the most charming being in my opinion hollie point, a lace built up of tiny buttonhole stitches, the gaps in the solid stitching form-

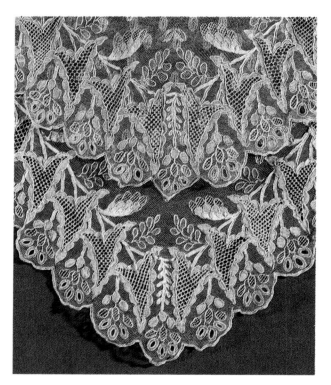

Part of a French needle-lace collar associated with Marie Antoinette, 1780s.

evidence suggests an early date, such as the famous gravestone of James Rodge in Honiton churchyard inscribed 'Bonelace Siller, died 1617'.[10] Certainly Flemish craftsmen fled to Devon from the persecutions of the Spanish Duke of Alva in the sixteenth century and presumably continued to exercise their trade once settled. The problem is that there are no pieces of lace known that can with certainty be ascribed to Devon prior to the eighteenth century. These earliest examples bear a strong resemblance to contemporary Brussels bobbin laces. The Honiton Museum and its associates are currently engaged in interesting work on this subject.

Still to be mentioned is probably the most important lace-producing area, the cradle of laces, Italy. A large proportion of the earliest surviving laces is of Italian origin. Italy shows perhaps the most uninterrupted development from the sixteenth century to the present day. It has followed an almost entirely independent course, with France and to some extent Flanders developing the Italian ideas. The initial impetus was given by underlinen and shirts becoming a visible fashion accessory for the first time in the second half of the sixteenth century; the need for fine trimming arose for the first time with the popularity of linen partlets and, above all ruffs.[9] To begin with, tiny cutwork holes were used to form a pattern, and seams were decorated with open-work insertions, either in white, or sometimes in coloured silks. A great deal of time was spent laundering linens to give them a variety of surface textures. However, the most effective process of monochrome or textural decoration was the use of cutwork patterns and the pulling of fabric to form holes with

ing patterns. This is a lace much used on baby clothes and occasionally for small samplers which are very rare. The most common English bobbin lace is Honiton lace, which by the nineteenth century is very easily confused with Brussels lace. It is produced in Devon, in south-west England. Like Brussels lace, the leaves have raised veining, but Honiton roses often have open centres worked with cross-hatching and have a ground of *brides* rather than a net *reseau* as is common in contemporary Brussels. Roses, shamrocks and thistles are also common motifs. Occasionally birds and animals are to be found too.

There is some debate as to the beginnings of Honiton lace production. Circumstantial

Border of Honiton bobbin lace border, mid 19th century. The roses and birds are typical motifs.

Mrs Vujdags van Vollenhoven, about 1615–20, painted by J. van Ravenstyn. Her ruff, cap and cuffs are trimmed with Flemish bobbin lace.

minute stitches known as *punto tirato* or drawn threadwork. The effect is of a strictly geometric network of linen threads, with patterns built on to the linen skeleton. At some point, a piece of inspired lateral thinking impelled a lacemaker to work in reverse – instead of starting with a plain piece of linen and either removing or pulling the fabric to form patterns, a groundwork of linen threads was pinned to a parchment strip and the pattern *built up* on them with buttonhole stitches. The result looks very similar, but the lacemaker has been freed from the necessity of working from the geometric grid of the linen fabric (as is typical throughout the sixteenth century), and can make the curved shapes characteristic of many seventeenth-century laces. This new process is known as *punto in aria*, literally 'stitches in the air'. The earlier method, cutting and pulling a linen ground, is known as *reticella*.[11] This is really the

starting point of the lace industry – it is the basic building block on which the development of lace rests.

The main centres of these new laces were, as in other European countries, large trading cities inhabited by a newly wealthy merchant class with money to spend and positions to maintain, foremost being, of course, Venice. Typically, in the sixteenth and early seventeenth century production centred on borders and collars with vandyked or pointed edges, whereas in the seventeenth century, Venice developed the speciality of padded raised needle laces of very fine flax, with many *picots*. *Gros point de Venise* was the largest scale lace, designed for furnishings, usually for church or boudoir. The smaller and more delicate variant suitable for costume is known as *rose point*, and the finest of all is *Point de neige*, positively bristling with snowflake *picots*. When Venetian lace has no raised work, it is known as

William Lotton, about 1630, wearing a Flemish bobbin lace collar, painted by Geoffrey Jackson.

coraline or *point plat*. The motifs of all these laces echo motifs found in the sumptuous silks of the time, being composed of scrolling foliage and flowers. Occasionally a figurative piece was commissioned. The feel of these laces is very cool and slippery, as is characteristic of such finely spun flax.

These Italian laces were designed to lie flat and were supremely suited to the fashions of the seventeenth century, that is to say for falling bands and large cape-like collars and cuffs. It is *extremely* rare to find unaltered seventeenth-century collars and cuffs still intact, on their linen supports; however, you will often find pieces that have been reassembled into nineteenth-century shaped collars. It is possible to tell the difference by trying to trace the pattern of the scrolling leaves with a finger. If the movement of the finger is continually interrupted, the lace has very likely been recycled. It is also worth being aware that in nineteenth-century Italy, a lace revival took place, producing exquisite copies of sixteenth- and seventeenth-century laces using original pattern books. The only difference between the originals and the copies lies in the quality of the thread used. By the nineteenth century, thread was machine-spun, resulting in a

coarser, less creamy coloured yarn. The most important such movement in Italy is known as *ars aemilia*.

Italian bobbin laces were a little slower to develop. They derive from the already existing *passementrie* and braid crafts. In the mid-sixteenth century, weighted bobbins (*piombini*) were attached to the threads to prevent them tangling when plaiting. The differences between sixteenth- and seventeenth-century pieces is therefore one of degree, rather than of kind, as is the case with needle laces. Bobbin lace was more likely to be made by professionals, whereas needle lace was also the province of the talented amateur – it was a proper occupation for gentlewomen.

Designs of both bobbin and needle laces of this early period have a strong resemblance to one another, partly due to the importance throughout Europe of pattern books. The earliest probably dates from 1524. It was published in Zwickau by Schonsperger as '*Ein neues Modelbuch*'.

It was firstly meant for embroiderers, but could be adapted for lacemaking. In 1542, Matio Pagano published *Gardinetto Novo di Ponti Tagliati*, and in 1543 the immensely popular *Ornamento de le Belle et Virtudiose Donne* appeared. In 1545 Giovanni Andrea Vavassore published *L'honesto Essempio* and *La Gloria e L'honore de ponti Tagliati et ponti in Aere*.[12] The book most widely disseminated throughout Europe was by Vinciolo whose patron was Catherine de Medici. This was *Les Singuliers et Nouveaux Pourtraicts et Ouvrages de Lingerie* which showed *reticella* patterns for the first time. Bobbin lace patterns only appeared in 1592, with Bindoni's *Il Monte II*, although it is fairly certain that bobbin lace was being made by professionals before that date. In museums throughout the world there are surviving examples worked according to these model books. The influence of pattern books on many of the decorative arts of the sixteenth, seventeenth and eighteenth centuries should not be underestimated. Originality was not at the premium we like to think it is today.

There is one other branch of Italian lace-making which might appear to be the precursor of all types of lace, being of very ancient origin and of which you may find small fragments. I refer to *filet* and to the related *buratto* laces, some of which can be traced back to the mediaeval period. Throughout the ages, a knotted net has been darned with various colours to form simple and effective patterns. It is tempting to speculate whether *filet* and *buratto* were at the height of their technical potential far earlier than bobbin or needle laces. *Filet* and *buratto* laces continue almost unchanged from the fifteenth century to the present day.

With these very early *filet* panels we have arrived at the bottom of the trunk. We started with needlerun net stoles and end with needlerun *filet* panels, with nearly 400 years of lace in between. I hope that this survey, telescoped by its very nature, will nevertheless stimulate readers to make further enquiries of their own. Curiosity is, after all, what collecting is all about.

Late 16th- and early 17th-century trimmings; from top to bottom: two whitework embroidered borders probably Italian, late 16th century; Italian bobbin lace with a pattern of perching birds, late 16th–early 17th century; Flemish bobbin lace, the vandyke edge is typical and the motifs include flowers, bows and stylised human figures.

The Creation of Eve worked on a filet lace altar frontal panel,
Italian, inscribed and dated 1596.

171

'Vulcan and Venus', silk and wool tapestry woven at Mortlake, early mid 17th century.
The flower-wrapped columns suggest the framing of a picture.

TEN

Tapestry

Diana Fowle

'The workshops at Gobelins in 1840', a watercolour by Jean-Charles Develly.
The tapestries are being woven on a high warp loom. Gobelins had been a centre for
tapestry manufacture since the 15th century.

THE term tapestry is often used indiscriminately to describe any patterned textile, whether painted, embroidered or woven. However, it should be limited to the description of a textile woven on a loom and created by the entwining of the warp and weft to make a patterned cloth. There are two types of loom, the high and low warp loom; and several types of weaving method. Tapestry and embroidery are often confused, but they are fundamentally different. An embroidery is patterned with a needle and thread rather than the interaction of the warp and weft, the design being worked after the original cloth is woven rather than during weaving as with tapestry.

Tapestries are normally woven with wool or linen warps, and the wefts are of wool although high-quality tapestries have a large proportion of silk or even gilt thread. European tapestries are rarely entirely of silk, although the Chinese have perfected a very fine form of silk tapestry weaving known as kossu or kesi silk. This is made using the same technique, but the material produced is more fragile and delicate than that of the European tapestry.

The value of European tapestries lay partly in their strength and durability. They were originally used in the Middle Ages as moveable furnishings and they had to be strong enough to withstand being transferred from place to place without damage. They could convert a cold castle hall with stone walls into a cosy, draught-free room with elaborate decorations. Originally they were not designed to fit a certain space as they were intended to be temporary. But by the seventeenth century they were beginning to be adjusted to fit each new room; often tapestries were cut to allow for a fireplace or window and they were sometimes led on round a corner if they were too big for one wall. With the gradual disappearance of the itinerant life style, tapestries began to be seen as permanent parts of a room's furniture. By the sixteenth century they were occasionally designed for specific rooms and were sometimes given elaborate borders which defined the tapestry as a fixed architectural element.

The appearance of borders on a tapestry is quite a useful pointer in their dating. They do not occur in early tapestries. By the early fifteenth century the picture space tended to be finished off by a subtle vertical such as a column or tree. This gradually developed into an actual border by about 1500. Slowly they become more elaborate and by the mid-sixteenth century are often divided into compartments full of decorative details. Grotesques and scroll ribbon ornaments are common by the end of the century. Often the borders especially of late sixteenth- and seventeenth-century tapestries are extremely wide and sometimes they seem to dominate the main subject of the tapestry. They display the Mannerist love of abundance and richness of detail. By the late seventeenth century the borders become narrower and are often composed of floral wreaths entwined with arabesques. The narrowing down is continued in the eighteenth century when the tapestry border is reduced to an imitation of a picture frame. By the nineteenth century tapestries tend not to have borders, unless they were deliberately in an earlier style as can be seen in some Merton Abbey tapestries.

Tapestries were not just used as wall hangings. In the Middle Ages they were sometimes used to decorate the streets for important events such as coronations or

'The Virgin with Musician angels', a silk and wool tapestry, 1500–1515, woven at Chaumont, France.

'Nobody is my name that beyreth everibody's blaim' (Wynkyn de Wore, about 1533), a silk and wool verdure tapestry, Franco–Flemish, mid 16th century. An emblematic figure, he has a winged cap, wears spectacles, carries an ear trumpet and overlarge patterns. His sack leaks money. His waterbottle is holed. The woodland background is conventional.

processions. They were even used to decorate tents on military campaigns. They were also used for upholstery and by the eighteenth century manufactories such as Aubusson and Beauvais specialised in producing tapestry chair seats and backs and helped make them fashionable. Tapestry is still used for this today to a certain extent, although from a conservation point of view it is not very kind to the fabric. Another eighteenth-century fashion was the tapestry portrait.

During previous centuries, tapestries were not merely attractive works of art. They were important as status symbols and capital investments. Tapestries were luxury items and ownership of a set of fine tapestries was a visible demonstration of wealth and consequent power. Tapestries could also enhance the owners' prestige by their subject matter. They were commissioned to commemorate a specific event, such as the triumph of the Duke of Burgundy at the battle of Liége in 1407, or as a form of more subtle propaganda. Louis XIV used tapestries from Gobelins to enhance his image as the Sun King. He gave tapestries to other monarchs depicting himself and his chateaux in the best possible light. They were an effective form of self-publicity.

Nowadays, tapestry owners are less grandiose in their ideas. Few private people have the space to display a large set of old tapestries. Unfortunately, even if they did, it would hardly be possible, as many sets of tapestry have been divided and even destroyed. This is because they have not always been treated with due respect, and attitudes towards them have changed. Early on in their history they had an important practical use but some were only used temporarily for special occasions. By the sixteenth and seventeenth century tapestries were regarded as permanent parts of a room's decoration and were highly valued. However, by the end of the eighteenth century tapestries were so unfashionable that they were often thrown away. Sometimes they would be destroyed in order to obtain the gilt threads. One of the most famous early Gothic tapestries, the Apocalypse of Angers, was used to

A hunting tapestry, French, about 1450–1480: the peasant attendants pause for refreshment.

protect fruit trees from the frost, and part of it had been cut up for use as bed covering. It was finally saved by the Bishop of Angebault who bought it back for the church in 1843 for 300 francs. It is now considered priceless. It was not until the nineteenth century that there was a renewal of interest in tapestries stimulated first by the Gothic Revival, and then by William Morris.

The earliest recorded tapestry fragment was found in Egypt in the tomb of Thotmosis IV. The piece has an inscription which dates it to 1503–1449 BC. The piece is of good quality and implies that tapestry weaving had long been established in Egypt. The Copts were highly skilled weavers. They wore linen tunics worked with decorative bands woven in silk or wool. These tapestry bands and other fragments were woven in a simple fashion and are characterised by the use of the free shuttle. This means that instead of keeping the weft at right angles to the warps as in European tapestries, the weft was used with a greater freedom. It was sometimes used to outline masses in a way similar to needlework, rather than in the series of steps that European weaving uses. Coptic tapestries are of high quality and sometimes have great realism although the subjects may seem rather naive. In the Graeco-Roman period the drawing is bold

and correct. By the fourth century AD, Christian details are apparent and the drawing becomes a little cramped and overcrowded with symbolism. During the Roman period tapestry portraits were popular. Coptic tapestries are not as rare as one might expect, given their age. The dead were often buried in clothes and the dry atmosphere of the tombs and their sanctity has protected these textiles from damage and disintegration.

Chronologically the next important group of tapestries are those of the Gothic period. Tapestry weaving in Europe on a large scale took a long while to emerge but the technique was well known and practised on a small scale in monasteries. It has been suggested that the Crusades and influence from Moorish Spain stimulated demand for and

'The Harvest', wool, Coptic tapestry, 6th–7th century.

'The Apocalypse of Angers' illustrates in a series of seven tapestries the revelation according to St John, who is seen standing on the right. The series was woven by Nicolas Bataille to a design by Hennequin of Bruges for Louis I, Duke of Anjou, Paris 1379–81.

provided the knowledge of tapestry weaving. Other theories hold that it was changes in domestic architecture that were responsible, as it is not until there is a large wall space, such as that of a castle hall, that a tapestry is useful. The growth of rich and luxury-loving courts must also have been a factor. Whatever the case, by 1295 reference is made to 'tapissiers Nostrez' living in Paris. By 1313 there is a reference to weavers in Arras. These references imply that tapestry weaving was firmly established in France at this period. Religious houses in Germany were producing tapestries by the fourteenth century. Many are the work of professional craftsmen and woven on small looms. Consequently they are often only about a yard long but very wide as the warps are always horizontal when a tapestry is hung. These tapestries were used as back cloths behind choir stalls or friezes. They often relate to manuscripts and have elaborate scrolling inscriptions. Unfortunately few of these tapestries survive.

One of the earliest major tapestry series to survive is the Apocalypse of Angers woven about 1380. Until about 1360 tapestries were mainly simple designs with either geometric or heraldic patterns. By the 1370s more figurative tapestries were being produced, possibly due to the increase in courtly patronage. The Apocalypse series was commissioned by Duke Louis I of Anjou from the Parisian weaver and merchant, Nicolas Bataille. Charles V's court painter, Hennequin of Bruges, prepared the designs which reflect the influence of various illuminated manuscripts including some lent by the King. The series is composed of seven hangings divided into two tiers of scenes depicting the revelation of St John. They are quite stark in design with the figures placed against a plain ground, and like most medieval tapestries have a limited colour range. The figures have an impressive monumental feeling and great dignity.

Paris was not the only tapestry centre at this period. The town of Arras was extremely important, so much so that their products became synonymous with the word tapestry (arras in English and *arrazo* in Italian). Tournai and other Burgundian towns were also important by the mid-fifteenth century; the emphasis had shifted from Paris to Burgundy after the English occupation of the capital in 1420. The Burgundian tapestry industry was also stimulated by the patronage of the Dukes of Burgundy; Philip the Bold owned at least seventy-five high-quality tapestries. These Franco-Burgundian tapestries promoted his prestige by depicting scenes from court life, such as hunting, or relevant episodes taken from mythology or history, though some had religious themes. They were characterised by a high skyline and often depict many figures and a profusion of detail; even the material of the clothes is carefully shown. Little perspective was used and the impression of a rich, surface decoration is achieved. The Devonshire Hunting tapestries at the Victoria and Albert Museum are characteristic of this period. Mille fleurs tapestries were also popular. These are highly attractive tapestries woven with many flowers in which the figures take second place to nature, and were popular c. 1450 to 1550.

By the late fifteenth century, the effects of the Renaissance were beginning to be appa-

'The Procession of a Chinese Prince', a Chinoiserie
pastiche woven at Beauvais, 1711.

rent in tapestries. Classical details gradually began to be seen in the architecture even though perspective was still not used. However, the real break with the Gothic style in tapestries happened in 1515–9 when Pope Leo X sent the cartoons Raphael had designed to be woven in Brussels. The first tapestries had been woven in Brussels in 1450, and after the collapse of Burgundy in 1476, the city had become the most famous centre of production. 'The Acts of the Apostles' designed by Raphael increased this reputation. They illustrate the break with the Gothic concept of a tapestry as they treated it as a three-dimensional picture space, rather than a flat decorative surface. They depicted realistically modelled figures in a deep landscape; the lowering of the skyline giving a feeling of distance and recession. Raphael had used tapestry to imitate Renaissance painting. This realism in tapestry designs required a much larger colour palette than was necessary for earlier tapestries. Subtle shading rather than flat areas of colour became the norm. The gradual increase in numbers of colours used over the period we are dealing with can be seen by the fact that the Apocalypse of Angers only uses twenty colours whereas the eighteenth-century tapestry, 'The Hunts of Louis XV' uses three hundred.

Flanders retained its important position throughout the sixteenth century, although under pressure, as weavers migrated during the Spanish invasion, but by the seventeenth century England initiated a challenge when in 1619 Charles I founded the tapestry workshop of Mortlake. Previously the only English tapestries had been produced in Worcestershire at William Sheldon's workshops. These tapestries were mainly small panels used for furnishings and cushions, although the famous Sheldon maps in the Victoria and Albert Museum are full size.

A formal landscape ('Verdure') woven at Oudenarde, Flanders, late 17th century.

The Mortlake factory was a much larger enterprise than Sheldon's founded by James I and was very successful during the first half of the seventeenth century. The weavers received many commissions from the court and used high-quality designs. The tapestries were on the grand scale and often depicted elaborate mythological or historical scenes. The sets 'Hero and Leander' and 'Vulcan and Venus' are good examples.

Gobelins and Beauvais became important tapestry manufactories during the second half of the seventeenth century and were strong rivals to Mortlake. Gobelins had been re-organised by Colbert, Louis XIV's minister, in 1662–63, to form the French crown's personal factory. Tapestries were woven to furnish the royal palaces and provide gifts for other monarchs. They were on a grand scale. One series illustrates scenes from the life of Louis XIV, including the 'Coronation of the King' and the 'Entrance of the King to Dunkirk'. Many of the cartoons were designed by the artist Charles Le Brun with the specific aim of glorifying the crown.

Although the products of the manufactor-

Screen panel from a set of tapestries woven with different birds, Savonnerie, mid 18th century.

179

Tapestry designed for Aubusson by Jean Picard le Doux.

of the preceding century. John Vanderbank, a royal arras maker of the late seventeenth and early eighteenth centuries, was famous for his Chinoiserie sets, which depict groups of exotic figures and vegetation against a dark ground in imitation of contemporary lacquer work.

By the late eighteenth century few tapestries were being produced as they were not really in accordance with the Neo-classical taste. The fashion for wallpaper also contributed to their decline in popularity. However, the factory at Aubusson continued to produce pieces. Aubusson was an old tapestry centre which had been re-organised in 1664. It was not as prestigious as Gobelins or Beauvais and aimed at a different market; often the weavers merely copied designs from other centres. By the nineteenth century it began to specialise in decorative hangings with no narrative. These *portières* and *entre fenêtres* are very popular today. They are characterised by their subtle colouring, often with pale pink grounds, and may depict large hanging baskets of flowers within scrolling wreaths and cartouches.

In England it was not until 1876 that the tapestry industry began to revive. In that year the Old Windsor Tapestry Company was established. Many of its pieces depicted contemporary Victorian life; others were historical but it was not long lasting. The workshops of William Morris at Merton Abbey were much more successful and lasted for over sixty years. The tapestries were designed by artists such as Henry Dearle, Morris and Burne Jones and attempted to revive the Gothic style, often depicting figures against a floral ground.

In America the renewed interest in tapestry at this period stimulated William Baumgarten to found one of the first American workshops in New York in 1893. Weavers from Windsor and Aubusson were employed there, weaving mainly curtains and furnishings. Contemporary American tapestries are very innovative and technically unusual; sometimes the warps are exposed or the tapestry is produced as a three- rather than two-dimensional piece.

ies overlapped, Beauvais tended to produce tapestries which were a little less monumental. They were usually of more informal subjects as they were not woven for the crown, but for private clients. By the eighteenth century these more light-hearted tapestries were very fashionable. The artists Oudry and Boucher exercised a strong influence over eighteenth-century French tapestries as they produced many successful designs such as 'The Love of the Gods' and Chinoiserie scenes. These tapestries all have a feeling of lightness and elegance and are very typical of the Rococo.

In England the Rococo taste is apparent in the London tapestry workshops. There were many workshops in the Soho area of London during the first half of the eighteenth century. One of the most important was that of Joshua Morris. He specialised in decorative and elaborate floral scenes often with parrots and arabesques against brightly coloured grounds. His designs make a sharp contrast to the heavier Mortlake tapestries

Nowadays tapestries are mainly used as decorative wall hangings. We no longer expect a tapestry to copy a painting, but admire it for the skill required in the actual technique and the way the modern weaver exploits the texture of the material, and, of course, the colour and design.

This change in attitude is due to the revolution in tapestry production led by Jean Lurçat working in France earlier this century. Lurçat felt that tapestry production was in decline and not being taken seriously. He wanted the art of weaving to return to its decorative purity and renounce its attempts at realism. Consequently, he reduced the colour palette and banished the use of perspective, the two props essential for realism in tapestry. Tapestry was to be a modern mural with the design based on the interaction of colours and the texture of the weave. Lurçat revived the weaving community at Aubusson and received much international support. In 1945 the Association of Tapestry Cartoon Painters was founded in conjunction with Picart le Doux and Saint Saens and in 1962 the first Tapestry Biennialle was held at Lausanne where contemporary tapestries were exhibited.

Although a large proportion of tapestries must have been lost through the ages, many do survive in public collections. The Victoria and Albert Museum have a large collection of tapestries, one of the most famous sets being the Devonshire Hunting Tapestries (c.1430–40). The Cloisters at the Metropolitan Museum in New York have another important collection, including the set 'Hunting of the Unicorn', and the Cluny Museum in Paris also has a fine collection, including the '*Dame à L'Icorne*' series. There are also rich collections in castles and country houses throughout Europe.

Although one would be extremely lucky to find tapestries of this quality on the market today, many do come up for sale. They are still relatively good value. When they were originally woven some were very expensive due to the intensive labour required in their production and the cost of materials. A modern buyer does not have to take this into consideration. Although so many fine tapestry sets and individual pieces are already in public collections, good examples are to be found both at auction and at specialist dealers. Coptic fragments sometimes appear in general textile sales as do small upholstery pieces. It is unfortunate that many fine tapestries are now in fragments though still with great decorative appeal. It is mainly seventeenth-century verdures and eighteenth-century tapestry pieces for upholstery that appear for sale. French nineteenth-century tapestries are also quite common. In particular, large decorative hangings from Aubusson are very fashionable with tapestry buyers. Nevertheless, whatever the prevailing fashion, all tapestries are worthy of the collector's attention. They should be admired not only for their decorative and design qualities, but also for the patience and skill of the weavers who created these masterpieces and who have provided us with so many examples of the greatness of their craft.

'Black Furrows' (Sillons noirs), designed by Alexander Calder for Pinton Frères at Aubusson, 1965.

Brocaded silk, English (Spitalfields) with a 'lace pattern'
design fashionable in the early 1720s.

ELEVEN

Collecting, choosing and buying

Susan Mayor

Chair upholstered with tapestry woven panels in
designs from Aesop's fables, French, mid 18th century.

COLLECTING textiles is never bor-
ing. It is one of the fields in which
one can still find rare, even important, items at reasonable prices.
Sometimes articles have lain forgotten in
chests or attics for decades. Over the last
twenty-three years I have catalogued Textile
sales at Christie's, and some extraordinarily
rare items have passed through our hands.
Many are now in museums – but not all and
more exciting objects will certainly appear
in the future.

The market is an international one, but
currently it centres on London. For instance,
Christie's South Kensington holds more
Textile sales each year than anywhere else in
the world – about twenty sales per annum.
There are several serious textile dealers in
London, and two more in New York. At the
time of writing there is particular Japanese
interest in western textiles. The Japanese
have organised several important exhibitions of costume, and there is continuing
interest in France and most European coun-

tries, as the museum and collecting world expands. This was not always so. During the early part of this century Venice, Munich and Paris were the main centres, not London. Sadly, great collectors of the past seem rarely to have kept records as to the provenance of their treasures so that it is difficult to establish historic links with their original maker or source. For instance, Mrs Walter Hayes Burns (J. Pierpont Morgan's sister) whose collection of Textiles and Lace was sold in 1980 on behalf of her granddaughter, the Hon. Mrs Mulholland, left no records at all, even though her collection included the important Renaissance Bed Tester of blue silk applied with yellow silk grotesques now on display at the Victoria and Albert Museum. Possibly she acquired many textiles through the decorators Lenygon and Morant as they furnished her house, North Mymms Park in Hertfordshire.

Again, the same is true of the collector who amassed the Important Collection of seventeenth-century English Needlework sold by Christie's in June 1986. We know this collection was formed from 1909 onwards, but no full records were kept. We were, however, able to trace one or two items through saleroom catalogues, contemporary articles in *The Connoisseur* and illustrated reference books such as *Domestic Needlework* by Seligman and Hughes. However, two important fragments of Opus Anglicanum from the same collection, embroidered with scenes from the life of St Thomas a Becket, which were acquired by the Victoria and Albert Museum, can be traced back to 1932 when Adolph Loewi, the Venetian textile dealer, exhibited them in Basel at the Gewerber Museum in '*Dokuments der Textilkunst*'. Fortunately, Mrs Loewi Robertson of San Francisco has kept her father's archive, so there is a chance that research may establish their original ecclesiastical source.

Few records survived of Belgian collector Baron Armand van Zuylen's collection, although we know that some of his treasures were exhibited in Brussels in 1883. Almost equally elusive are sources for the Iklé

Border from a complete set of bed hangings embroidered in wool and silk with vignettes of peasant life based on paintings by David Teniers linked by Baroque motifs. Franco–Flemish, late 17th– early 18th century.

Collection, which Christie's sold in 1989. Leopold Iklé, the lace manufacturer of St Gallen, Switzerland, began collecting one hundred years ago. Some of his hoard was bought at auction sales in Germany but few details of provenance survive. However, it was helpful to have the 1923 auction catalogue of part of it, from which one of his children had bought back a number of lots.

It is an exciting field, and there is still much to discover. Many amazing and rare objects that appear in Christie's sales are

Embroidered picture, 'A Visit to the Tomb of Rousseau', French, about 1800.

Chasuble with orphrey embroidered with silk and gilt thread, German, early 16th century. From the Van Zuylen Collection.

virtually unknown until they reach us.

In their time, early textiles were rated very highly, if only for their cost of production. They were therefore very carefully looked after – that is why so many have reached us in remarkably good condition. It was really only during the second quarter of the twentieth century that there was an almost total disregard for the textile arts. Luckily this was a period when American collectors such as Mrs Walter Burns and the Founders of Colonial Williamsburg – to say nothing of the American who had acquired the magnificent vestments Christie's sold in 1976 – were all building up their holdings.

Now things are very different. There are some serious collectors – but still not enough – so with luck little of interest will ever again get thrown away or burnt.

Particularly at risk is the costume, too apt to be worn out and altered as fancy dress, and couture clothes which still have fashion potential or are regarded as personalia or trivial with built-in obsolescence. Sir Cecil Beaton, searching for Haute Couture, the nucleus of the Victoria and Albert Museum Fashion collection, came across many instances where important designers' work had been discarded. However, this was twenty years ago: people are now much more aware and many specialise in this area.

There have been some superb exhibitions

of Costume and Textiles recently, in particular 'The Age of Napoleon', at the Costume Institute of the Metropolitan Museum, New York early in 1990 and the 'Belle Epoque' Exhibition at the Brooklyn Museum. Curators such as Christa Mayer Thurman of the Art Institute of Chicago and Naomi Tarrant of The Royal Scottish Museum, Edinburgh, have built up very fine collections in recent years. This must surely spur on more and more people to collect. And the catalogues of the exhibitions have become text and source books.

Coptic tapestry panel, late 4th–early 5th century, woven with a goddess holding lotus blooms. From the Iklé Collection.

If you are interested in textiles, you must get into the habit of visiting as many textile collections in Museums as possible, as well as antique shops specialising in the same field. Then, of course, there are the salerooms. Christie's sell the most at their South Kensington branch; fine American needlework pictures, samplers and quilts also appear in their auctions of Americana in New York. Phillips hold regular sales in London at their West Two saleroom, and Sotheby's include textiles in their Collector's sales. Bonham's sell textiles at their Lots Road saleroom in South-west London. The auctioneers at the Hotel Drouot in Paris also cover textiles, occasionally holding specialised textile sales. Many country auctioneers

also deal in textiles. Most auctions in Britain are advertised in the *Antique Trade Gazette*. Sales abroad tend to have different regulations from those in the United Kingdom, so it is as well to check conditions of sale beforehand.

No collector can do without regular subscriptions to sale catalogues. Christie's are published two-and-a-half to three-and-a-half weeks in advance so that they can be despatched in time to overseas clients. The items are normally 'on view' to prospective purchasers for a day and a half beforehand.

It is really only by looking at as many textiles as possible that a new enthusiast will 'get his eye in'. Only by comparing textiles in both good and bad states can you accurately gauge condition, possible alteration and quality. It is also very useful to have a good visual memory. Rarity, condition and quality are all important considerations in buying textiles. But many other factors come into play too, such as usefulness and supply and demand. Perhaps these last points are most important of all.

When cataloguing textiles at Christie's we do not normally mention condition unless a Lot is illustrated. But should you not have time to come and view an item yourself you can always write, fax, or telephone and we will check for you. You should also bear in mind that our estimates are based partly on condition: so if something appears to have rather a low estimate, that very often means that it is in a poor state.

What should you buy? People always say 'buy the best you can afford'; and many do. But once they find something they want even more, they then sell some of their earlier purchases to finance their new acquisition – thus upgrading their collection.

What should you choose? As you will have gathered from other contributions in this book, there are so many types of textiles from which to select. Over the last twenty-three years I have handled many specialised collections. They always generate more interest and often higher prices. One fascinating series of samplers was formed by a lady who had attempted to buy dated examples

Valance embroidered with a Chinoiserie design, French, late 17th century,
from hangings from a château in the Dijon area.

to cover each year for 100 years from 1760 to 1860 – and she almost succeeded.

Dr Iklé was a textile manufacturer himself, so the strength of his collection was techniques, weaves and stitches. The owner of the Very Important Collection of Needlework we sold in 1986 hardly ever strayed from English seventeenth-century needlework, and he seemed particularly interested in raised (or stump) work. Today I know of people who are building up collections of printed commemorative handkerchiefs and of seventeenth- and eighteenth-century damask table-linen – both of which are fascinating and involve endless research.

Where there are authoritative, well-illustrated reference books on a subject, this is of immense use and encouragement to collectors. Notable in their particular fields are Santina Levy, *History of Lace* (1986) and Nathalie Rothstein, *Flowered Silks* (1990). Other useful books are Linda Parry's *Textiles of William Morris* (1988) and Josette Bredif's *Toiles de Jouy* (1989). Exhibition catalogues especially those that are comprehensive provide guidance on identification and dating as well as an introduction to the subject. Among textiles recently examined are damasks, otherwise very difficult to research. These are treated in A.C. Panwell's *Damask*, Museum voor oud Heidkunde en Sierkunst, Kotrijk (1986). *Raoul Dufy* was the subject of a Hayward Gallery Exhibition with catalogue in 1987, and Linda Parry wrote a useful book, *Textiles of the Arts and Crafts Movement* for the Victoria and Albert Museum Exhibition in 1988.

Textile art is not normally a field where

Portfolio embroidered with The Three Fates in coloured silks and metal thread, English, mid 17th century.

you will find forgeries, although a great many eighteenth-century designs were pirated in the nineteenth and early twentieth centuries. This occurred particularly in furnishing textiles and in silks used for vestments. Such nineteenth-century church silks woven in eighteenth-century style, are termed *drap d'eglise*. It is only from experience, and knowing how textiles were woven, that one can tell the difference – sometimes it is even difficult for specialists.

At the end of the nineteenth century there was a revival of interest in the medieval, and at Krefeld in Germany they wove silks recreating ninth-century fragments excavated from the tombs of early Saints. Some of these were deliberately aged and the selvages were removed by unscrupulous dealers with intent to deceive.

When buying silks it is obviously important to buy a piece with at least one full repeat of the design and if possible a piece with both its selvages.

Most damage to textiles can be repaired but repair work is very labour-intensive and thus highly expensive. A tear, for example, on an otherwise sound piece will discount that piece by some 10–20 per cent. A series of such tears, which indicates that the fabric

structure is weakened, probably removes half its value or more. The most extreme case is shattered silk, which occurs in fabrics of the late nineteenth to early twentieth centuries. Here, too much lead weighting has been applied in order to give a lustrous effect so the silk begins to fall apart. Such items lose almost all their value.

Dyes fade, and of course this sometimes produces a pleasant effect – but otherwise it affects the value considerably. White silk stains to a dull pale brown. This can sometimes be bleached out – but not only does this often weaken the silk, it also bleaches any colours which have been applied. A faded and stained silk-embroidered picture is worth only about one third of a bright one. A good way to test the degree of fading is to look at the reverse of the fabric.

If you are intending to use any textiles be sure that they are sound. It matters less if you are going to frame them, and less still if you are going to keep them stored in the dark for reference. In any case, they should never be left in the light for a long time.

What could you collect? Tapestries and carpets tend to be a specialised market. Romanesque figured silks never appear on the market – well hardly ever – and few

'The Monuments of Paris', a French (Jouy) printed cotton, dated 1818.

Tapestry with fanciful hunting scene of wild men and women, Swiss, 1468–76. The arms of
the Breitenlandberg and Flachslandt families for which it was originally made can be seen
in the corners.

pieces of Opus Anglicanum. Eighteenth-century woven carpets are highly expensive, as are embroidered shoes. Silk dresses dyed with Perkin's Purple, the first aniline dye, are rare and sought after. Also they can fade in a short time. It would be difficult today to collect these in good condition. When the Science Museum bought one at Christie's, the editor of this book sent over a large black bag to cover it on its journey across two London streets, for fear of fading.

There are certain subjects that are already collected seriously, and these tend to be more expensive than others: printed commemorative handkerchiefs and shoes, for instance. It might be easier to select something plentiful such as samplers, quilts, Berlin woolwork, nineteenth-century *drap d'église* silks, perhaps even William Morris textiles, eighteenth- and nineteenth-century vestments, needlework tools, parasols, hats, gloves, stockings. You might select embroidered pictures of all forms. Pretty, late eighteenth-century – early nineteenth-century silkwork pictures are readily available. You could choose biblical themes, topics from literature or subjects involving shepherdesses. If they are in their original oval frames, these command a premium – sometimes of over 100 per cent. A clue can

be the framer's label – that occasionally survives on the back. These are sometimes easier to date than the frames themselves. If the label is interesting it can, of course, add to the value. Some of the 1820 French chenille-work pictures come in their original black and gold glass mounts, *verre eglomisé*, which if marked with the name of the Lyonnais framer are enhanced in value.

Woolwork Sailor's pictures are much sought after, particularly if they have elaborate details. There were some copies of these produced in the early 1980s, often backed with old newspapers and deliberately aged – so one should be on one's guard. Berlin woolwork can be very decorative, particularly items featuring dogs and flowers, sometimes combined with plushwork and beadwork.

There are a considerable number of different types of shawl. A collector today could buy them from many parts of the world. For instance, the European centres for shawl-making were Edinburgh, Norwich, Paisley, Vienna, Lyons, Nimes and Paris. You might choose textiles from a particular region – where you come from or where you go on holiday. The scientific-minded enthusiast might collect textiles for the dyes used.

If you want a smaller field you must think

189

Patchwork quilt made of wool from Crimean war uniforms, possibly by convalescent soldiers. English, about 1860. Plain woollen fabrics are rare survivals.

harder. Here are a few possibilities: embroidered purses, the very finest seventeenth-century examples can fetch thousands of pounds, but pretty eighteenth- and nineteenth-century versions could cost about £100; embroidered regional hats, which make a most decorative display; damask, Liberty textiles or twentieth-century textiles designed by artists such as Fortuny, Gallenga, Dufy, Michael O'Connell, and Henry Moore.

For those with fuller purses there are Polish sashes, seventeenth-century beadwork, and, at the most expensive end of the market, eighteenth-century embroidered clothes and embroidered leather shoes, and Renaissance vestments.

Stirring events in Eastern Europe may now turn up fine 'peasant' embroidered costume. Indeed, the long-term economic improvement in these countries should force prices up eventually.

Many subjects are under-explored: bed linen, for example. I do not know anyone who actually collects bed linen seriously. Brooklyn Museum has a marvellous display showing a bed with all the accoutrements. If you happen to build up a serious dated collection, your collection would surely be in great demand when exhibitions were being mounted.

Finally, lace comes in many forms. You could collect lace of a particular period or place or involving a particular use such as fans, collars, lappets or handkerchiefs.

Who buys what and why? Museums collect most important examples. These can be surprisingly cheap, especially if no-one else is interested. A parasol of great technical importance – but of little aesthetic merit – cost the Victoria and Albert Museum only £55 at Christie's, South Kensington. Had a keen collector been there the price would, of course, have been higher. Other buyers include collectors themselves, dealers buying for clients, as well as for stock. Decorators look for cushion covers, tassels and tie backs. Some like embroidered pictures for their clients' walls. Then there are designers of textiles, wallpapers and dresses, for films and the theatre – all looking for inspiration. You will also find general antique dealers buying textiles and needlework as stock to make their shops look more attractive. National variations exist among collectors' preferences: Americans have a particular fondness for the work of Fortuny and Gallenga. As in every other market, different people want textiles for different reasons.

Prices are still rising. A skilled collector can do better than the market by building up a collection which, when sold, can be seen to be especially interesting. The best is usually 'variety around a theme'. If exhibition organisers want to borrow your goods, then encourage them, providing they will be displayed and handled under museum conditions. Make sure you keep a catalogue of every item you own – notes of where you bought it, when and for how much. Any clue as to identification and provenance might help you in the future when you have acquired a greater knowledge about the sub-

Ladies shoes, early 18th century: on the left, embroidered, and on the right, made from brocaded silk.

ject. Should you decide to sell, any detail of provenance or history adds significantly to the value. An inventory, with photographs, is also important should you happen to be burgled.

Even if there is no antique textiles dealer near you, you are probably within reach of antique collector's fairs. Because textiles are still reasonable in price, you will find them in antique markets such as London's Portobello Road and Le Marché aux Puces in Paris. If they are not too busy, antique dealers are delighted to talk about their goods and you can learn much in this way. As your experience increases you can possibly even find good textiles in jumble and car boot sales. Some of the rare objects sold at Christie's South Kensington were found by vendors in this manner, including a Jacobean nightcap bought for only £10 which sold for £2,300; a pair of rare early Georgian shoes and a Fortuny dress bought for 50p which sold for £800. Some items for the specialist collector can be bought more cheaply in country auctions than in London – costume springs to mind. It fetches reasonable prices even in the usually very expensive country-house dispersals. On the other hand, decorative embroidery sometimes

fetches as much or more in a specialised London saleroom.

It is well worthwhile buying exhibition catalogues while exhibitions are in progress. They are always harder to find later on and usually expensive. However, to find catalogues of exhibitions that have already taken place, it is worth visiting antiquarian or specialist art bookshops, or libraries, or contacting the museums concerned. Once you let specialist booksellers know of your interest, you can ask to be placed on their mailing lists. Textile reference books also appear in book auctions and Christie's sometimes include sections of them in textile sales. So far we have sold several textile reference libraries – in particular a Swiss collection which formed an entire sale in 1987 with many rare tomes long out of print. The sale fetched £75,000. We also sold the late Mrs Doris Langley Moore's Archive of Fashion Plates and reference books which contained many fine and rare items.

These are just a few hints for the budding collector of antique textiles and costume. As time goes on you will build up your own expertise – and perhaps your own secret sources of supply!

Fan of Brussels lace mounted with mother of pearl, French, about 1862.

A horseman on a felt-hanging from Pasyryck in the
Caucusus, 2nd century BC. It has survived in the sealed
stable conditions of the burial mound.

Caring for your collection

Karen Finch with Danielle Bosworth

Fungus obscures this silver thread embroidery
but is removable under laboratory conditions.

I N COMPARISON with other historic artefacts, very few textiles have survived to
become collectable, possibly because
they are the only artefacts that could
ultimately end up as dusters or − in the case
of the Apocalypse tapestries now at Angers
− as cover blinds for greenhouses. Fortunately they were rescued to give continuing
delights as works of art.

Convincing proof that prevention of damage is the best form of conservation comes
easily to mind, because of the traditional

image of family heirlooms, such as wedding
dresses, christening robes or embroidered
samplers, stored in old chests. Heirlooms
have special significance in people's lives,
not least when they have been treasured as
mementoes of family events together with
letters, diaries, sketches, or photographs
showing them as they were used or worn.
The way they have been kept has a particular importance, beginning with the chest
itself, which was often made from cedarwood, with its legendary reputation for

The Adoration of the Beast from the Apocalypse of Angers tapestry series, Paris 1379–81;
forgotten and in the late 18th century used to cover a greenhouse,
it has now been rescued and restored.

keeping things safe and free of insects. Only the best was ever deliberately put away and the wrappers, often consisting of old sheets, table-linen or even old petticoats, were considered expendable. They were used as protection from dust and contact with bare wood and it is to this practice that we owe the continued existence of some plain utilitarian textiles that today are even rarer than the objects they were used to protect.

The survival of heirlooms depended on family sentiment and space for storage, but collections are conscious, not chance, accumulations, often put together for the purpose of comparing and studying one particular aspect of human endeavour or natural phenomena. In the past, institutional care of collections owed much to the precepts of Cathedral treasuries with, for example, their custom-built storage shaped to fit copes and chasubles. Their precautions have preserved untold wealth, and the corresponding care given to their archives can sometimes yield essential information relating to the source, date and purpose of the objects themselves.

There can be no doubt that family heirlooms as well as religious relics such as the Turin Shroud have survived because of the care taken of them. They have both benefited from good 'housekeeping' which has provided clean surroundings free from moth and mould. In a domestic context, it was customary to have blinds and lined curtains for keeping out the light when rooms were unoccupied and loose covers, which would only be removed on very special occasions, to protect fine furnishings from wear and tear. We should not forget that when Mrs Beeton wrote her book *Household Management* in 1858, it was based on practices of good housekeeping that derived directly from the medieval housewife's desire to protect precious hangings and covers. This daily care and common sense have preserved many treasures of the recent past for our delight and curiosity today. Now modern scientists, by studying the conditions that have preserved ancient textiles, have helped us to gain a further understanding of the factors affecting the survival of organic materials over a long period. Their work has given important guidelines for the establishment of better conditions in present-day textile collections.

Conditions of survival

The reasons for the survival of textiles from early times have varied but have always depended on the characteristics of their fibres, dyestuffs and finishing treatments and the reaction of these to one another as well as to their environment.

The most destructive influence on all organic materials is light. A damp atmosphere such as prevails in Britain is the next most serious danger. High relative humidity activates any problem present in the composition of an object. Separately, each fibre survives according to its built-in characteristics and earlier treatment, but when together in a weave, under conditions of high relative humidity, fibres tend to degrade in the following order: silk – linen – cotton – wool. Silk does not tolerate being with any other fibre – linen is damaged by cotton and wool. Wool lasts the longest – except in alkaline conditions.

Wool lasts well in damp and slightly acid conditions which tend to destroy bast fibres such as linen in a relatively short time, but, of course, wool succumbs to moth. Thus it is the conditions in which they are kept, not age, which govern the survival of textiles. Those of both plant and animal origin have survived in the dry dark tombs of Peru and Egypt, in deep caves with a similar environment, in the ice and permafrost of Asian tombs, or on embalmed or mummified bodies buried in churches and graveyards.

The Turin shroud; a relic carefully preserved in a cathedral treasury. Made from linen, it is now considered to be not from the time of Christ but mediaeval. This photographically enhanced image brings out the cryptic staining.

195

A 16th-century brocaded silk faded and destroyed by excess light.

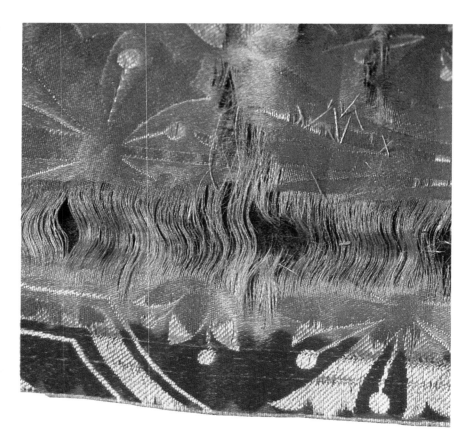

Some have even been retrieved from refuse heaps where a substrate of sand may have been the prerequisite for survival. Woollen fabrics alone as well as complete bodies have been found in peat bogs in Denmark, Ireland, Scotland and Sweden, and in the oak coffin burials of the Danish Bronze Age. Their survival stems from the conditions of their keeping combined with their built-in properties and characteristics.

In *Bockstensmannen och hans Dräkt* (The Bocksten Man and his Costume) by Margareta Nockert, peat formation and the degradation of organic substance in a swamp is described by Dag Fredriksson as follows: 'The Bocksten bog began with the eutrophication of a lake. The raised bog which evolved was cut off from the surrounding groundwater and thus became entirely dependent on the poor nourishment supplied by precipitation. The peat in these strata is made up predominantly of sphagnum moss. Most bacteria and fungi are aerobic. Consequently a poor supply of oxygen will mean slow humification. In stagnant bog water, the oxygent content is so low that the process of bacterial humification comes to a standstill only a few decimeters (less than a foot) below the surface of the water. Most humification therefore takes place in the superficial strata of the peat'. The Bocksten man was found in 1936. The book quoted is a re-evaluation of this 600-year-old find.

The conditions that led to the preservation of the contents of oak coffins are described [in translation] in *Bronzealderens Dragter* (Bronze Age Dress) published by Viborg Stifts Museum, Denmark:

'For a grand burial a large oak was felled for the coffin, which would be about ten feet long. The oak was halved lengthwise and each piece hollowed out as for a boat. The bottom part was placed on a bed of stones with large stones supporting the sides. A layer of fresh green plants that often included wild chervil was placed inside and covered by a cowhide with the hair inside. The body was dressed and laid on the cowhide, weapons or jewellery and other grave goods were put in place, such as vessels containing mead and food and perhaps extra clothes and blankets. Finally, the edges of the cowhide were folded over the body and the top part of the oak bole tightly fitted so that no earth could get in during the subsequent work of building the barrow. The coffin would be covered with layers of moss and peat, or seaweed and heather interspersed with grass turves. More grass turves would be put on top till the barrow had reached its planned size – this might use up the grass and topsoil of several acres of land. Large stones would be placed round the circumference of the barrow with smaller stones filling the gaps in between.

'The process that led to the preservation of some of the oak coffins and their contents started right away. The peat and grass turves contained a certain amount of moisture, which could combine with the humic acids that are particularly common in the soils of some areas of Jutland; when humic acids make contact with oxygen, iron is produced, and iron would knit with grains of sand to form impenetrable layers of hard pan. Layers would form below the coffin because of the oxygen from the original field under the barrow as well as above because of the oxygen from the rainwater seeping through the grass turves. When the layers eventually joined up, they would form a shell or capsule around the coffin that would provide a relatively constant degree of humidity. Oakwood in humid surroundings produces tannin which destroys vegetable fibres but has a preserving influence on wool, wood, horn and leather. Skeletons are rarely found, because acid conditions precipitate decomposition of the calcium salts of bones. Should the shell get broken through digging or a collapse of the barrow the coffin and the capsule and its contents will quite rapidly disappear.'

The National Museum of Denmark has conducted investigations of a number of burial sites in Denmark and Greenland. One such investigation concerned the coffin in the crypt of Faarevejle church that is believed to contain the mummified remains of the Earl of Bothwell. The Earl was kept prisoner in Malmø Castle and later Dragsholm Castle by the King of Denmark from September 1567 until he died on 14 April 1578. When the coffin was first opened in

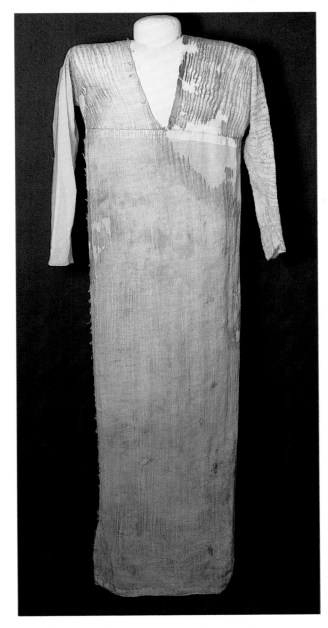

A tunic of pleated linen, a woman's funerary dress, Egyptian, about 2400BC, which has survived in the dry sealed conditions of an Egyptian burial. On discovery, it was an enigmatic crumpled bundle; skilful restoration has restored its contours. Only part of the sleeve and skirt have needed replacement.

1858, its contents were in good condition. It was opened again in 1915, when the head was x-rayed. The report of the 1915 investigations states that the Earl had been laid to rest on straw mixed with chrysanthemum flowers (C. parthenium) and that the straw, which normally would be quickly eaten up by insects, was still there and in good condition because the alkaloids of the flowers had killed the insects.

In 1975 the coffin was again investigated and the National Museum invited to analyse the textile fragments: silk, linen, cotton. Only a few tatters remained of the white linen shroud of the 1858 description but remnants of the green silk coffin lining, the linen shirt and knitted stockings, a piece of cotton and flower shapes cut from black paper and used for decoration were still present. The mummification of the body and the preservation of the silk and plant fibre including the chrysanthemum petals is attributed to the fact that the church was built over a layer of sand. Sand is alkaline and allows any moisture to drain away very quickly.

Other conditions in which textiles have survived include underwater environments of silt and clay and postholes from ancient buildings where lack of oxygen and a consequent anaerobic atmosphere has prevented the growth of most bacteria, moulds and fungi.

The underwater excavation of the sixteenth-century ship the *Mary Rose* brought to light textiles of both plant and animal origin preserved by the wave of grey clay which had engulfed a large part of the ship and had excluded oxygen. Textiles have also survived as impressions on metal objects such as brooches or on sites of chalk and limestone. In such impressions the fibres have been replaced by metal corrosion products or mineral salts. Fibres and weaves that remain only as casts of their original structure may sometimes be identified under an electron scanning microscope. Identification may also be possible of textiles or yarns incorporated as decoration on clay before it is fired.

Above: A woollen hood of the 14th century from a burial in a bog in Bocksten, South Sweden, where the chemical conditions of the soil have preserved the textile; and *right*: the hood after careful restoration.

Conditions of display and storage

All matter must eventually return to its original components but understanding the ways of delaying the inevitable is without doubt the greatest element in preventive conservation.

We have learned that organic materials bleach and age through photo-chemical reactions to oxygen, humidity, light and airborne pollution, that high temperatures accelerate all reactions and that high temperatures and humidity together encourage the growth of fungi, bacteria and other pests that feed on textile fibres. In caring for and displaying a collection, we make use of data collected from organic survivals, but even with the most careful application of scientific principles we seem unable to simulate the happy accidents of history. Preven-

tion of damage takes account of all the hazards, including those of display, storage, handling and documentation.

It is a sad truism of a collector's life that all display is destructive, and this applies whether the object is shown under open conditions or in a showcase. Also dangerous are unsuitable storage environments, careless handling and the loss of identity and information that stem from imperfectly kept records. Since none of these hazards may be totally avoidable we should concentrate on how to minimise their potential damage, beginning with the environment.

Textiles should be kept in darkness – except when viewing at general light levels of 50 Lux. Since displays need to be seen and since individual assessment of light intensity inevitably varies it is essential to make an individual assessment by using a 'lux meter',

especially as damage occurs in direct proportion to the light intensity multiplied by the duration of exposure. It is not recommended that an ordinary photographic light meter be used instead of a lux meter, as its results are not sufficiently accurate nor intended for this purpose. 'Dosimeters' are used to measure and record the total amount of illumination and duration of exposure.

Daylight with its ultra-violet radiation is the most damaging type of light. Crawford uv monitors measure the amount of ultra-violet radiation in lighting: the recommended level for textiles is 75 microwatts per lumen.

Filters of colourless or near colourless ultraviolet absorbing acrylic sheets are commonly available as Perspex VE, Plexiglas 201 and Oroglas UF 3. These may all be used in place of glass for showcases and picture-frames.

Colourless plastic sheet with ultra-violet absorbing additions may be used as roller blinds at windows, or window-panes may be varnished on the inside with ultra-violet absorbing varnish. Their ability to absorb ultra-violet radiation decreases as time passes so they should be constantly monitored.

No historic textile should ever be shown in direct sunlight, not even for a very short time, and rooms with displays should be darkened when unoccupied as they were in the past. Reflected light, on the other hand, is very helpful. White walls regularly painted can reflect more than 75 per cent of daylight, while also absorbing about 90 per cent of its ultra-violet content. It can also be directed by placing a white or light-coloured reflector screen close to the windows. However, aluminium and other metal reflectors do not reduce ultra-violet radiation. From the point of view of ensuring that the light is as safe as possible it is easier to control artificial light in a darkened room than to try to monitor daylight.

Tungsten incandescent lamps emit only a limited amount of ultra-violet radiation and need no filtering. Incandescent light is flattering to most objects because of its warm tones, but must never be placed inside a case

Unsuitable washing and storage have left an early 19th-century Christening robe with yellow discoloration and iron stains which have begun to destroy the fabric.

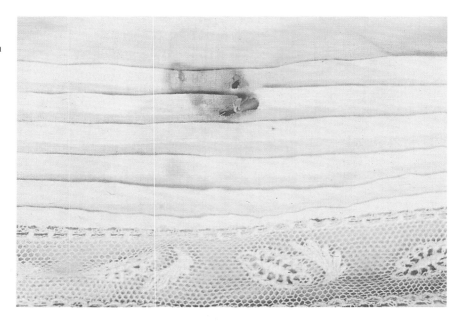

or close to an object because of the heat generated.

Conventional spotlights should be avoided. The climatic conditions created above them are like those of an oven, and spotlights not only destroy the organic materials they light but their effect on the relative humidity of the room as a whole is detrimental to all other objects in it. However, low-voltage tungsten halogen lamps used for spotlighting have high luminosity as well as low power consumption and are therefore safer, though they should be fitted with ultra-violet filters. Neon or fluorescent lights also generate little heat but emit a high degree of ultra-violet radiation and should therefore always be fitted with efficient filters. The safest form of lighting is undoubtedly fibre optics which generates no heat at all as it illuminates.

Stable conditions presuppose well-insulated rooms in which no windows face south. Temperatures between 12°C and 18°C are ideal but rarely possible outside museum store-rooms. In private houses, the temperature should never exceed 20°C in rooms with textile displays or the damage could be considerable. They also need a stable relative humidity of 50 to 55 per cent, and attention to the properties of display and storage materials. Unnecessary handling should be avoided.

It is not always realised to what an extent conditions are affected by the number of people in a room at any given time, and whether, for example, they have just come in from the rain and are still wearing their outdoor clothes. People generate heat and have humid breath. In winter, when outside temperatures are low, relative humidity levels are low, and heating cold air for comfort reduces levels of relative humidity even further. In summer, when outside temperatures are high, relative humidity rises. These changes force the hygroscopic

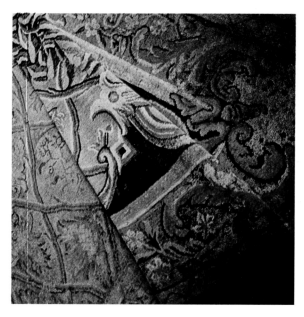

The original colours of this French Savonnerie carpet, about 1660, only survive where chance has protected them from the light.

I have a mother in the dust.
her mouldring body lies
i had a mother but i trust
her spirit in the skies.

Inexpert washing has caused the dye to run on this 19th-century sampler.

nature of organic materials to adjust their moisture content to achieve equilibrium with that of their environment.

As textile fibres absorb moisture, they expand, and as they release it, they contract. Continual adjustments of this kind lead to stresses that can totally destroy the already partly degraded fibres of a textile produced long ago.

Airborne dust and gases and atmospheric pollution pose problems for textiles as they do for human beings. Their influence was noticed as early as the thirteenth century in London when the use of coal for lime burning and other manufacturing processes became common, and in 1307 a commission was appointed to discover all persons guilty of burning coal. Nevertheless coal was increasingly used as fuel and the emission of the resultant sulphur dioxide and soot continued to grow. In spite of clean air legislation, such pollution still poses problems. Pollution was always worse in the towns. In country houses, silver in daily use did not tarnish until the seventeenth century.

Sulphur dioxide in the air can bleach dyestuffs, but worse, it converts into sulphuric acid in the presence of moisture and a catalyst such as iron, manganese or copper, and in a humid environment sulphuric acid may form on any dusty surface.

The presence of rust-spots on linen and cotton textile underlines the fact that these textiles are particularly vulnerable to damage by sulphur dioxide because of built-in iron impurities left over from imperfect finishing treatments. Iron impurities assist the conversion of airborne pollutants such as sulphur dioxide to sulphuric acid in or within the fibres.

Hydrogen sulphide is another airborne pollutant that converts into sulphur. It is emitted by wool, mixed fibre felts, rubber, rayon and some of the dark blue, black and brown cotton dyes; some leathers too are in this category. The presence of hydrogen sulphide gas tarnishes metals of all kinds, including silvergilt threads used for metalwork embroidery and brocades.

Soot comes from the burning of coal, oil and other fuels, and besides acting as a carrier of their corrosive substances it forms an acid compress wherever it settles.

Ozone forms in sunny climates by the action of sunlight on hydrocarbons and on the nitrogen oxides in car exhaust gases. Ozone is a strong oxidising agent that attacks all organic materials, in particular rubber and some dyestuffs.

Air conditioning with special filters needs ducted air-condition systems and is rarely appropriate except for museums with a well-trained maintenance staff. A private collector should ensure he has tightly fitting double-glazed windows or dustproof showcases with controllable airflow conditions.

Showcases

Fluctuations in temperature and air pressure are the prime causes of air exchange. When air in a showcase is temporarily heated, some will escape because of expansion. When it cools off, the outside air is sucked in. Similarly, when the air in the outside room is heated some will be forced into the case until the air pressure inside is equal to that without.

But since the circulation of clean air is necessary to counteract the effect that the materials of the objects on display may have on one another, a well-constructed showcase should have an opening that permits a slow exchange of air filtered through activated carbon filters. A hole about 5 cm in diameter per cubic metre of space is large enough. The hole may be placed in an inconspicuous position, but it should be convenient for checking and exchanging of filters.

A properly designed, well-constructed dustproof showcase should have controllable air exchanges and maintain a constant relative humidity. If it is necessary to compromise and use an ordinary showcase or picture frame, acidic airborne pollutants such as sulphur dioxide and hydrochloric acid may be rendered harmless to the objects on display by incorporating paper or cloth impregnated with magnesium hydroxide or calcium carbonate impregnated cardboard. This could be placed under the display or at the back of a framed textile.

Hygroscopic display materials such as wood, textiles and paper stabilise the relative humidity in showcases, but not instantly. As an added precaution, containers of Silica Gel granules are commonly incorporated in calculated amounts in every type of case. Like the filters they should be exchangeable without the case having to be opened.

Illumination, except in the case of fibre optics, must come from outside but spotlights or sunlight must be avoided, because these would seriously endanger objects in showcases by causing violent fluctuations in relative humidity. The same obviously goes for glazed picture frames.

A showcase should be made of glass and metal − not transparent glass substitutes such as the acrylic sheets of, for example, Perspex® and Plexiglas,® because they build up an electrostatic charge which attracts dust. These materials are easily scratched and are slightly more permeable to air than glass.

Removing dust by polishing causes damage to the objects by pulling the fibres towards the glazing, so that they eventually break. The best way to deal with cleaning is by use of a damp cloth and no polishing.

Low-reflecting glass whose surface − like that of a camera lens − has an anti-reflection coating is increasingly being used when displaying textiles and is certainly quite flattering.

Display and storage materials and techniques

Pins of any sort, stainless steel, dressmakers' pins, lace brass pins, glass-headed or even entomological pins, should never be left in any textile for long enough to cause damage by corroding metals or tearing of insufficiently supported and mostly fragile fabrics. If attachment is considered essential for temporary display, then either minimal tacking to a backboard or entomological pins might be considered.

Materials with a deleterious effect on other materials include all of the Polyvinyl chlorides − the PVCs − because in decomposition these release corrosive products such as hydrochloric acid. PVC is used as PVC film, PVC adhesives, PVC disperse pigments and bubble-wrap plastic. Polythene bags should not be used in long-term storage (more than a few days) as they attract dust and become porous with age. They also retain moisture. Already mentioned as emitting hydrogen sulphide are woollen fabrics, mixed fibre felts, rubber, rayon and some of the dark cotton dyes. Mixed fibre felts also give off peroxide.

Among other display and storage mate-

Light damage to a silk patchwork of the early 19th century.

rials to avoid are those made from wood pulp paper, some modern textiles with synthetic finishes, any plastic film or adhesive that include plasticisers and textiles of any kind rinsed with fabric conditioners.

Wood from which display or storage cases are made should be tested for acidic by-products that would promote corrosion of every type of metalwork, including gold embroidery and metallic brocades. Oak, sweet chestnut, and Douglas fir are known to be acidic and to cause this kind of damage. Their finishes are also often injurious, if they involve cellulose acetate films and fresh oil paint. Silk, wool and leather are damaged by adhesives used for plywood, chipboard and hardboard.

The advice concerning exposure to light, and materials that are safe, is even more applicable to storage, because sound storage conditions are a long-term investment in survival. Handling and touching must be reduced to a minimum by careful organisation, including the placing of each object on its own strong silkpaper or well-washed

An embroidered 18th-century silk, damaged along the fold lines.

203

Left: the larvae of the brown house moth, about 16mm long, which feeds on and pupates in textiles and other organic materials; and *right*: the brown house moth adult (*Hofmannophila Pseudpretella*).

unbleached calico wrapping for the dual purpose of keeping the objects separate and as a support when lifting them for inspection and study. Small objects may be stored in individual cellophane or 'acid-free' tissue paper envelopes. Yellowing indicates that they need to be replaced. When handling, clean cotton gloves should be worn, since salts forming naturally on the skin by perspiration will corrode metals, stain photographs and slides and attract moisture to all organic materials and, as anyone will know

from their seaside holidays, salty moisture not washed out will inevitably lead to mould growth. Since this is as much for the protection of the wearer as of the objects, they should only be worn once before washing and never kept loose in a handbag or pocket.

Storage furniture should include chests with large shallow drawers such as architects' plan chests. Cedarwood and mahogany are considered to be relatively safe woods for storage furniture, but because of the problems concerning modern wood pro-

Left: the varied carpet beetle (*Anthremus verbasci*); adults, and the 'woolly bear' larvae. A major textile pest which benefits from central heating and fitted carpet. The 'woolly bear' eats holes especially on folds and seam lines; and *right*: silver fish (*Lepisma saccharina*), adults and young, are voracious destroyers of textiles and other organic materials.

ducts and adhesives, the metal variety of plan chest may be preferred.

Preventive conservation begins with good storage that allows each piece to relax and shed its creases, so that it will be readily available for occasional exhibition. As much of the collection as possible should lie flat; larger pieces may be rolled on well-washed calico-covered lightweight 'acid-free' rollers, but hanging is best avoided because of the strain it puts on deteriorating fibres. Remember that strained materials may tear and will certainly develop creases and distortions.

For storage of dresses in good condition hanging may be permitted provided stress is minimised by using padded hangers and supporting the weight of heavy skirts. Liberal use of 'acid-free' tissue paper is recommended to prevent sharp creases when a textile is folded. Polyester wadding can also be used to pad garment sleeves and bodices, shoes, hats and bonnets.

It is advisable to have a large surface like a dining table to use for examination and preparation for storage and display. A washed cotton mattress cover may be used over padding and there should be enough spare covers elasticated at each corner to have a clean cover for each working session.

Preventive conservation includes choice of colour for display because even very faded and worn textile objects can be made to look well by flattering display and lighting arrangements.

A smooth textile will reflect light even at the low levels of illumination recommended and this fact, together with careful choice of display colours, will help to divert attention from any stains and missing parts.

Flattering display colours for old and faded textiles are dull blue shades – the general rule is that shades should be duller than those they are intended to flatter. Browns and beiges though, while also quite dull colours, tend to be picked up by the colours of stains and so accentuate these. The most flattering light by far comes from incandescent tungsten lamps whose yellow light is reminiscent of candles.

Pests

Before being integrated with the collection every new acquisition must be inspected for moths and other pests and thoroughly vacuum-cleaned inside and out through monofilament screening. This is particularly relevant to carpets, tapestries and military uniforms. Extra care should, of course, be taken when dealing with fine or fragile textiles. Vulnerable items made from fur,

Wool damaged by the larvae of the common clothes moth (*Tineola bisselliella*). The hole is surrounded by excreted fragments.

feather, hair or wool should be kept in isolation for several months. The temptation to make use of toxic chemicals to kill moths and prevent re-infestation should be resisted because they have been known to cause irreversible damage to textile fibres and dyestuffs, though both reputable pest control firms and regional museum services will give guidance on new developments.

Light has destroyed a tapestry weft dyed with a light-sensitive black mordant.

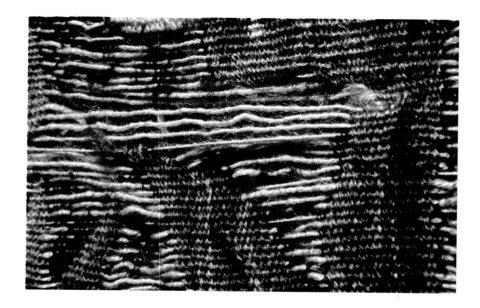

In the past museums used to fumigate suspect objects with ethylene oxide, but reports on cancer risks have encouraged the study of alternative methods; one non-contaminating method that has proved effective involves freezing for about three weeks at temperatures of 20°C below. There can be no doubt that the most effective precaution against pests is good housekeeping with regular thorough vacuum-cleaning into all corners and under all shelving to remove all types of dust. Pests feed on the organic particules of dust shed from dead skin-cells.

Repairing a tapestry in which the weft and some of the warp have been destroyed.

Cleaning and remedial conservation

Washing and drycleaning are drastic operations that could cause rapid deterioration, and should be avoided as much as possible. This type of work is best left to a qualified textile conservator with all the necessary facilities for the preliminary investigation to ascertain the safest procedures. Remedial conservation is also best avoided unless done under qualified guidance – except possibly for garments still in use such as christening robes and wedding veils. In the long term, these, and any other form of dress and furnishings still in use, have to be considered expendable.

If you decide you need a conservator or qualified guidance then, in the United States, the American Institute of Conservators and, in the United Kingdom, the Museums and Galleries Commission, can provide information.

Textiles in a collection should be respected for themselves and for their intrinsic value. It cannot be stressed too often that handling should be done with care. A 'stitch in time' does not usually save an ancient textile, but is more likely to cause stresses in the surrounding areas and break the fragile fibres. Adhesives or adhesive tapes should never be used, as the total removal of most glues is impossible without causing further damage to a decaying textile.

Tapestries, wall hangings and carpets often have a deceptively sturdy appearance. When hanging them, Velcro® hook and loop fastening is usually recommended because the weight of the tapestry can be evenly distributed along the loop strip stitched to the top of the textile. Another method is a sleeve of strong cloth stitched to the back of the top edge through which a rod can be passed. This provides regular weight distribution but does not allow for minor adjustments in the hang as does Velcro®.

Before display, textiles should always be lined. A well-scoured sympathetic fabric will give good support. It is important to catch it to the back evenly with spaced lines of stitches. Some excess material should be allowed in both directions in order to cope with the gravitational pull when a textile is hung vertically but it should never be so loose as to defeat its purpose.

The silk weft of this tapestry has been destroyed,
leaving bare the woollen warp.

Documentation

Preventive conservation and care of objects should always encompass the documentary information that accompanies the objects and provides evidence of the past. This knowledge keeps our history alive – but only if it is properly recorded and the records kept safe and easily retrievable.

Whether using a computer or an index card system the documentation begins with the accessioning and recording of all the information given by an object's donor or owner. The information required includes the name and address of all known owners or sellers, any connection with the original owner or maker, the professional status of the maker with name and dates, country of origin, photographs or other illustrations preferably showing the object in use, date and purpose of original acquisition, purchase place and price, present-day value, the use made by subsequent owners, and the reports of any known restoration and conservation. This should all be recorded in a permanent form and each entry should commence with the accession number, date and name of recorder. In all cases a copy disk is essential.

Cataloguing and photography for records and insurance purposes should come next with the object shown alongside a ruler or scale and a colour guide. Basic data should be recorded, commencing with the simple

A mid 17th-century stump-work casket, a victim of
mould and excessive light.

name of the object, its purpose, shape, dimensions in centimetres, colours, materials, techniques (woven, non-woven, surface decoration such as embroidery or printing, handmade, machine-made, etc). Signs of wear and built-in damage caused by weighting of silks and black dyestuffs as well as any special features, repairs and conservation treatment, should be noted. Holding objects up to the light will reveal areas of weakness. The reverse, with seam lines, may also provide a clearer indication of any joins or alterations.

Photography should provide complete coverage of the object including the reverse side but it is also important to draw it in every detail in the course of cataloguing, because the nature of drawing ensures total familiarity with an object. Photographs are useful, but the information they can convey is rarely comparable to drawings and diagrams, even when inexpertly done; in any case the principles of drawing can be learned in the same way as writing and practice makes master.

For ethical and scientific reasons the watchword should be 'no interference' with objects of historic value because interference will lessen their value as historic documents. To be a collector means assuming the temporary guardianship of a part of history, and though curiosity may have killed the cat it also helps to develop new forms of research which might reveal significant information, even from previously well-researched objects. Provided that no evidence has been removed by zealous cleaning or the excessive demands of display every collection will continue to reveal new facts of interest to captivate and enthrall its guardians.

The mid 17th-century stump-work casket, illustrating the unfaded colour protected by the doors and the lid, restored but still faded.

GLOSSARY

Magdalena Abakanowicz Born 1930 Poland. Fibre Art designer. Associate Professor Fine Arts Academy, Warsaw, since 1965. Has exhibited all over the world at major exhibitions and has also had 38 one-person exhibitions since 1960.

Acanthus decoration Stylised pattern of curling acanthus leaves frequently seen on Italian velvets and damasks.

Acrylic fibres Based on polyacrylonitrite, obtained from coal carbonisation and natural gas found in oil wells. This is made into a polymer which is dissolved in a solvent so that it can be spun into filaments. Acrylonitrite polymers were discovered before the Second World War but no suitable solvent was available. The first polyacrylonitrite fibre to go into commercial production was Orlon, developed by E.I. Du Pont De Nemours & Co. in the USA. Others now include Acrylan, Chemstrand Ltd. and Courtelle, Courtaulds Ltd. and Dralon by Bayer used in knitwear and dress fabrics. Acrylics mix and blend well with other fibres including wool and cotton.

Activated carbon filters Used to exclude gaseous pollutants from showcases.

Aerophane Fine thin crepe-like silk, popular in early 19th century for decorative applications, as raised motifs or applied and re-embroidered, and for pleated and gathered dress trimmings.

Anni Albers Born Germany in 1899, she studied and worked at the Bauhaus 1922–1930 and became head of the Weaving Workshop. In 1933, she and her husband, Josef Albers, emigrated to America where she continued to promote the craft of weaving by teaching and writing.

Album or Friendship Quilts Patchwork quilts worked in squares or sections by individuals as part of a quilting bee for combination into a presentation. Often inscribed.

Alençon Fine French needle lace introduced in s17th century. Has characteristic raised cordonnet with picots, and tight looped net ground. Takes name from its centre of manufacture in France.

Almeria Important port on the southern coastline of Muslim Spain, a major centre of silk production, 9th–11th centuries.

Alpaca Prepared from the wool of a member of the South American camel family. The fibre is fine and strong with rich silky lustre.

Alsace and Mulhouse Important for production of printed cloth towards the close of the 18th century, to serve the Parisian market after the lifting of a French ban on manufacture of printed textiles in 1759.

Altobasseo Splendid velvet of the Italian Renaissance woven in different coloured silks on a gold background. The height of the pile was varied for further decorative effect.

Amish Communities of strict Mennonite Christians, in Pennsylvania. Their patchwork quilts are much admired for their combinations of dark muted and brilliant colour tones in large-scale geometric designs with intricate quilting stitches. Until the orthodox communities dispersed, patterned textiles were avoided and the quilting was in black thread.

Anatolia Asian territory of what is now Turkey with a long tradition of carpet weaving. Earliest extant examples date from the 13th century. Often depicted in European paintings from the 16th century, such carpets were highly influential, inspiring the start of carpet weaving in the West.

Anilines Group of dyestuffs based on coal tar developed by O. Unverdorben in 1826. Often referred to as the first synthetic fabric dyes. From 1856 range increased with benzine purple (W.H. Perkin 1837–1907) and French mauveine and magenta, 1860.

Angora Soft wool of the angora goat, woven into the luxury fabric 'camlet', imported from the Near East in the Middle Ages. Strong, lustrous and resilient, it is now known as mohair and produced in South Africa and the South West of the United States.

Appliqué Applied work: a technique of ancient origin in which one fabric is applied to another forming a surface decoration. It is a major element of stumpwork and 19th-century bed covers. In modern embroidery it is an aspect of collage and can be stuck rather than stitched to the ground.

Arabesques Scrolling decorative motifs with entwining leaves and branches; often found in Rococo embroidery and tapestries.

Arcading Decorative scheme of pillars and arches dividing a large cloth into smaller sections. Device common in medieval Opus Anglicanum embroidery and on copes from Piacenza, Bologna and Toledo.

Richard Arkwright (1732–1792) Invented the spinning frame in which cotton fibres are passed through a series of drafting rollers, producing a strong even thread used first for stockings, then as warp for all cotton cloth, securing relief from duty for printed calico in 1774. From 1769 he worked with Jedediah Strutt. In 1775 he combined all processes for yarn production, in the first factory powered by water. Became a successful manufacturer notable for factory organisation.

Argentan Fine French needlelace similar to Alençon until early 18th century when it adopted heavy *brides bouclées* and *tortillées*.

Argentella Fine French needlelace of late 17th and 18th centuries. Variant of Argentan, worked with an elaborate mesh composed of a series of hexagon-like spiders' webs, a rarity because it is so fragile.

Arras Important Flemish centre of production for tapestries. High-loom weaving first mentioned there in 1313. Arras tapestries and craftsmen highly regarded during the 14th and 15th centuries, so much so that the word arras and tapestry were interchangeable in the English language.

Art Needlework Product of the later 19th century, a reaction to the garish commercialised patterns of Berlin wool work. Associated with the works of designers such as William Morris, Norman Shaw, James Sedding, Herbert Butterfield and Candace Wheeler, and practised at the School of Art Needlework. Its aesthetic was based on a combination of mid 17th-century crewel-worked motifs and naturalistic observation, with emphasis on the role of the individual in interpreting designs. The techniques employed were simple with much use of running and satin stitch, and muted colours. Soon commercialized.

Art Nouveau Introduced in the 1880s when designers in Britain and Europe were looking for a new style specific to the 19th century instead of archaic revivalism. Based on the natural and organic line, with curves and asymmetry being a strong feature. Reached the height of its popularity in 1900. The term derives from 'L'Art Nouveau', the Paris shop of Samuel Bing (1838–1919).

Art Workers' Guild Formed initially in 1883 by some pupils of the architect Richard Norman Shaw as the St George's Art Society, combined with similar group called The Fifteen. First combined meeting as the Art Workers' Guild took place in 1884. Many Arts & Crafts designers were affiliated and it existed to provide a forum for discussion between craftsmen, architects and designers such as Walter Crane, Lewis F. Day, C.F.A. Voysey, A.H. Mackmurdo, Edwin Lutyens and Roger Fry. An offshoot of the guild formed the Arts & Crafts Exhibition Society.

Arts & Crafts Exhibition Society Group of artists and craftsmen who created their own exhibiting society because the Royal Academy would not admit applied art to its annual exhibitions. Founded by a splinter group from the Art Workers Guild including W.R. Lethaby, W.A.S. Benson, T.J. Cobden-Sanderson, William De Morgan, Lewis Day and Walter Crane. The first six exhibitions, between 1888 and 1899, were very successful and the ideals of the society, disseminated by such magazines as *The Studio*, became very influential in Europe and the USA.

Associated Artists Interior decorating firm founded in 1879 by Louis Comfort Tiffany (1848–1933), Samuel Colman (1850–1932) Lockwood de Forest (1850–1931), with Candace Wheeler (1828–1923), who was responsible for textile and embroidery designs. The partnership was dissolved in 1883; Tiffany began a new venture under his own name, and Wheeler continued in charge of Associated Artists.

Association of tapestry cartoon printers Founded in 1945, a group of artists interested in painting tapestry cartoons including Jean Picart le Doux and Marc Saint-Saens, with Lurçat as president. Held exhibitions in an attempt to revive interest in tapestry weaving.

Atelier, Martine Decorative art school and workshop founded by the couturier Paul Poiret in 1912 to produce and market a wide range of objects, including textiles.

Aubusson With the nearby centre of Felletin, an important French centre of tapestry and carpet production. Tradition suggests a 13th-century origin, but tapestries from Felletin are first recorded in 1514 and from Aubusson in 1560. Then probably cheaper versions of Flemish tapestries, woven on low-warp looms with relatively thick warps and wefts. In 1665 Colbert issued letters patent and chartered them as a 'Royal Manufactory', laying down standards and marks, the letters MRD or MRDA woven into the blue (for Aubusson) or brown (for Felletin) selvedge. In 1742, a school of design was set up and in 1744 tapestry-woven pile carpets on vertical looms were introduced. Tapestry landscapes, Chinoiseries and subjects after Oudry and Boucher were popular, as were furnishings, often woven with subjects from the Fables de La Fontaine. The carpets, cheaper than

Savonnerie, were the mainstay of the centre as the tapestry vogue declined in the 19th century. Despite the introduction of the power loom, succumbed to oriental competion. Currently a centre for the weaving of artist-designed tapestries.

Axminster Small town in Devon, South West England, locale of Thomas Whitty's carpet manufacturing business in 1755 that gave the town its fame. Until 1835 this was the most important centre of hand-knotted carpet weaving in Britain, when it closed, relocating to Wilton. The term is now used nonspecifically for many types of machine-made carpets with a knotted pile.

Ayrshire embroidery White cotton embroidery worked on fine muslin mainly in satin stitch with open work fillings.

G.P. & J. Baker Ltd London Textile printers founded by the brothers George Percival and James Baker in 1884, famous for 1890s Art Nouveau fabrics. George formed important collection of historic textiles; many were adapted and translated for printing. Now owned by Parker Knoll.

Bargello work Hungarian, Florentine, Irish, flame or cushion stitch: canvaswork technique based on a straight stitch worked in subtle-coloured silk or wool in a zig-zag pattern, giving a ripple or rainbow effect.

Baroque Style that flourished in Europe in the 17th century. The style is one of bold exuberance, of large scrolls and rich colours often offset by an abundance of gold.

Barron & Larcher Phyllis Barron (1890–1964) and Dorothy Larcher (1884–1952), partners from 1923 until 1952, re-created the old traditions of hand block-printed textiles in Britain.

Nicholas Bataille One of the few weavers of the medieval period known to us by name. He was a tapestry merchant working in Paris who is first recorded in 1363. Responsible for weaving the 'Apocalypse of Angers' in 1379.

Batik Textile craft, originating from Java, which consists in drawing a design on cloth with liquid wax and immersing the fabric in dyes which resist the waxed areas; when the wax is melted this leaves the drawn pattern visible in the original ground colour; this process is repeated for each colour.

Bauhaus Weimar art and architectural schools known collectively as Das Staatliche Bauhaus Weimar. The 1919 manifesto stressed the unity of all decorative arts under the primacy of architecture and called for a reconsideration of the crafts, ideas seminal to the Arts & Crafts Movement in Britain from the last quarter of the 19th century. Closed down by the Nazis in 1933.

William Baumgarten American responsible for establishing some of the first tapestry workshops in the USA at Williamsbridge, New York in 1893.

Bayeux Tapestry Remarkable embroidered hanging commemorating the Battle of Hastings in 1066. Thought to have been commissioned shortly after the battle by the French victors from English embroiderers. Embroidered on linen over 70 m long and 50 cm wide in different coloured wools. Can be seen in the museum in Bayeux, France.

Beauvais French tapestry manufactory founded in 1644 by Louis Hinart, in conjunction with the Crown. Hinart was succeeded by Philippe Beghale in 1684 and later the artist Oudry became director. Mostly associated with 18th-century Rococo tapestries, mainly designed by Oudry, Boucher and Huet.

Bed hangings Curtains which trimmed the fourposter bed, providing privacy and protection from the cold. On state beds they were elaborate and expensive. At their most ostentatious, in the 17th century, they consisted of two large and two small curtains, with a cantoon (Fr *cantonnière*) to cover gaps at the corners, a tester or canopy with inner and outer valances, a headcloth (Fr *dossier*) and coverings for the head and footboards. Counterpane usually made to match.

Bedfordshire Maltese A cotton bobbin lace, usually black, with many wheatears and no mesh ground. A straight bobbin lace, mainly 19th and 20th century.

Jean Berain (1637–1711) French architect and important Baroque interior designer, son of a Lorraine goldsmith.

Berlin Woolwork Canvaswork counted stitch embroidery, very popular in 19th century. Worked from widely available coloured paper patterns printed with motifs on a grid mesh, to be copied exactly. Main stitches were tent, *gros point* and cross stitch.

Férier Bianchini One of the largest French silk manufacturers, based in Lyons since 1870s with branches in Paris, London, Montreal Hall and New York. Produced printed and woven artist-designed silks, particularly some by Raoul Dufy, during the 1920s and 1930s.

Erastus Bigelow (1814–79) Inventor and economist born Massachusetts. Invented a power loom for making coach lace, tapestry velvet carpet and improved ingrained carpeting as well as looms for counterpanes, gingham, silk brocatel, pile fabric and wire cloth. Instrumental in founding the factory village at Clinton, Mass., but then moved his establishment to Lowell. The firm became a household name. Copies of his patents are lodged in the Massachusetts Historical Society.

Samuel Bing (1838–1919) Born in Germany but made his name as an art collector in Paris. His shop called *L'Art Nouveau* christened the style of decorative art.

Bizarre silks Woven with exotic designs fashionable in Europe from the late 17th century to *c.*1720, they reflect the influence of Oriental, Indian and Persian designs, but appear to have originated in Lyons, though often imitated.

Blackwork (Spanish or Holbein work) Monochrome, mainly black silk embroidery fashionable in the early 16th century and in England associated with Catherine of Aragon, although an international style known from the Middle Ages and stylistically related to Arabic and Moorish designs. Small-scale with angular, formal repeated motifs mainly carried out in double running stitch. From the later 16th century designs based on printed sources and included flowers, birds, animals and insects. Stitches varied and sometimes enhanced with metal thread and spangles. Best known from collar and cuff details in period portraits.

Block Print Hand process which allows images to be stamped onto cloth with the use of incised wooden or metal blocks.

Blonde Natural colour of undyed silk. The term used for early 19th-century laces made from silk and sometimes dyed black.

Bobbin lace Generic term for lace formed by the plaiting of threads usually held with pins as the lace progresses, worked over a pattern on a pillow. Each thread weighted with a bobbin. Also known as 'pillow lace'.

Bobbins For pillow lace, each thread being weighted with a bobbin of wood, bone or Murano glass. Generally hung with a gingle or spangle, a ring of glass beads for identification and extra weight. Some are decorative, inscribed with tokens or messages.

Bonnaz (or Cornelly) embroidery machine Based on the sewing-machine principle but using a hooked needle above and a thread below manipulated by a handle. Invented in 1865 by Antoine Bonnaz, the system was taken over by Ercole Cornelly. Adaptable for all materials and threads as well as strung sequins. Still in use.

Book of the Prefect Document issued by the Byzantine Emperor Leo VI in 911–12, detailing the activities and restrictions placed on the manufacturers and merchants in the city of Constantinople. Valuable source on the Byzantine silk industry.

François Boucher (1703–1770) French painter especially of Arcadian and mythological scenes and most typical of Rococo decorations. Produced many designs for tapestries. Influenced Aubusson and Beauvais and appointed director of the Royal Gobelins manufactory in 1755, though mainly associated with the Beauvais manufactory.

Bradford Principal centre for the spinning and weaving of worsted, profiting from its proximity to Yorkshire wool. The first mills established in 1798 and at the beginning of the 20th century over 40,000 people were employed in 300 mills.

Brides Generic term for bars on needle lace links between motifs. For instance: *Brides Picotées* associated with *Point de France* and early Argentan, a type of buttonhole stitch with ribbed edges; *Brides Tortillées* associated with later Argentan, being simple whipped mesh; *Brides Bouclées* buttonhole stitch as in early Argenton and late Alençon.

Broadcloth Woollen fabric (traditionally 54 in or over in width) in plain weave, the wool being carded beforehand and fulled after weaving. The finest were produced in the west of England on a broadloom necessitating two weavers to throw the shuttle from one side of the web to the other.

Broadloom Carpet of a width greater than six feet, woven in a single piece.

Brocades Heavy dress and furnishing fabrics, today usually Jacquard woven, in which figured patterns are raised against a ground cloth by use of a supplementary weft.

Broderie Anglaise Embroidery popular in the mid 19th century and consisting of petal shapes and eyelet holes overcast with a padded satin stitch. Popular for underwear and household linen; a speciality of the island of Madeira, hence the name by which it was known in the late 19th century.

Broderie Perse Applied work of 19th century, using printed cottons cut into naive figurative or floral shapes. Early in the century there was a vogue for specially printed commemorative cottons featured as the centrepiece in coverlets.

Bromley Hall Situated on the river Lea in East London, Talwin and Foster installed their printworks there from 1694 to 1823; it was one of the most important printed fabric centres in England in the 18th century.

Moses Brown (1738–1836) Quaker merchant and manufacturer of Rhode Island, concerned with developing industry as an antidote to poverty. Manufacturer of fustian, worked with Samuel Slater on mechanising the early American textile industry.

Ivan da Silva Bruhns (1891–1980) French carpet designer of Brazilian ancestry active from the 1920s. He devised his own system of knotting and concentrated on colour and design control. Also employed as a designer by the Savonnerie workshop. Most of his work is geometric with sombre colours. For Savonnerie he includes animals and more curvilinear motifs.

Brussels Appliqué lace Muslin floral motifs applied to net ground generally machine made, outlined by chain stitch; a 19th- and 20th-century lace.

Brussels Carpet Machine technique for making loop-piled carpeting. The coloured threads used for the pile are run between two layers of wefts, pulled through in loops to the surface when the appropriate colour is required. The reverse shows the lines of coloured threads. Two or three colours is usual, over six becoming expensive. Characterised by the short pile.

Burano Needle laces both in the late 18th and late 19th centuries, produced on the Venetian island of that name.

Buratto Form of lace consisting of a base woven gauze with darned decoration. Very similar in appearance to filet, but with twists instead of knots at cross-over points in mesh.

Buratto work Darned patterns on sheer ground fabric such as gauze or leno with patterns similar to those of the net laces, filet and lacis popular in the 16th century.

Bure Coarse woollen cloth commonly used in Medieval times as clothing for the poor.

Edward Burne-Jones (1834–98) Pre-Raphaelite artist who designed tapestries and embroideries for his friend William Morris.

Buser flat screen printing Extremely accurate flat-bed printing machine which uses the conventional squeegee as a method of applying dye. Produces high-quality printed fabrics.

Lydia Bush-Brown (1887–1984) American textile designer specialising in batik work.

Lindsay Butterfield (1868–1948) UK designer of textiles and wallpapers. Closely associated with and influenced by the Victoria & Albert collections of historical textiles. He designed for most of the leading manufacturers and taught at various art schools.

Calico A plain weave cotton of varying quality although usually lightweight and often bleached. Originally from India, it was printed extensively in the west from the 17th century onwards when hand-blocked, resist and dyed methods were used. It was also known as 'calicut', named after the Indian city Calcutta from which it was shipped.

Camlet Soft luxury fabric made of angora, imported from the Near East to Europe in the Middle Ages.

Candlewick Thick soft cord originally made from several candlewicks twisted together (tufting). Pattern worked in large-scale running stitch with loops subsequently cut, forming tufts. After washing shrinkage held the threads in place. It was popular in the later 19th century for white bedcovers.

Canvaswork (US – Needlepoint) Embroidery on canvas, which is a strong unbleached tabby woven cloth made from hemp, jute or flax, available at all periods for many types of embroidered object. Its stitches are varied but most make systematic use of the regular weave, tent stitch being the most popular.

Carbon Dating Technique establishing the age of carbon-containing specimens. With ageing, carbon nuclei increase their atomic mass from 12 to 14.

Carrickmacross Guipure lace, appliqué on net. Consists of muslin flowers and frequently shamrocks outlined with a running stitched cordonnet (whereas similar Brussels Appliqué lace is outlined by chain stitch).

Cartoon Design for tapestry. Sometimes monochrome allowing colour choice. Often re-worked several times, they were sometimes actual size. The most famous are by Raphael, in the Victoria and Albert Museum.

Edmund Cartwright (1743–1823) Clergyman, poet, farmer and secretary to Royal Society of Arts. Invented power loom (1785–90) and wool combing machine (1789–90), central to textile industrial revolution.

Century Guild Formed in 1882 by A.H. Mackmurdo (1851–1942) and Selwyn Image (1849–1930). The aim was to involve artists in designs for all products of interior design.

Chantilly Fine black and also blonde silk bobbin lace, with fond chant ground. First popular in 18th century, and little survives.

Now made at Le Puy, and other centres around Paris.

Chemical Lace Machine embroidery on silk ground which, when dissolved with a chlorine or caustic solution, leaves distinct fuzzy edges. Introduced in late 19th century.

Cheney Brothers American silk-weaving firm, founded by Frank and Knight Cheney, in Manchester, Connecticut, who had a studio in Paris during the 1920s. They took advantage of the improved dyes for man-made yarns to promote the use of co-ordinated colours for the full range of textiles used in household decor.

Chenille Thread with a soft fuzzy surface. Usually of silk but also wool or cotton. Introduced in the 17th century and often couched on the surface of the material, woven into rich silk brocades or used for fringing. From Fr *Chenille* = Caterpillar.

Chevron Patterns Decoration similar to herringbone, bands of diagonal lines lying in alternating directions. Often formed a background motif in Opus Anglicanum, worked in gold thread attached by underside couching.

Chinoiserie Western blend of oriental and Chinese design, increasingly popular after import of decorative wares from the East in the mid-17th century. Reached its peak in the 1760s and was applied to all forms of decorative arts including textiles.

Chintz Generally a glazed cotton cloth of plain weave construction with printed design. Hand-painted and starch-finished chintzes were initially imported from the East during the 17th and 18th centuries as dress and furnishing fabrics. An unglazed chintz is known as a cretonne.

Joyce Clissold (1906–1984) Artist-textile designer. From the late 1920s she managed the printing studio, Footprints, at Hammersmith, and two London West End shops employing thirty assistants designing, producing and selling hand block-printed textiles.

The Cloth Very popular design group set up in August 1983 by four ex-students of the Printed Textile Department of the Royal College of Art: Helen Manning, Brian Bolger, Fraser Taylor and David Band.

Jean-Baptiste Colbert (1619–83) Assistant to Cardinal Mazarin and from 1665 Louis XIV's Controller-General of Finance. He practised a protectionist, economic policy referred to as mercantilism which discouraged the importation of manufactured goods and encouraged home production. He aimed to build up the luxury and textile trades such as the silk and lace industries. Point de Colbert – a type of lace – is named after him.

Colefax and Fowler Lady Sybil Colefax with John Fowler in 1938 established the interior decorating firm of Colefax and Fowler perfecting the 18th-century style interior. The Company is well known for its chintzes.

Colifichet Embroidery worked in silk floss on paper or parchment and reversible. Introduced from China in the 17th century and popular until the 19th century, it was often made in convents, and examples are often in a double-sided glass frame.

Constantinople Capital city of Byzantine Empire founded by Constantine the Great in 328 AD. City of immense splendour strategically situated on the Bosphorus between Europe and Asia. Many textile crafts centred there, but particularly famous for silk weaving. In 1453 captured by the Turks.

Copperplate Printing Incised copper plates used to print intricate and detailed images. Essentially a hand technique introduced in 1762, narrative and figurative scenes were popular using one colour for each. Suitable for handkerchief squares and large-scale furnishing fabrics.

Coptic Textiles produced in Egypt from the introduction of Christianity to the Arab conquest of 640 AD. Many survive from burial sites, typically of linen with woollen tapestry decoration, but woven silks and resist-printed cottons have also been excavated.

Coptic Tunic Typical garment worn by men and women in early Christian Egypt. Woven in one piece and slit at the neck. Decorative tapestry panels from shoulder to waist or hem ('clavi') were frequently applied.

Coraline Flat form of Venetian needle lace dating from the 17th century, characterised by loose patterning and comparatively crude workmanship.

Cordoba Capital of Muslim Spain from 756, first Spanish centre of silk production. Reached the height of prosperity in the mid-10th century. Renowned for its silversmiths and leather craftsmen as well as weavers.

Cordonnet Thicker gimp thread used to outline bobbin and needlelaces with raised effect. Can be *picoté* as in Alençon where it is stiffened with crin (horsehair), or part of the fabric as in Brussels laces.

Cotton Produced from the seed fibre of a subtropical shrubby plant. The fibre is classified by staple length. The pods are ginned to remove seeds, carded, combed and spun.

Courtaulds Ltd Samuel Courtauld (1793–1881), the principal founder, ran the Bocking silk mill in 1861. Courtaulds Ltd was incorporated in 1913. Famed for the production of crêpe and as pioneers in the manufacture of rayon by the viscose process. In 1939 in conjuction with I.C.I. began production of nylon yarn. By 1940, together with its associated companies, it was one of the world's largest textile concerns.

Walter Crane (1845–1915) UK artist and designer, trained as engraver. Made his name as a book illustrator but after working with members of the Arts & Crafts movement he diversified and produced designs for embroideries, printed and woven textiles and carpets and other applied arts. Founder member of the Art Worker's Guild in 1884.

Cresta Silks Ltd Founded in 1929 by Tom Heron who, following his interest in avant-garde art, decided to produce high-quality screen-printed fabrics from designs created by practising artists. Artists involved included Cedric Morris, Bruce Turner, Paul Nash, and Patrick Heron, son of the founder.

Crewel work Outline embroidery in wool on linen or linen mixtures, popular in the 17th and 18th centuries, revived in the late 19th and 20th centuries, and well adapted to large scale domestic textiles. It was often monochrome in blue or green. The most popular stitches were stem or crewel stitch, feather, satin and chain stitch, also French knots. The designs generally incorporate luxuriant leaf shapes deriving from Middle Eastern sources and sometimes animal motifs.

Crochet Made with a hook manipulating a single thread into knotted loops. Irish crochet a speciality, characterised by roses with raised petals and other motifs such as acorns.

Samuel Crompton (1753–1827) Weaver from Bolton who invented the spinning mule, patented in 1779. It combined features of Hargreaves' spinning jenny and Arkwright's water frame. The resultant yarn so produced was strong and of a high quality.

Cutwork Forerunner of needle lace. Form of linen embroidery especially popular in 16th century, consisting of small buttonholed openings forming a pattern, and linked by *brides*. A variant of reticella, it has least remaining ground fabric.

Cylinder Power Roller Printing Machine Cylinder printing was a direct progression from plate printing. The first machine was patented by Thomas Bell in 1783 and allowed an incised copper roller to print continuously lengths of cloth.

Damask Either a rich fabric usually silk or a twilled linen or cotton fabric with woven designs which show up by opposing reflections of light from the surface. Often involves a warp-faced satin background and a weft-faced satin weave. The name is derived from the city of Damascus and the earliest examples from the 4th century originate from the Middle East. Italy was to emerge as the most important centre for the production of silk damask in the 15th century.

Darning Samplers Popular in the late 18th, early 19th centuries and worked with darns simulating a variety of cloth textures. The floral motifs often incorporate varieties of needlepoint fillings.

Lucienne Day Born 1917, British textile designer. Studied at Croydon School of Art 1934–7 and the Royal College of Art 1937–40. Became a full-time freelance designer, establishing a studio in London in 1948 with her husband, Robin Day. Designed dress and furnishing fabrics, carpets, wallpapers and table linens for firms such as Edinburgh Weavers, Cavendish Textiles and Heals. Became known for her boldly coloured textiles in abstract patterns and her 'Calyx' pattern of 1951 was judged the best textile design on the American market in 1952.

Beryl Dean Active in ecclesiastical embroidery from 1958, working with the Needlework Development Council. Work includes five panels for St George's Chapel, Windsor (1974) and copes for the enthronement of the Archbishop of Canterbury.

Henry Dearle (1860–1932) Close associate of William Morris; was chief textile designer at Morris and Company; after Morris's death in 1896 he became the firm's art director.

Deerfield Embroidery Product of a workshop organised in Deerfield, Massachusetts by the painters Margaret C. Whiting and Ellen Miller from 1896 until about 1915. Inspired by Colonial blue and white embroidery, pieces are marked with a blue spinning wheel.

Sonia Delaunay (1885–1979) French artist and designer born in the Ukraine. She studied art in Paris c.1905, her style influenced by Rousseau, Matisse and the Fauves. Contrasting bright colours were a feature of both her painting and textile work.

Design & Industries Association UK Association of manufacturers, designers and distributors including Ambrose Heal and Harry Peach of Dryad Handicrafts, founded in 1914 advocating good design in industry and inspired by the 1914 Deutsche Werkbund exhibition. Its aim was the application of the ideals of the Arts & Crafts Movement to manufacturing industry. Exhibitions and publications encouraged a more intelligent demand for well-designed practical products.

Designers Guild Co-founded by Tricia Guild in London in 1970. Worldwide reputation for innovative textiles and printed fabrics, wallpaper design and home furnishings.

Deutsche Werkbund Founded in Munich in 1907 to improve industrial products through the combined efforts of artists, industrialists and craftsmen. Its moving spirit was Herman Muthesius (1861–1927), who had been influenced by and had published accounts of the Arts & Crafts Movement in England. The first exhibition held in Cologne in 1914.

Dibaj Silk produced in Muslim Spain. According to the Muslim historian Al Makkari, it was a durable, high-quality silk woven in Almeria.

Marion Dorn (1899–1964) Born USA, worked in England from early 1920s with the graphic artist Edward McKnight Kauffer as successful textile designers, particularly of rugs with a dominant modern motif which were used as works of art to decorate an interior. Developed a style using the textural quality of cut wool pile to create variations in depth giving a three-dimensional quality.

Double Cloth Fabric which combines two separate cloths worked simultaneously on the loom. Two warps are woven with weft fillings that construct the back and face cloth individually or allow the cloths to interchange and bind in an integral piece.

Drawloom Introduced from the Near East, renowned for production of figured silks in the 8th century. Individual warps were threaded through linen heddles weighted from the bottom and connected to an overhead harness. This was controlled by a drawboy and allowed free grouping of warps lifted in any combination. Forerunner of Jacquard's mechanised loom which was in operation by the early 19th century.

Drawn Thread, Pulled Work or Punto Tirato Form of early embroidery on linen consisting of pulling threads apart with stitches to form a pattern of holes. Fashionable in late 16th–early 17th century. Revived in 19th century.

Dresden embroidery Also known as 'Point de Saxe'. Fine whitework characterised by exquisite drawn threadwork and darned fillings creating areas of light and shade, 18th century and later.

Christopher Dresser (1834–1904) UK designer who entered the government-sponsored School of Design in 1847 and subsequently worked in virtually every medium.

Raoul Dufy (1877–1953) French artist influenced by the work of the Fauves, especially Matisse, and a prolific textile designer; he designed for Paul Poiret.

E.I. DuPont de Nemours Ltd (US); Du Pont UK Ltd Chemical conglomerate founded by French immigrant in USA. By late 1800s had turned from nitrocellulose to cellulose and its derivatives, including textile fibres. Its rayon technology was derived from France. In the 1930s via research on synthetics it developed nylon (1938), in the 1950s purchased polyester technology from the Calico Printers Association, producing acrylic fibre. The elastane fibres (lycra) were developed in 1960.

Edinburgh Tapestry Company (Dovecot Studios) Founded in 1912 by the fourth Marquis of Bute at Corstorphine where the studios are today. Aimed to produce traditional figurative tapestries. After the war translated the work of British artists such as Sutherland and Spencer into domestic-scale tapestries.

Edinburgh Weavers Established in 1928, was a department of Morton, Sundour Fabrics Ltd, an offshoot of the Scottish family firm, Alexander Morton & Company. New weaving venture formed to evolve and design woven fabrics which would complement modern architecture and interior design.

Elastane Fibres Made from segmented polyurethane which is obtained from the petro-chemical industry. First made in the USA as 'Spanolex' yarns, but in Europe referred to as elastomeric yarns. Du Pont manufacture Lycra and Courtaulds Ltd. make Spanzelle. Fabrics have a high degree of stretch and elasticity and unlike rubber do not perish. The fibres are used in foundation and support garments and are incorporated into stretch fabrics for sportswear, where rubber threads were used.

Embroidery Decorative surface stitching common to all cultures and in use since the Neolithic period. Although designs differ, stitches throughout the world have great similarity. They are usually grouped as outline, filling or couching stitches and there are many guides to appearance and formation.

Fabric Conditioners Chemical substances used for softening and discouraging static build up. They work by coating fibres.

Kaffe Fassett USA designer, born in 1937, now living in Britain. Fassett taught himself to knit after he had moved to Britain. He concentrated on hand-knit commissions but has also designed for needlepoint.

Filet Net formed by knotting, usually with a darned pattern; early examples of filet purses and hair nets date to medieval period. Also known as lacis.

Finishes Treatment of textiles by impregnation or surface application to improve their appearance or properties eg. starch, wax, glazes, flame proofing, moth proofing, water repellants, anti-static finishes.

Flanders Alternatively known as the Low Countries and comprising areas of Holland and Belgium. Using fine quality wool mainly imported from England, the Flemish cities of Ypres, Ghent and Bruges were the major producers of luxury woollen cloth in early medieval Europe.

Flatweave General term relating to carpets. Encompasses a variety of different weaves including *kilim, verneh* and *soumac*. It differentiates carpets woven with continuous threads running over the surface from those employing a cut or looped pile technique.

Florence One of the most important cities of the Italian Renaissance, with a sizeable weaving community. Initially concentrated on fine woollen cloth until the industry's decline in the 15th century when silk, introduced in the 14th century, took over as the main product.

The Flowerers Professional whitework embroiderers in Ayrshire from 1780–c.1820, trained by Luigi Ruffini as tambour embroiderers, and, from 1820–1870s specialists in 'sewn muslin'.

Forms Made of wood, these gave the required shape to woollen knitted garments such as stockings, gloves, socks, caps or hats during drying after fulling.

Fortuny Mariano Fortuny y Madrazo (1871–1949) was born in Spain, brought up in Paris and studied painting and worked in Venice. His technically unique textiles were inspired by his collection of historic textiles from many countries. The firm still exists.

Frame knitting machine Makes one row of loops at a time. As invented by William Lee in 1589, it depended on a bearded needle, but this is now replaced by the common latch needle introduced in 1847.

Framework Knitters Company Organisation of English machine knitters chartered in 1655.

Roger Fry (1866–1934) UK artist-designer, Director of the Metropolitan Museum in New York 1905–1910 but returned to London to introduce the Post-Impressionists to the British public. He founded the Omega Workshops to produce decorative arts responsive to modern art trends. Designers who were involved with the workshops included Vanessa Bell, Dora Carrington, Duncan Grant and, initially, the Vorticist painter Wyndham Lewis. The workshops produced furniture, much of it painted, textiles, stained glass and pottery.

Fulham Where the first large carpet factory following the French Savonnerie model was established in West London, England. Founded in 1753 by Peter Parisot.

Fulling mill Trough with furrowed bottom in which the woollen fabrics were kneaded, while hot water mixed with fuller's clay or soap was poured over it to felt and make the fibres thicker and more waterproof. In Europe the process was mechanized from the 13th century but mills were not introduced to

America till 1624.

Maria Monaci Gallenga (1880–1914) Italian textile designer who opened her Rome studio for artistic textiles and fashions in 1908, closing in 1938.

Anna Maria Garthwaite (1690–1763) Daughter of a Lincolnshire parson, a professional designer of silks, active from the 1720s to the mid 50s in the Spitalfields area of East London. Over a thousand designs by her from 1726 to 1756 survive in the collection of the Victoria and Albert Museum.

Gimp (Guimp) Thick thread or cord often used as outline of lace motifs.

Glasgow On the Clyde Estuary, an important port especially for the Americas and manufacturing centre from the late 18th century. Cotton weaving commenced in 1780 at Anderston and in 1783 David Dale with Richard Arkwright set up the water-powered New Lanark mills outside the city. The proximity of coal mines facilitated the change to steam power. It was also a centre for machine carpet manufacture.

Gobelin stitch Small stitch twice as high as it is wide worked closely over a lengthwise cord simulating the look of woven tapestry.

Gobelins Royal tapestry manufactory founded by Colbert in 1663 working specifically for royal palaces on prestige state commissions. In 1733, Oudry became artistic director at Gobelins, succeeded by Boucher in 1753. Factory closed in 1794 after the French Revolution.

Gold work Usually couched embroidery, popular at all periods and the work of professionals. The earliest membrane gold or silver thread, probably of Chinese origin, consisted of fine strips of gilded fish skin or animal gut. Afterwards it was made at Cologne. Other types consist of wire, or flat strip which is often wound around a core thread. Purl or pearl was the wire twisted to resemble strung beads. Although precious metals were used they were often adulterated with base metals.

Grisaille Embroidery in shades of grey, black and white popular in the early 19th century and associated with mourning pictures. It merges with 'printed embroidery' which attempted to produce engravings.

Gros Point de Venise Large-scale needle lace originating in 17th-century Venice. Contains scrolling motifs with characteristic raised and padded *cordonnet* with *picot*.

Grotesques Renaissance decorative motif, derived from classical designs discovered in Roman remains (grotte). Often found on formal decorations of the early 17th century and on 18th-century tapestries they consist of masks, animals, humans and floral motifs.

Guipure 19th-century term for lace formed by cotton or muslin floral motifs linked by *brides*. It is used generically for any lace without a mesh ground including crochet and tape lace.

Hairwork or Point Tresse Embroidery worked with hair or very fine silk. Popular in the mid 17th century for mourning pictures, especially commemorations of the 'Martyr King', Charles I, and in the early 19th century.

Handrun Outlines Machine-made laces especially Pusher lace shawls have a thick *cordonnet* threaded through by hand to give the appearance of a handmade lace.

Hardwicke Hall Built between 1591 and 1597 for Elizabeth, Countess of Shrewsbury (Bess of Hardwicke). It contains one of the finest collections of Elizabethan embroidery and is presently owned by the National Trust.

James Hargreaves Invented spinning jenny designed for multiple spinning of yarns in 1764. Initially the apparatus only produced weft thread of a limited count and strength.

Hargreaves' frame could be worked by one person and consisted of several spindles linked together.

Heals, London Large furniture and interior design store established in the late 19th century under Ambrose Heal. Heals became the arbiters of trade on all contemporary interior design matters from the 1930s onwards.

Heal's Fabrics Ltd (HFL) Heal's Fabrics Ltd succeeded Wholesale & Export Ltd (established in 1941) in 1944. Designs were economical, with few colours. Freelance designers responsible for the variety, among them Jane Edgar and Lucienne Day.

Hennequin of Bruges Artist responsible for designing the tapestry series the 'Apocalypse of Angers' in 1376 for Louis Duke of Anjou.

John Hewson (1744–1821) Founder of the American printed textile industry. Trained in England, he emigrated to America, set up a printworks in Philadelphia producing handkerchiefs representing George Washington on horseback, and coverlets.

M. Jose Heilmann Inventor of the first embroidery machine in 1828, later installed by the textile company Messrs. Koechlin of Mulhouse, France. Heilmann's machine achieved multiple stitching by simultaneous working of up to 140 needles.

High-warp loom (haute lisse) This holds the warps in a vertical position with the frame secured to the roof and floor. It is the loom that most tapestries were produced on, including the medieval Flemish and Gobelins tapestries.

Catherine Holliday Wife of Henry Holliday, painter and designer, a friend of William Morris and one of his most skilled embroideresses.

Hollie Point English needle lace mainly 18th century. Worked with dates and occasionally names. Commonly found as inserts on baby shirts or caps, and on samplers, usually showing a flowering shrub. Pattern formed by holes in solid buttonhole toile.

Honiton English bobbin lace. Thought to have originated in 17th century, but no provenanced pieces survive from before 18th century. Usually white, occasionally black, characterized by cross hatching in flower centres, usually with *brides* rather than *reseau*. Commonly applied to machine net. Degeneration of motif after 1860s. Still produced today. Named after Honiton, Devon, original centre of manufacture.

Jean-Baptiste Huet (1745–1811) French painter and textile designer. One of the main designers of printed cottons employed by Christopher Oberkampf. His most famous design represents the processes of manufacture at Jouy.

Huguenots French Protestants whose persecution by successive French monarchs culminated in Louis XIV's revocation of the Edict of Nantes in 1685. Many were skilled artisans. Protestant countries such as Holland, Prussia or England benefited from their immigration; they provided an important stimulus for the development of the English Spitalfields silk industry.

Alec Hunter Joined Warners in 1932 as production manager. He controlled the style and design of their output until his death in 1958. He encouraged experimentation for power loom production of modern designs.

Ingrain Describes type of flat-woven machine-made carpet which involves two levels of warps around which the coloured threads used for the surface (and which also act as the weft) are tightly woven. The pattern is achieved by bringing the colour at the back up to the front. It produces a two-coloured cloth where the pattern on the front is the reverse of that on the back. It is also known

as 'Scotch' or 'Kidderminster'. In the 18th century, handwoven, it was machine made from the early 19th century. See also *Kilmarnock, Kidderminster*.

Fugiwo Ishimoto Born 1941, Japanese who lives in Finland. Trained as a Graphic Designer, he became interested in textile design and designed fabrics for Ichida from 1964 to 1970. In 1971 he went to Finland and since 1974 has created printed fabrics for Marimekko.

Jacquard Loom Combined the harness mechanism and versatility of a drawloom with a punch-card system, thereby giving mechanised warp and shed control. At the time of invention (1801), Joseph Marie Jacquard (1752–1834) presented a loom which cancelled any need for a drawboy and gave control to the weaver alone. Using punched holes and blanks, the card roll defined each warp combination for a pick, and lifted individual threads from the harness. This gave speed to the production of intricate and fine cloth although threading-up the loom remained a time-consuming process.

Jute Bast fibre, strong but not elastic or resistant to damp, used mainly for carpet backing and sacks.

Edward McKnight Kauffer (1890–1954) born in Great Falls, US poster artist and rug designer, who moved to England in 1914. Working from 1923 with Marion Dorn. Through her he became interested in rug design, holding, in 1929, a joint exhibition in London. In 1940 both left for New York, but despite a number of commissions Kauffer never managed the success he had achieved in England.

John Kay (1704–64) Invented flying shuttle, which he patented in 1733. This facilitated the handweaving of broadcloths over thirty-six inches wide by allowing one person to do the work which previously had been done by two. The weaver propelled the shuttle through the warp from side to side by pulling buffers or pickers along a slide-rod in a box fixed to each end of the sley.

Kekolymena Byzantine term meaning 'Forbidden Cloth'. Referred to the highest grade of silk cloth produced by the Byzantine Imperial workshops which was reserved for the use or gift of the Emperor. A policy of hierarchy through clothing was enforced in the Empire, and complex weaves, particularly those with purple threads, were forbidden to ordinary citizens and foreigners.

Kells embroidery Celtic-type designs embroidered mainly in linen thread on wool and flannel, very popular for furnishings. Introduced in 1883.

Kersey Medieval woollen cloth produced in England and named after village in East Anglia. Cheap, coarse fabric with very good weatherproof qualities.

Kidderminster Town in Worcestershire, still largest centre for machine-woven carpet in Britain. In the 16th century *Kidderminster stuffe* was mentioned in inventories of great houses to specify a low status, heavy duty textile sometimes used on the floor. This was probably the ingrain that was also sold in the 18th century as Kidderminster carpet. The hand weavers at Axminster and Wilton were adversely effected by Kidderminster's machine-driven competition; this was the eventual reason for their downfall.

Kilmarnock Most important carpet-weaving centre in Scotland. Principally renowned for the ingrain carpets known as 'Scotch', it was also from 1831 the base for a small group of hand-knotting weavers too far from any rich potential purchasers to prosper. Carpets were originally hand-woven but machine-woven from the early 19th century.

Gustav Klimt 1862–1918 Avant-garde Austrian artist who was the first President of the Vienna Secession. He designed some textiles and inspired many more.

Kloster stitch Form of couched embroidery used for large-scale German and Swiss hangings of the 15th and 16th centuries.

Knitting Textile technique involving the formation of elastic rows of stitches made from a thread of unlimited length, using two or more needles or, more recently, a machine.

Knitting stick Made from wood, metal or bone with a fork or eyelet. It supported a knitting needle in fixed position, relieving one of the hands of the knitter. This implement appears in many European countries where hand knitting is well established.

Knoll Associates Set up originally as Knoll Furniture Company in 1943. Florence Knoll (b.1917) help to popularise the International Style through the firm's editions of Classic Bauhaus design from the late 1940s. She also developed a textile division and produced woven fabrics designed by Anni Albers, Evelyn Hill, Eszter Haraszty and Suzanne Huguenin in the 1950s.

Knotless netting technique Involves working with one needle and the fingers of the other hand and is linked with home production of knitted garments for personal use. This ancient technique created fabrics of great strength, compactness, smoothness.

Knots One of the three basic components of any pile carpets together with warp and weft. The warp and weft form the structure around which the ends of the knots are tied, the ends forming the soft upper surface. In hand-knotted carpets they are usually individually tied. With machine-made carpeting, individual knotting is possible, but more frequently encountered is the technique of cutting a series of loops, as in Wilton carpeting. The separately tied knots are of a number of different types, most of which are tied around two warps.

Kossu/kesi Chinese silk tapestry weaving.

Lacis See *Filet*

Laid work Embroidery in which a cord or thread is held to the surface of the cloth and not threaded through.

Lancashire The most important centre for cotton weaving and printing in England during the Industrial Revolution. Its geography was particularly suited to mechanised mass production of cotton cloth with a damp climate and fast running water to power mill machinery. Raw cotton was imported in bulk from America via Liverpool and woven for the calico industry. Between 1810 and 1850 the print works at Banister Hall were renowned for fine blocked prints. However, restricted imports during the American Civil War left the area depressed in the late 1860s. Its subsequent revival, particularly marked in the late 19th and early 20th centuries, was checked by the development of mechanised cotton cloth production in the Far East.

Lappets Two 'streamers' attached to either side of a lady's cap, fashionable in the 18th century and informally in the 19th century.

Jack Lenor Larsen Born 1927, American textile designer. In 1952 he opened his own studio in New York, receiving major commissions for textiles for the Lever building, and other large-scale projects such as upholstery for Pan-Am and Braniff. Larsen is well known for the technical ingenuity of his fabrics and his adaptations of traditional styles and processes. He is also a teacher and writer on textiles.

Philippe de Lasalle (1723–1805) Leading Lyons silk designer and manufacturer. Originally trained in Paris as a painter under Boucher.

Marie Laurençin French artist and designer, associated with the avant-garde circle in Paris in the first decade of the 20th century. The rugs and textiles she designed were made up in pastel shades and owed much to the floral art deco style in which she painted.

Charles Le Brun (1619–90) One of the principal designers and painters during the reign of Louis XIV and artistic director of the Gobelins tapestry factory.

William Lee Invented the Hand frame knitting machine (1589) but refused patent and monopoly rights by Queen Elizabeth I, emigrated with his invention to France.

Leeds Yorkshire centre for wool weaving since the Middle Ages when sheep were a major crop developed by the Cistercian monks on the Yorkshire Wolds (hills). It continues as a major producer of woollen goods and ready-made clothes.

Leek Embroidery Society Founded 1879 by wife of Thomas Wardle, silk printer and dyer and friend of William Morris. The embroideries, mainly designed by Thomas Wardle but also by J.D. Sedding and Norman Shaw, were usually worked on ready-printed silk tussore grounds.

Liberty & Company Limited World-famous shop in Regent Street, London was founded by Arthur Lasenby Liberty (1845–1917) in 1875. Its original specialities were imported oriental goods and products in historical and revivalist styles popular with the English artistic intelligentsia. Liberty became a leading figure in the English Arts & Crafts Movement and many artists and designers were employed by the firm including C.F.A. Voysey and Archibald Knox who created the 'Stile Liberty', a successful blend of the stylistic features of both the Arts & Crafts and the Art Nouveau movements. The company did much to link art and industry and to foster progressive design and their textiles in traditional and modernist styles remain a feature.

Light In conservation the quantity of light and its colour are crucial. It is important to measure both visible and invisible (ultraviolet) light, the latter is potentially more damaging. The amount of (visible) light falling onto an object is measured in *lux*. The *lumen* expresses the amount of light being radiated from a light source. For ultra-violet light the convention is to specify the energy of the ultra-violet component per lumen. Current conservation specifications suggest sensitive objects like textiles should be illuminated below 50 lux with light with a UV content below 10 microwatts per lumen. Two instruments are used to take measurements: the lux meter, and the UV monitor.

Light: Sources The nature of each source affects the characteristics of the emitted light, notably with regard to the quantity of visible and ultra-violet light and the various proportions of each spectral component (i.e., roughly the colour). Tungsten light, for example, contains much red and yellow (as well as infra-red, which is heat, because the light source is an electrically heated filament) but relatively little of the more energetic blue and ultra-violet components, while fluorescent tubes may emit light with high levels of ultra-violet. Unwanted ultra-violet light may be removed by the use of UV filters. Tungsten lights may heat the object because they give off so much infra-red light. Fibre-optic lighting offers benefits including removal of infra-red and ultra-violet components at source but is more expensive.

Lille Bobbin lace now produced in Mechlin- and twistenet ground and Valenciennes-style with thin spidery floral motifs.

Limerick Machine net darned with elaborate patterns, a product of late 19th-century lace revival in Ireland.

Linen Produced from treated stalks of flax, herbacious annual native to Mediterranean and temperate climes. Known in ancient Egypt, the best comes from Germany and the Low Countries. Cool, lustrous, absorbent but not elastic, fabric is excellent for lace and household textiles.

Lindsey Wooley Cloth made of linen and woollen yarn. It originated in England and was much in use in the American colonies.

Mary Linwood (1755–1845) Embroideress born in Birmingham (UK) who imitated paintings in embroidery. She outlived her popularity, but there are important collections of her work in the Birmingham Museum and Art Gallery.

Elizabeth Anne Little UK painter and textile designer, who opened the shop, 'Modern Textiles', in London in 1926 to sell her own and other's designs including those of Paul Nash who helped her in the venture.

Lolol Spanish silk mentioned by the 13th-century writer Al Shakandi, who described it as a striped silk produced in Malaga.

Loom Apparatus for weaving cloth made by interlacing yarns at right angles; the warp being under tension, and the weft threaded through. Looms, traditionally a wooden frame, can be horizontal or vertical. In both hand and machine processes, the weft, wound on the shuttle, is threaded through the warp, separated or shed by a heddle or heald, a comb-like frame of wires perpendicular to the warps and pressed or beaten into place. The basic weaves are plain or tabby, the weft passing alternate warps; twill, two over, two under forming diagonal lines; satin, with a long floating warp. Patterns are drafted with dots on point or squared paper.

Loom-woven Its literal meaning describes almost any carpet and most textiles. In the field of carpets, it is used for convenience to define those that have not been hand-knotted.

Low-warp loom (*basse lisse*) The warps and loom frame lie horizontally. The weaver is unable to see the progress of his design as the finished surface is facing the floor so quality control is difficult. Faster and cheaper than the high-warp loom as warps are parted by harnesses attached to treadles. In the past it was considered inferior to the high-warp loom. Was and is used at Aubusson where a high-warp loom is used for carpets.

Lowell Historic centre of the US textile industry, situated on the Merrimack, close to New Chelmsford. Founded by Francis Cabot Lowell, as an organised factory community, a safe haven for his young largely female workforce. It flourished until 1840, and though its paternalistic spirit then waned, the town remained a focus for textile industry, including the introduction of the Jacquard loom and the mechanised carpet industry.

Francis Cabot Lowell (1775–1817) Introduced the power loom to the USA in 1814, establishing a factory at Waltham and in 1822 moving to Pawtucket, at East Chelmsford, Mass., which became the Merrimack Manufacturing Co.

Lucca In the 13th century became the first town in northern Italy to admit Muslim weavers and develop silk weaving. It remained one of the most important silk weaving centres throughout the Renaissance, producing fine cloth for the Italian market and for export.

Jean Lurçat (1892–1966) Artist and from 1915 tapestry weaver who revitalized the craft. In 1940 he joined Aubusson. In 1951 he founded the Association of Tapestry Cartoon Painters. Designed carpets for Savonnerie.

Lyons French silk centre. Originally a centre for trade in Italian silks, but weaving was encouraged by Louis XI and expanded under Colbert who imposed a ban in 1667 on the importation of all foreign woven silk. In the 1780s it employed 20,000 craftsmen; its superiority remains.

Machine Net and Lace Introduced from late 18th century. Bobbin net machine was invented in 1809 by John Heathcote, exactly reproducing twist net. Curtain net machine making distinctive square mesh ridged laces, invented by John Livsey in 1846. John Leaver's machine a variant bobbin net machine, invented in 1813 was very important and widespread, Pusher lace machine variant of bobbin lace machine invented in 1820, for lace mainly finished by hand.

Machine-woven carpets In which the loom or any part of the pile process is facilitated by mechanical power. Most textile machine processes were adaptable to some aspect of carpet weaving but machine woven pile carpet was not introduced until 1846.

Charles Mackintosh (1766–1843) Chemist and manufacturer. Patented the first rubberised and fully waterproofed cloth in 1823 by binding two fabrics with a naphtha solution of crude rubber to form a 'double-texture' cloth for coats subsequently made by Thomas Hancock. Mackintosh's name later became synonymous with rainwear. He also worked on dyes and bleaching powder. Eventually taken over by Dunlop in 1925.

Charles Rennie Mackintosh (1868–1928) Scottish architect and designer. As one of 'The Four' with his fellow architect, H.J. MacNair, and their wives the Macdonald sisters, Margaret and Frances, inaugurated the 'Glasgow Style' of decorative art, which covered a vast range of products, including textiles, especially embroidery.

Ethel Mairet (1872–1952) UK weaver who worked in Ceylon and became interested in natural dyes. She married Philip Mairet in 1913 and established the 'Gospels' Workshop in Ditchling, Sussex close to the craftsman Eric Gill and his commune. Mairet exhibited widely and sold her textiles from her own shop in Brighton, where she also taught weaving at the College of Art. She published books on dyeing, weaving and education.

Malaga City on southern coastline of Muslim Spain, an area of sericulture, silk spinning, weaving and dyeing. By the 10th century, its fabrics were regarded as of equal quality as those of Almeria.

Maltese Lace Heavy silk bobbin lace usually cream (blonde) also found in black, silk, characterised by short wheatears often in the form of a Maltese Cross. Mainly 19th century, but still made today on the island to the same patterns.

Manchester, New Hampshire, USA Textile town modelled on Lowell, developed under William Amory from 1820, flourishing until 1920s. At its height it housed 125,000 spindles, 3,500 looms, providing work for 1800 women and 900 men.

Map samplers Geographical outlines, drawn or ready printed and embroidered in silk or chenille. Popular in the late 18 and early 19th centuries for their dual educational function.

Enid Marx UK textile designer who worked for a time with Barron & Larcher. Opened her own studio in 1927, and her stylised patterns of crisp geometric shapes became well known when she became part of the Utility Team of designers at the start of the Second World War.

Mary, Queen of Scots (1542–87) Cousin to Elizabeth I and had aspirations to the English throne. During her imprisonment she became noted for her embroideries, especially those now at Oxburgh Hall, Norfolk.

Luidmila Mayakovskaya Artist and textile designer from the USSR who perfected a special type of airbrush (the aerograph) which she used to apply her designs to a wide range of textiles, using subdued colours and curving lines rather than the bright colours and geometric motifs of most Soviet-designed textiles after 1917.

Althea McNish Born Trinidad. Remained in London after training at the Royal College of Art. She designed vivid boldly drawn, influential textiles and supplied a number of firms in the 1960s and 1970s including Liberty's, Heal's, Cavendish textiles.

Mechanisation of Textile Production Basic mechanisation of textile techniques took place in Europe and America between 1730 and 1830. Advances were made in yarn preparation, spinning, weaving, finishing and all areas of printing. The majority of inventions concentrated on increased speed of production thereby reducing manual labour.

Mechlin Straight bobbin lace with characteristically thick gimp outline and hexagonal mesh ground.

Memphis Group Founded in 1981, its first avant-garde collection was launched in autumn 1981 during the Milan Furniture Fair, displaying diverse influences which brought together clashing colours and exaggerated patterns – now the hallmark of this group. Founding members included Ettore Sottass and Andrea Branz' both architect designers.

Mercerisation Chemical treatment of cotton fibres to give them lustre, more absorption to dyes, and fibre strength. The process, using caustic potash or soda was invented by John Mercer, an Accrington (UK) dyer in 1844, patented in 1850 but not used till 1895.

Merton Abbey Workshops of Morris and Co., opened in 1881, situated on outskirts of London.

Metallic Fibres A metal sheet laminated between two sheets of plastic, e.g. cellulose acetate – butyrate foil, then split into yarns of the desired width which can be incorporated into a variety of woven and knitted fabrics. Used for embroidering and also as a sewing thread. Lurex is the trade name for the Dubeckmum Co. USA.

Milanese Lace Bobbin lace of 17th to 19th centuries, easily confused with Flemish laces but the threads of the *reseau* pass underneath the *toile* in Flemish lace and resume at the other side. In Milanese lace, there is no thread passing underneath the *toile*.

Mill and Die Engraving Allowed mechanical incising of copper rollers for fabric printing.

Mille fleurs tapestries Literally translated as a thousand flowers, this term refers to tapestries with the ground decorated with many scattered flowers, often depicting courtly subjects typical of the international Gothic style. Mainly produced during the 15th and 16th centuries; one of the most famous sets is the series 'La Dame à l'Icorne.'

Modernism Term for new style of architecture and design pervasive throughout Europe and America in the 20th century, also known as the International Style. Dominant characteristics functionalism, the relationship of form and function and simplicity. New designs and materials were used for textiles compatible with modern buildings. Textural woven fabrics in natural colours were favoured more than printed patterns for soft furnishings and wall surfaces.

Mordant Chemical substance used in dyeing which allows dye stuffs easily to migrate and bind with fibre to create a stable pigment.

Joshua Morris Tapestry weaver with a workshop in Frith Street, Soho, from 1720 to 1728. He is associated with decorative Rococo tapestries with Chinoiserie motifs.

William Morris (1834–1896) Friend and associate of the Pre-Raphaelites and Philip Webb, the architect. Morris, Marshall, Faulkner and Co, his decorating firm, was founded in 1861, and successful in the 1862 Exhibition. Concentrated on natural dyes and hand-worked textiles including carpets and tapestries. His textile designs have an enduring popularity and are frequently re-issued. His conviction of the indivisibility of art, craft and spiritual values was seminal to the Arts and Crafts Movement.

May Morris (1862–1938) Daughter of William Morris and from the 1880s increasingly the supervisor and designer for his embroidery workshop. Although she worked much in her father's style, her designs are stiffer and more formal. She continued to supervise his craft workshop after his death.

Mortlake tapestries Manufactory founded by James I in 1619; the first major tapestry workshop in England inspired by Henry IV's attempt to encourage the industry in France. It subsequently declined closing in 1703 unable to combat competition from France and independent weavers working in London. The Mortlake mark was a red cross on a white shield (this also occurs on other London tapestries).

Morton Sundour Fabric Ltd Textile manufacturers, Carlisle. Set up in 1914. Except for lace and carpet production the firm took over all the manufacturing process of Alexander Morton & Co. It specialised in 'Sundour' unfadable fabrics researching and manufacturing synthetic vat dyestuffs.

Mulham Cloth with silk warp and cotton weft produced in Muslim Spain.

Paul Nash (1889–1946) UK artist and designer, his textile designs were produced by Footprints Workshop, Cresta Silks and the Old Bleach Linen Company Limited of Northern Ireland.

Needle lace Generic term for lace built up with buttonhole stitches usually on a framework of thread pinned to a parchment-pricked pattern. When magnified the basic construction can be seen. Also known as Needlepoint, but not in USA where it is an embroidery term.

Needle Painting Realistic depiction in stitchery, usually carried out in long and short stitch. Its quality depends on its drawing and the subtlety of the shading. A well known executant in the early 19th century was Mary Linwood.

Needlerun Net Usually of machine net with a hand darned pattern. Very popular for wedding veils and stoles. Much was made at Limerick from mid 19th century and is known as Limerick lace.

Needlework pictures Pictorial embroidery especially the ready drawn or printed pictures on a satin ground with additional painted detail popular in the late 18th early 19th centuries.

Jessie Rowatt Newbery UK embroiderer, a teacher of decorative art at the Glasgow School of Art, wife of the principal, Francis Newbery. Her innovative embroidery classes, from 1894–1908, set the standard for needlework education in Britain. Inspired by universal excellence, she promoted the use of strong, inexpensive materials decorated with simplified designs for everyday use as an alternative to the rich fabrics and more elaborate style of the Royal School of Needlework.

New York Decorative Art Society Formed in 1877 by committee of philanthropic women and encouraged by Candace Wheeler, it was modelled on London's Royal School of Art Needlework and the first secretary was Elizabeth, General Custer's widow. It aimed to educate and instruct, set standards and find outlets for women who wanted to earn a living in the decorative arts. Similar societies in other American cities soon followed.

Nancy Nicholson (1899–1977) UK illustrator and designer, who ran her own business, the Poulk Press, to design and print fabrics.

Francis Nixon Irish portrait engraver, responsible for introducing the copperengraving technique in the printing of fabrics in 1752 at Drumcondra printworks near Dublin. The process was introduced into England in 1756.

Christophe-Philippe Oberkampf (1738–1815) On the removal of the ban on the manufacture of printed cottons in France, in 1759 he set up a successful factory for the manufacture of printed cottons at Jouy. Designs typically consisted of chinoiseries or bucolic scenes.

Old Windsor Tapestry Manufactory Set up in 1876. Specialised in tapestries depicting contemporary scenes, as well as historical subjects, including the 'Mort D'Arthur'. It closed by the end of the century.

Olefin Fibres Consist of polyethylene and polypropylene. Both derive from the petroleum industry. The fibres have specialist uses. Polyethylene was the first to be used as a textile by Courtaulds, who produced a fibre called 'Courlene', for upholstery and car seats. Woven in gay patterns, it is used for deck chairs and can also be used for bathroom covers and shower curtains. Polypropylene, also non-absorbent, has a low melting point. It is used to make the knitted backing for 'fur fabrics'. ICI manufacture a staple polypropylene fibre called 'Spunstron' and British Celanese Ltd a monofilament called 'Cournova'. ICI also produce a polypropylene fibre called 'Ulston' used for making blankets, protective clothing, upholstery fabrics and carpets.

Opus Anglicanum Magnificent embroideries of gold and silk threads made in England from Anglo-Saxon times until the craft's decline at the end of the 14th century. Famed throughout Europe, and considered at least as precious as goldsmiths' work.

Opus Teutonicum Whitework linen embroidery produced in Germany in the Middle Ages, primarily for church use. Colour is rare. The variety of stitches and use of openwork and drawn-thread techniques created interest.

Or Nué Gold laid work embroidery in which the gold thread is held by being caught from the back at intervals rather than couched on the surface. It gives a smoother line.

Jean Baptist Oudry (1686–1755) Painter, closely associated with the French tapestry industry. Became director of the manufactory at Beauvais in 1734, as well as artistic director at Gobelins.

Paisley Pattern and Paisley Shawls Pattern of oriental origin based on Indian motifs. Design adapted by and named after the town in Scotland, where shawls were made throughout the 19th century inspired by shawls from Kashmir, using fine worsted wools, rich colours and closely packed motifs.

Palampore Coverlet named after a town in Gujarat in India. It is composed of a single chintz (painted cotton) panel. Very fashionable by the late 17th century. In the years 1695–6 the East India Company imported 20,000 large 10,000 middling and 10,000 small palampores.

Pantograph Adjustable device for the copying and rescaling of designs and in a textile context a tool for repeatedly engraving printing rollers capable of altering the scale of the original cartoon.

Peter Parisot Born Pierre Norbert in Lorraine. A disillusioned priest, he fled to London before 1748 and became naturalised as Peter Paddington. Opened carpet workshops in

Paddington, then Fulham. The factory closed in 1755.

Passements French for braid or trimming (passementerie), also refers to early metal thread laces of the 16th century, originally designed to lay on top of fine silks.

Patchwork Pieces of fabric joined to form a pattern, usually an assemblage of geometric shapes cut with a template. Although it existed from early times as a basic method of recycling fragments, the earliest extant British examples are from Levens Hall, Cumbria, early 18th century. Krazy patchwork was particularly popular in the 1980s.

Elizabeth Peacock (1880–1969) UK weaver who worked with Ethel Mairet before establishing her own workshop at Clayton, Sussex from 1922 to 1969. Peacock exhibited and demonstrated in London and provincial galleries; she taught weaving and was a co-founder of the Guild of Weavers, Spinners and Dyers in 1931.

Pencilling Hand technique used with block printing to colour in outlined motifs. Prior to the introduction of copperplate and roller printing, 'pencillers' were regularly employed in workshops. Women applied ink with a horsehair brush blocking in colour and overlaying areas to give a tonal effect.

Marion Pepler Designed rugs in the 1920s and 1930s. She executed designs for Wilton, and many of her rugs were sold by her brother-in-law's firm, Gordon Russell Ltd.

Charles Percier (1764–1838) Designer and artist born in Paris. Worked with Pierre Fontaine. On their return to Paris, they created a new classical style adopted by Napoleon as the official style of the Empire, publishing their ideas in 1801 as the *Recueil de decorations interieures*. They made brief forays into the Renaissance and Gothic styles.

William Henry Perkin (1837–1907) Invented in 1856 the first fast aniline dye derived from coal tar, benzine purple (from 1858 Tyrian purple).

Philip the Bold (d.1404) First Duke of Burgundy. Notable patron, whose marriage brought the tapestry centres of Artois into Burgundian dominion.

Photochemical Reaction Chemical reaction caused by light. Significant for conservation of textiles.

Jean Picart Le Doux (1902–1982) Paris-born tapestry designer. Contributor to the 1944 exhibition at the Salon des Artistes Decorateurs of contemporary tapestries. His work serene, tidy and logical concentrates on landscapes, birds and animals.

Picots Needle lace elaborations usually to *brides*, but also to raised needle laces such as *Point de Neige* and *Gros Point*.

Pile Threads that protrude on the surface. Usually loops of thread or in carpets cut ends of separate knots.

Jean-Baptiste Pillement (1728–1808) Painter and designer. Born in Lyons, the son of a textile designer. There are good examples of his decorative in chinoiserie style work in Poland, Italy and Vienna.

Plasticisers Substance added to a synthetic resin to retain its flexibility.

Point D'Angleterre Lace, bobbin or needle point, made in Belgium in the 18th century, for export to England, hence the name. The term revived late 19th century for different types of Belgian lace.

Point de France Made from soft linen thread. A speciality of Mechlin, Belgium, in the 18th century. Industry established by Colbert in Alençon in 1665 with a monopoly to supply the French court. The monopoly expired in 1677. Point de France became associated with needle lace with the figurative on heraldic designs and a hexagonal *picoté* mesh.

Point de Gaze Fine 19th-century Brussels needle lace worked with flowers especially roses with raised petals on a net ground.

Point rentré Method of shading introduced by textile designer Jean Revel in the early 18th century, the shades of colour are dovetailed in weaving to give an illusion of three-dimensional form.

Polyamide Fibres The first entirely chemical fibre. Created by H. Carothers, an American chemist, at E.I. du Pont de Nemours & Co. in the USA during the 1930s. Created by a process of polymerisation – a method of linking atoms and groups of atoms to create long molecules which are linked to form a larger molecule – the polymer. Nylon is the generic term and includes Nylon 66 produced as Bri-Nylon by ICI Fibres Ltd. and Blue-C Nylon by Monsanto Textuli in Luxembourg. Nylon 66 (originally developed in Germany under a different chemical process) is produced by Courtaulds, and Enkalon by British Enkalon. Celon is used for knitted fabrics, i.e. lingerie, nylon shirtings, dresses, stretch slacks and socks.

Polyester Man-made fibre produced from petroleum and its by-products, invented and developed in Britain by J.R. Whinfield and J.T. Dickson of the Calico Printers Association and is produced by ICI in Britain. Dacron based on the same polymer is manufactured by E.I. du Pont de Nemours & Co. in the USA. (Polyester fibres produce both filament yarn and stable fibre.) It is extremely hardwearing mixing well with cotton, wool and viscose. It is used in all types of dress and furnishing fabrics.

Polyvinyl Chloride Discovered in the last century, but successful conversion to a spinning material suitable for fabrics is recent. Waterproof, non-absorbent, with a very low melting point, the range is limited. As a plastic sheeting it can be obtained in various thicknesses, it is non-porous and can be printed in bright colours and patterns or can be self-coloured throughout. The surface can be moulded into different textures.

Portières From the French, curtains hung over a doorway to prevent draft or decoratively around it.

Pouncing Method of copying patterns which predated tracing. The 'pounce', commonly powdered juniper gum, coloured chalk or pipe clay, was pressed through pin-holes in the design outline onto the cloth beneath and the spots then joined with pen or paint brush.

Power Loom Launched with limited success by Cartwright in 1790, steam powered by 1791 and commercially viable in 1809.

Pulled work Form of open work embroidery consisting of a decorative drawing together of the warp threads after the weft is removed.

Punto in Aria From the Italian for 'Stitches in the Air'. Needle lace formed by pinning threads to a parchment pattern and then elaborating by building up patterns with buttonhole stitches. Similar in effect to *reticella*, but without the restrictions imposed by the weave of linen ground cloth. First mentioned in pattern books in 1587 though probably produced by professionals before that date.

Mary Quant Born 1934, in London. Fashion, household furnishings and product designer. Freelance since 1955, she was the first to use PVC in fashion and was the first designer of tights for the Nylon Hosiery Company.

Quilting Materials interlined for warmth or stiffness and held together with lines of stitching, regular and or decorative. Although known from mediaeval period, most surviving examples are from the 18th century. Corded quilting is known as *Trapunto*. Hand sewers use running or back stitch but since late 19th century attachments for the sewing machine have been available.

Raphael Cartoons Set of tapestry cartoons designed by Raphael (1483–1520) in 1515. Woven for Pope Leo X in Brussels, and intended for the Sistine Chapel in Rome, they depict scenes from the lives of the apostles. They mark an important point in the history of tapestry design, as they were among the earliest to be conceived as three-dimensional pictures, drawn in the Renaissance style, as opposed to the flat decorative Gothic schemes. They were purchased by Charles I in 1619 for £300 in Genoa. Now on permanent display at the Victoria and Albert Museum.

Rapier Loom In 1947 Dornier, the German aircraft manufactures, started making textile machines, producing their prototype rapier loom in 1963. The operation of the shuttle is replaced by two carrier rapiers from each side of the loom which transfer the yarn in mid-shed. The weft is supplied from cones on the right-hand side only. When the carriers meet one weft yarn is transferred from the right-hand to the left-hand carrier and that then reverses direction and returns to the side.

Regenerated Cellulose Fibre Viscose became the first man-made fibre to be produced commercially. In 1644, Robert Hooke an English scientist suggested that it should be possible to make fibre in a similar way to the production of silk by the silkworm, but not until 1855 was a patent was taken out by George Audemars from Switzerland. His invention of a nitrocellullose fibre was limited because of its flammability. Sir Joseph Swan in 1883 patented a process for extruding nitrocellullose from wood pulp but applied it to electric light bulbs. Artificial silk was successfully manufactured by Count Hilaire de Chardonnet for the Paris Exhibition of 1889, using cotton waste, sulphuric acid and nitric acids. However large-scale production was never realised. In 1892 a process for the manufacture of viscose (viscose became known in America as rayon in 1924), wood pulp dissolved in caustic soda and carbon bisulphide, was patented by Cross, Bevan and Beadle.

Reseau Mesh or net ground. This varies according to the characteristics of the place of manufacture, and is bobbin e.g. *Droschel* in Brussels lace, bobbins mesh; *Fond Chant* short for *Chantilly*, bobbin mesh also known as *Point de Paris*, a six-pointed star mesh; *Fond Simple* with four sides with two twists, two sides with one cross over, also known as *twist net*; *Reseau rosace* hexagonal needle mesh as in Alençon or Argentan, where it is strengthened with buttonhole stitches on all sides; *Valenciennes* with plaited sides; *Mechlin* partly plaited hexagonal bobbin mesh.

Reticella Needle lace formed by removing threads from a panel of linen, leaving a geometric grid, which is then elaborated with buttonhole stitches. The earliest pattern books recorded it in 1587; Continues to be made in the 20th century as a peasant lace (*Erzgebirge*).

Zandra Rhodes Textile designer who designs clothes to complement her fabrics. Her inspirations are varied, thematic, romantic and ethographic, their effect on the sheer floating fabrics she prefers, highly romantic.

Rieter Embroidery Machine Invention that combined the action of an industrial sewing machine with earlier embroidery models. Stitching was achieved by a shuttle and needle which looped two continuous threads through a layer of cloth.

Rococo Artistic style current in the early to mid 18th century. Its dominant design elements are C scrolls and countercurves, also shell motifs. It is seen at its most developed in France and Germany rather than the UK.

Rosaline 19th century variant of Brussels bobbin lace in imitation of Venetian 17th-century needle lace, consisting of bobbin lace scrolls linked by *brides*.

Muriel Rose (1897–1986) Important figure in the craft revival of the inter-war years in Britain, she promoted the best in craftsmanship at her Little Gallery in Sloane Street, London.

Rotary (Roller) Screen Printing Rotary machines for screen printing have been in commercial use since 1954, but it was in the late 1960s that they gained popularity in the textile industry and today 90 per cent of all fabrics worldwide are rotary printed.

Royal School of Needlework Originally named the Royal School of Art Needlework, established in 1872 as part of the Art Embroidery movement in England. Princess Christian of Schleswig-Holstein stood as president with a committee of renowned needlewomen including Lady Marion Alford. It aimed to 'supply suitable employment for poor gentle folk' and undertook commissions for conservation and design. William Morris and Walter Crane were among their clientele. They successfully participated internationally in the late 19th-century exhibitions of work. They are now housed at Hampton Court Palace, Isleworth.

Emile Jacques Ruhlmann (1879–1933) French designer who established the firm Ruhlmann & Laurent in 1919. He designed textiles and carpets as well the high-quality luxury furniture which the firm exhibited at the 1925 Paris Exhibition.

John Ruskin (1819–1900) UK philosopher and aesthete whose influential work on aesthetics, was to inspire William Morris. He was a champion of the Gothic Revival and established the St George's Guild in the hope of recreating medieaval artisan practices.

Rya Name used for a group of Scandinavian rugs first mentioned in the Middle Ages, continuing in production until the 19th century. Small and typified by long shaggy pile on a coarsely woven foundation, they are suitable for the cold temperatures and were used as rugs and bed coverings. Early designs often include the date and the initials of the weaver. Revived in the 20th century as a vehicle for imaginative artistic production.

Sable work French term for very fine bead work popular in the third quarter of the 18th century. The beads were as small as grains of sand (Fr *sable*) hence the term.

St Petersburg Tapestry Factory Founded with the help of French workers in 1717, it survived until 1859. At its best, its output was of extremely high quality, mostly influenced by the French designs of the period, but with local variations, especially a fondness for tapestry portraiture. From the end of the 1820s production was almost entirely of flat-woven carpets.

Thomas Saint London cabinet-maker, who patented a sewing-machine in 1790 when he registered his invention for stitching leather apparently never used, along with other specifications for a braid-making machine and woolcombing mechanism.

Sir Titus Salt (1803–1876) Textile manufacturer. From 1834 he pioneered the use of alpaca in the woollen industry creating a strong lustrous fabric in universal demand. Between 1850–72 he built his model industrial town Saltaire outside Bradford to accommodate 3000 workers, producing 30,000 yards of cloth daily.

Sampler Piece of fabric used to practise embroidery or show off skills. The earliest known example (200–500AD) is Peruvian. They were common educational tools between 16th and 19th centuries and in addition to motifs and stitches usually include letters, numbers and sometimes a verse, and were often signed.

A. Sanderson & Son Wallpaper and textile manufacturer. Established in 1860 by Arthur Sanderson (d.1882). Furnishing printworks build at Uxbridge in 1921, and the weaving mill started in 1934. It offers a huge range of fabrics, some of the best known designs being the William Morris prints. Sanderson also has the William Morris wallpaper blocks.

Savonnerie Name of products of the 'Manufacture Royale de la Savonnerie', the old soap factory on the outskirts of Paris, an offshoot of that founded in the Louvre by Pierre Dupont in 1608, established by his former pupil, Simon Lourdet in 1627. It has always been under the control of the central power in France, owing all its commissions to that source. Each was designed by an artist, either a designer for the factory or, especially in recent years, an outsider for a commission. Quality of output has always been extremely high. Principally known for its pile carpets, it also produced a number of furnishing items. The highpoint was a series of carpets ordered by Louis XIV for the palace at Versailles in about 1675. The factory is still in production, although it has moved further out of Paris.

School of Design for Women Founded in Philadelphia by Mrs King Peter in 1844.

Screen Printing A form of stencilling, carried out by hand. Originally silk was stretched over a wooden frame, but this has changed to either nylon or a glass-fibre fabric. The design requires a screen for each colour, and various methods can be used to apply the design. Simple methods include painting out the background with wax or varnish to more advanced photo-mechanical processes. Hand screen printing has many advantages including set up costs and it is easier to change a set of colours. It is favoured by designers as a method for more experimental work.

Sewing Machines Initially introduced for industrial use and although patents were registered in England as early as 1790, the majority were taken out in America between 1845 and 1854. The American industry had grown to include 200 companies by the early 1900s. Domestic machines were common from the 1860s onwards operated by hand or treadle, and greatly boosted interest in home dress-making. Later developments enabled most households to own an electrically-powered machine. Today computerised models are available to industrial and home users.

William Sheldon Founded the first English tapestry workshops at Barcheston in Warwickshire, c.1560. The Sheldon workshops were continued under his son Ralph, but had closed down by c.1613.

Sicily Sericulture was introduced into Norman Sicily by the Arabs. Most raw silk was exported to other weaving centres, but silk cloth was produced for the court, particularly during the 12th century under the Norman king, Roger II.

Silica Gel A dessicant in the form of granules or beads. Some types are 'indicating', changing colour when saturated. Can be regenerated for re-use.

Silk Produce of the caterpillar of the silk worm moth which spins cocoons of continuous lengths of silk, 600–900 metres long, basically a fibroin or protein. The threads of several cocoons are thrown as thraw-twist into a yarn from which the sericin or gum is removed in hot water. Native to China, the silk worm is now also cultivated in the Mediterranean. Silk is strong, elastic, absorbent and lustrous.

Silver Studio Arthur Silver (1853–1896) founded the very successful Silver Studio in

1880. Although conducted on firm commercial lines, the ideals of the Arts & Crafts Movement, the decorative art of Japan, the textile collection of the Victoria and Albert Museum, and the work of designers such as Mackmurdo, Crane, Voysey and Morris were all influential. Silver blended these various influences into an assured art nouveau style which helped to popularise and extend the appreciation to a wider public. His sons, Rex and Harry Silver succeeded him. Textiles and wallpapers were exported to Europe and America and the studio survived to 1963; excellent archives exist at Middlesex Polytechnic, London.

Isaac Merrit Singer (1811–1875) Founder of the sewing machine firm, born New York, a self-taught engineer who invented an improvement of the Elias Howe sewing machine, and went into operation in Boston Mass in 1850. Disputes over patents were settled by the patent pool of 1854. Singers were active in promoting the domestic as well as the industrial sewing machine, and made a feature of advertising and hire purchase. By the late 19th century they had opened factories world wide.

Samuel Slater (1768–1835) Born Derbyshire UK, apprentice and factory manager to Jedediah Strutt and Richard Arkwright, emigrated to USA in 1789, working with Moses Brown until 1793 on establishment of Arkwright spinning mill at Waltham, then at Pawtucket Rhode Island and finally at Lowell on the Merrimack.

Slips Embroidered motifs cut out and applied to large pieces of material and much used in the late 16th and 17th century, especially on heavy silk or velvet grounds hangings.

Smocking Embroidery on a regular tight pleated ground which takes its name from the Old English for shirt or shift for which it was first used, though by the 19th century it was principally applied to agricultural overalls. By the end of the century it was popular for aesthetic dresses and children's clothes. Back-stitch or running stitch holds the pleats in place which are then re-embroidered generally in chain, feather stitch or herringbone.

Soho Tapestries Generic term often used incorrectly to describe all 18th-century English tapestries; should refer only to tapestries produced in the Soho area where several independent workshops existed then (c.1689–1770), all producing Rococo-style tapestries.

Spain and Silk Weaving The techniques were introduced after the Islamic invasion of 711–2. The raw silk had to be imported, but sericulture was soon introduced. Very fine silks were woven and exported to Muslim and Christian countries.

Spitalfields District in East End of London, in the 17th and 18th centuries, the most important centre for the manufacture of silk in England. With the revocation of the Edict of Nantes in 1685 many Huguenot weavers settled there. The skill which they brought was an important stimulus in the development of the industry.

Spinning Twisting of threads so as to strengthen, lengthen and variegate them. The manual process employs a drop spindle or wheel. The process was first mechanised by the cotton gin.

William Sprague Carpet manufacturer born in Kidderminster, moved to Axminster to learn his trade from Thomas Whitty. He emigrated to Philadelphia in the 1780s setting up narrow looms to weave pile carpets, probably in 1790. His most famous commission was undertaken in 1791; a carpet for the floor of Congress Hall, Philadelphia that measured 17 feet by 15 feet.

Sprang Ancient form of decorative looped mesh.

Stehli Silk Corporation, New York Influential in novelty design from 1925 into the early 1930s when artistic director Kneeland Green collaborated with among others photographer Edward Steichen and tennis star Helen Wills Moody.

Varvara Stepanova 1895–1958 USSR artist and textile designer who was, with her husband Alexander Rodchenko, a Russian Constructivist who felt that art should be socially aware. Stepanova answered the call for artists to join factory unions and help to revolutionise textile design; to discard the traditional floral designs for those of geometric or abstract designs. Because textiles were mass produced and mass consumed they were seen as a potent force for socialist propaganda.

Gustave Stickley (1857–1946) The foremost Arts & Crafts furniture manufacturer in the United States. He followed precepts of Ruskin and Morris disseminating their views in *The Craftsman* (1901–1916).

Stocking stitch Plain-knit structure when all the loops are on one face of the fabric and the two faces are dissimilar.

Straight Lace Generic term for bobbin lace in which the pattern-linking bars or mesh ground are made at the same time.

Marianne Straub Textile designer, born in Switzerland 1909. She moved to England and attended the Bradford Technical College (1932–33) after which she worked briefly with Ethel Mairet. From 1950–1970 she worked for Warners.

George Edmund Street (1824–1881) Ecclesiastical and domestic architect and designer, Street carried out numerous church embroideries worked by Jones and Willis of Birmingham, a number of which were displayed at the 1851 Great Exhibition.

Jedediah Strutt (1726–1797) Invented a device for making ribbed garments on the stocking frame in 1758, later known as the Derbyshire patent rib. From 1769–1782 he was partner to Richard Arkwright in the development of the spinning frame, to which he contributed, opening factories at Cromford and Belper, in Derbyshire.

Stumpwork Mid 17th-century embroidery, usually figurative and worked from figures derived from stamps or engravings, hence the term. Often applied to pictures or caskets, it involves much raised work, appliqué, needle-point and beadwork.

Sulzar Machine Machine based on a high degree of precision engineering and a revolutionary weft insertion system developed by the Swiss Sulzer brothers in the 1950s. A shuttleless loom utilises a number of tiny projectiles, 90mm long, with gripper attachments which are fired across the loom at tremendous speed by the reflex action of a torsion rod. Each gripper projectile picks up yarn from a cone and takes it through the warp where it is severed by a cutter motion. In the return cycle the loose end of the weft is tucked in to form a selvedge while the projectile returns to its former position.

Ann Sutton Born 1935, British. Studied for National Diploma in Design in Embroidery and Weaving at Cardiff College of Art. Along with teaching, she has worked in freelance designing and as consultant designer to the Welsh Woollen Association. Responsible for the International Exhibitions of Miniature Textiles between 1974 and 1980. Has presented television series on weaving and is the author of various publications.

Tambouring Chain stitch worked with a small hook over a tambour (or drum frame). A fast and effective method of embroidering large surfaces. Introduced from the East in the mid 18th century and much used in white-and bead embroidery.

Tapestry Biennale Exhibition first held in 1962 at Lausanne with the aim of encouraging interest in contemporary tapestries.

Tapestry loom Although tapestry can be woven on any loom, the specialised one does not need a batten for beating the wefts down. There are two types: the high-warp and the low-warp loom.

Tapestry Marks Interwoven in the border, the distinguishing mark of the workshop, sometimes the signature and initials of the designer and the date. Gothic tapestries are rarely marked. Current practice includes an identification tape stitched to the back, numbered and signed.

Tapestry weaving Differs in that the weft does not pass all the way across the warps but only where that colour is necessary. When the area is finished the weft is left hanging. Many different-coloured wefts are used to create the pattern by interlacing with and gradually covering all the warps. Each different weft area should be bound to the next to give a tapestry strength and stop it splitting.

Tatting Circular motifs linked together, made with a shuttle and single thread looped and knotted between the fingers.

Teasel Grows in Europe around the Mediterranean and in tropical Africa. The dried heads of the Fuller's teasel which have hooked bracts were used for raising the surface of woollen fabrics, usually fixed to a pair of small wooden hand frames.

Barthelem Thimonnier Successful in using sewing-machines for commercial production of military uniforms patenting his own model in 1830.

Louis Comfort Tiffany (1848–1933) US designer, trained initially as a painter before being involved with Candace Wheeler in the decorating firm Associated Artists. In 1885 he founded the Tiffany Glass Company following his early interest in stained glass. He benefited from a close commercial link with Samuel Bing. Tiffany designed and produced a wide range of art objects including textiles.

Tiraz Islamic fabric produced also in Spain. Very light-weight cloth with an open weave distinguished by its bands of Kufic inscriptions which were usually religious texts or the names of sultans or noblemen. Woven in gold or coloured thread, they formed a prominent decoration.

Toile Most solid and cloth-like (Fr. *toile*, cloth) part of lace as opposed to the net.

Toiles de Jouy Scenic or floral printed cottons manufactured at the factory of Christopher Philip Oberkampf at Jouy, near Versailles from 1760 until 1843. Popular throughout the late 18th century for furnishing purposes and the factory continued beyond Oberkampf's death in 1815 until 1843. Various innovations were incorporated: fast colours, prepared green ink and steam dyeing. Fabrics were characterised by engraved figurative vignettes showing domestic, industrial and picturesque scenes in an all-over repeat. Their popularity prompted many imitations.

Toledo Important centre for silk production in 15th–16th century Christian Spain. Silk weaving began there probably in the 11th century, before the city was captured by the Christians in 1085. Produced plain velvets, satins, figured silks and damasks.

Torchon Simple bobbin lace characterised by a ground set at 45° to the edge of the lace, i.e. diagonally, worked with only two bobbins and having rather straight geometric designs.

Tours Since the late 15th century, one of the most important centres for silk production in France. In particular patronised by Cardinal Richelieu who introduced protective laws to limit the importation of silk from Italy.

Transfer Printing Heat-transfer method of patterning synthetic fibres. The pattern is first printed onto a paper web with special inks, usually containing dispersed dyestuffs which sublime at temperatures between 160° and 220° F. Sublimation is the process whereby a solid is converted into a vapour by heat and back again into a solid on cooling. At these temperatures the dyestuffs being vapourised transfer to the fabric and are fixed at that temperature. The majority of polyesters, acrylics, Nylon 66, actate and triacetate fibres are suitable for the transfer process. The process is particularly popular in the knitting industry.

Turkey Red Synthetic dye originally created for use on cotton using a madder base which required time-consuming work. Came to Europe from India during the calico craze and by the 18th century Glasgow and the Vale of Levin in Scotland had become centres for dye manufacture. In 1785, George Mackintosh of Glasgow went into partnership with M. Papillon, a dyer from Rouen, and together they launched one of the largest dyeworks in Scotland. Output remained high throughout the Victorian period although madder was now replaced by synthetic alizarin invented by H. Perkin in 1865.

Turkeywork Form of pile embroidery on perhaps small scale domestic carpet weaving. It was popular for upholstery and floor covering in the 17th century.

Underside Couching Embroidery technique for attaching gold thread to the surface of a cloth, commonly used in Opus Anglicanum embroidery. Metal thread is secured at regular points with a loop stitch ensuring no gold thread is wasted on the back of the cloth.

Valenciennes Straight bobbin lace with either a plaited square or round mesh. The solid part of the pattern is characteristically outlined with pinholes. High point in early 18th century, revived in the 19th century.

Henri Van de Velde (1863–1957) Belgian painter, but inspired by the ideas of Ruskin and Morris he concentrated on design and architecture. The flowing curves of art nouveau were superseded by the functional Modern style in his designs and he became more of a writer and critic on design than a practitioner.

Velvet Thick, rich silk material produced by a pile warp which is raised in loops above the ground weave by the introduction of thin rods during weaving. When covered with pile it is referred to as 'solid' and when free as 'voided'. Velvet is used both for clothing and as a furnishing material.

Velvet Pile Loosely used to describe carpets that employ the cut- rather than loop-pile technique. It is also used to describe the best quality of Wilton machine carpeting. Sometimes referred to as 'veloute'.

Venice Important port and market-place for those wishing to acquire luxury textiles from the East and the Far East. Many Byzantine silks passed through Venice which had a very generous trading agreement with the Byzantines. By the 14th century Venice had a silk-weaving community of its own producing textiles and ribbons.

Versailles Palace of Louis XIV built outside Paris 1669–1710, Charles Le Brun responsible for much of the interior decoration. Its furnishings were largely provided by the *manufactures royales* developed by Colbert; these include tapestries from Beauvais and Gobelins and carpets from Savonnerie.

Vestments Worn by officiating priests in churches which follow the traditional rites of the Catholic Church. A full set will include a cope, chasuble, dalmatic, tunicle, maniple, mitre, pallium and stole. Usually highly decorative, applied bands of ornament being termed orphreys or apparels. The alb is white though sometimes decorated at cuffs and hem. Vestment colours vary according to the different festivals of the canonical year.

Victoria & Albert Museum, London Began life as the South Kensington Museum created by Henry Cole from the profits of the Great Exhibition. Opened in 1856. Houses the world's largest collection of decorative art. The aim of improving public taste in design matters and the application of art to industrial products was born out of despair at Britain's falling export trade but the concept inspired all subsequent decorative art museums. It includes a Department of Textiles and Dress with a large international collection.

C.F.A. Voysey (1857–1941) UK designer and architect associated with the Gothic Revival movement, internationally known for his many decorative artifacts including textiles. His own designs owed something to the Gothic influence of Pugin but were much simpler and more graphic.

Warner & Sons Operated as a silk-weaving company in Spitalfields, London, set up by Benjamin Warner in 1870. Family business renowned for high-quality furnishing fabrics, particularly silks and velvets. In 1895 the firm moved to Braintree in Essex and established an international clientele.

Warp and Weft Warp threads are spaced and set on the loom running the length of a piece of woven cloth. A selvedge or strengthened border is made at each side. The intersecting threads which weave the cloth are known as the weft; these cross the warp at right angles running from selvedge to selvedge.

Watts and Co. Ecclesiastical furnishing company formed in 1874 by architects G.F. Bodley, Thomas Garner and George Gilbert Scott the Younger. Furniture, woven textiles and embroideries produced for church use and interior decoration, all relying on Gothic motifs. Still in operation in London.

Weighting To add more weight in the processing metal salts are added e.g. tin, to improve the appearance of a thin silk, or natural gums or sugars to facilitate weaving.

West Dean Tapestry Studio Founded 1976, teams use low-warp looms. Established a policy of translation by weavers of paintings and drawings, including 'Mother and Child' by Henry Moore.

Wheatears Small bobbin lace motifs especially common in Maltese lace.

Candace Thurber Wheeler (1828–1923) US designer and founder with Louis Comfort Tiffany in 1877 of the Decorative Arts Society, in part inspired by the Royal School of Needlework, and in 1879, the decorative firm Associated Artists. She was a skilled embroideress and in addition to devising interesting and innovative textiles for interior decoration introduced embroidered tapestries on a silk ground.

Whitework Embroidery usually in white linen or cotton on a matching ground and often involving decorative openwork. Very popular in the 18th and early 19th centuries.

Eli Whitney (1765–1825) Born Westborough, Mass. inventor. On a visit to the Southern States he accepted a challenge to devise a cleaning method for the green seed cotton heads, hitherto very labour intensive, and devised the cotton gin, patented in 1794. This was instrumental in raising American exports of cotton fibre.

Thomas Whitty (1716–1792) Carpet manufacturer, trained as a weaver but taught himself the knotting technique. After a tour of Parisot's Fulham factory, he made a loom in his home town of Axminster where, in 1755, he wove his first carpet. Through influential local patronage and winning the Royal Society Prizes for the years 1757–1759, he managed to produce carpets as good as and cheaper than those of his rivals.

Wiener Werkstätte The Vienna Workshop was founded in 1903 specifically aimed at making and selling the best in modern design and craftsmanship. Founder members were the designers Josef Hoffmann (1870–1956) and Kolomann Moser (1868–1918) while wealthy textile manufacturer Fritz Waerndorfer (1869–1939) provided the backing. Two English guilds, Art Workers Guild and C.R. Ashbee's Guild of Handicraft, were direct ideological predecessors.

Wilton Small town in Wiltshire, where carpets were made from the 18th century. In 1836 a local maker of machine made carpets, Mr Blackmore, purchased the bankrupt stock of Whitty's Axminster hand weaving establishment, together with the good will, and moved to Wilton where he managed to re-establish the hand-weaving business. It changed hands a few times, was rescued from near bankruptcy in 1905, and was re-founded as the Wilton Royal Factory Co. Ltd. The hand-woven products continued to use the name of Axminster up until the last hand-loom stopped in 1957. The factory is still in production making machine-carpeting. Wilton is also used to describe a particular type of machine-carpeting, in structure almost identical to Brussels carpeting, but the pile is cut instead of being looped. This has the advantage in production that two carpets can be made face to face, the cutting of the pile splitting the two finished products.

Wool Fibrous coat of a living animal, insulating against extremes of temperature. Keratin, a form of protein, it is absorbent, elastic, resilient. For textile use, it is clipped, sorted, scoured or cleaned, carded to straighten, spun, woven, then checked or burled to remove knots, fulled or milled to shrink, finally washed, smoothed, sheared and pressed. Formerly a hand process, it has been mechanised since the mid 19th century.

Wool Trade Medieval trade in luxury woollen cloth was international. Fine quality fleece produced in England, in areas such as Yorkshire, the Cotswolds, Shropshire and Herefordshire, and also in Spain where Merino sheep introduced by the Berbers. Almost all fine wool was exported to the famous weaving centres of Flanders. This regular trade was known as the Wool Trade and continued until the English weaving industry became competitive in the 13th century.

Worsted Common type of lightweight smooth and strong woollen cloth made of long staple fleece which has been carded and combed giving a strong, even quality twist.

Wool Staple Medieval company of English wool merchants whose control over the export of English wool developed from early legislation at the end of the 13th century, until the eventual establishment of the Company of the Staple of Calais in 1399. Ensured that duty on wool, an important source of revenue for the Crown, was levied correctly, and enabled the Crown to raise loans on the security of the wool to be exported.

Zimmer Flat Bed Machine Uses 'magnet-roll' system for transferring colour through the mesh of the screen. This is a simple round metal roller placed loosely in the screen with the dye paste and moved along by means of a magnetic coil under the printing blanket, drawing the dye stuff through the mesh.

NOTES TO CHAPTERS

CHAPTER FOUR

1. Quoted in *The Edwardian Era*, edited by Jane Beckett and Deborah Cherry. Phaidon Press & Barbican Art Gallery, 1987.
2. Comment by Samuel Bing in 1898, three years after he opened his Galéries de l'Art Nouveau in Paris. Quoted in *Sources of Art Nouveau*, Stephan Tschudi Madsen.
3. Quoted in Peter Thornton's *Authentic Decor: 1620–1920*, Weidenfeld & Nicolson, 1984.
4. 'Textiles' by Sir Frank Warner and A.F. Kendrick from *Reports on the Present Position and Tendencies of the Industrial Arts as indicated at the International Exhibition of Modern Decorative & Industrial Arts, Paris 1925*, edited by Frank Scarlett.
5. See Alistair Duncan, *Art Deco*, Thames & Hudson, 1988.
6. 'Modern Art in Textile Design' by Brenda King in the catalogue for *Art & design at the Whitworth Gallery – The last hundred years*, 1989.
7. Paul Nash, 'Modern English Textiles – 1', *The Listener*, April 1932, quoted in 'Modern Textiles' by Hazel Clark, *Journal of the Decorative Art Society (1850 to the present)*, No. 12.

CHAPTER NINE

1. There are, of course, other types of black lace, in particular Chantilly. I am assuming that as Chantilly lace has become scarce, the likelihood of finding a shawl is remote.
2. The Venetian Ambassador to the English Court in 1695 mentions that Venetian lace is no longer fashionable and 'that called English Point which you know, is not made here, but in Flanders, and only bears the name of English to distinguish it from others'. Quoted from Mrs Palliser's *History of Lace*, 1902, p. 117.
3. 'The Exact Dress of the Head . . . 1725–86', Bernard Lens, V&A No E1652–1681 and 1672–1926, is a very useful illustration setting out all the contemporary variants of a 'head'.
4. Lingerie accessories from Dresden are usually included in discussions of lace. They are, however, strictly speaking, embroidery (see Glossary).
5. Anderson, *The Origin of Commerce*, 1681. Reynard remarks as he journeys through Flanders: 'The common people here as throughout all Flanders occupy themselves in making the white lace known as Malines'.
6. Cf Mme Despierres 'Histoire de Point d'Alençon . . .' (1886) and Mme Laprade 'Le Poinc de France . . .' (1904).
7. R Montague to Lord Arlington, Mss of the Duke of Buccleuch, Vol I, Hist. Mss Comm.
8. 1650, Letter of Favier Dubonlay, Intendant of Alençon: '*Points de Venise* were successfully being copied by "*une femme nommée la Perierre, fort habile à ces ouvrages*",' quoted from 7 September 1665, *Correspondance Administrative sous le Regne de Louis XIV*, Vol. 3.
10. Cf Hellowes 'Familiar Epistle of Sir Anthonye of Guevara', who claims to have seen a woman making pillow lace in 1577; and the complaints lodged by the London trade in 1620 against high-quality foreign artisans.
9. Cf portraits by Memling and Van Eyck.
11. Cf plate 110, in Santina Levy, *Lace, A History*, for an excellent illustration of this development.
12. This refers to a raised embroidery stitch, not to *punto in aria*, as yet.

SELECT BIBLIOGRAPHY

TEXTILES, GENERAL

Edwards, R. & Ramsay, L.G.G, *Connoisseur's Period Guides*, 1958
Geiger, A. *Textile Art*, 1979
Jacque, J. Thome (ed.) *Chez d'oeuvres du Musée de l'impression sur Étoffes, Mulhouse*, 1978
King, D. (ed.) *British Textile Design in the Victoria and Albert Museum*, 1980
London, HMSO, *Records of British Business and Industry 1760–1914, Textiles and Leather* n.d.
Lopez, R.S. *The Silk Industry in the Byzantine Empire*, 1945
Montgomery, F.M. *Textiles in America 1650–1870*, 1974
Parry, L. *William Morris Textiles*, 1983
Parry, L. *Textiles of the Arts and Crafts Movement*, 1988
Robinson, S. *History of Dyed Textiles*, 1969, Robinson, S. *History of Printed Textiles*, 1969
Rothstein, N. *Barbara Johnson's Album of Fashion and Fabrics*, 1987
Rothstein, N. *Flowered Silks*, 1989
Schoeser, M. & Rufey, C. *English and American Textiles from 1790 to the Present*, 1989
Stafford, C.L. & Bishop, R. *America's Quilts and Coverlets*, 1972
Thornton, P. *Baroque and Rococo Silks*, 1965
Tuscherer, J.M. (ed.) *Étoffes merveilleuses du Musée Historique des Tissus*, 1979
Volbach, W.F. *Early Decorative Silks*, 1969
Warner, F. *The Silk Industry of the U.K.: its origins and development* n.d.
Weibel, A.C. *Two Thousand Years of Textiles*, 1952
Ysselstein, G.T. *White Figured Linen Damasks*, 1962

GENERAL: TWENTIETH CENTURY

Atterbury, P. *Art Deco Patterns*, 1989
Benton, C., & Scharf, T.A. *German Design and the Bauhaus 1925–32*, 1975

Benton, C. & Scharf, T.A. *Modernism in the Decorative Arts, Paris 1810–30*, 1975
Constantine, M. & Lenor Larsen, J. *The Art Fabric: Beyond Craft*, 1973
Heals, *Catalogues, 1834–1934*, 1972
Srizenova, T. *Costume Revolution: Soviet costume, 1917–53*, 1987
Sutton, A. *British Craft Textiles*, 1982
Talley, C.S. *Contemporary Textile Art: Scandinavia*, 1982
Victoria and Albert Museum, *Ascher, Fabric, Art, Fashion*, 1987

CARPETS

Bennet, I. (ed.) *Rugs and Carpets of the World*, 1977
Faraday, C. Bateman *European and American Carpets and Rugs*, 1929
Jarry, M. *The Carpets of Aubusson: the Carpets of the Manufacture de la Savonnerie*, 1962
Tattershall, C.E.L. & Reed, S. *A History of British Carpets*, 1934–66

EMBROIDERY

Caulfield, S.F.A. & Saward, B.C. *Encyclopedia of Needlework, 1882–1972*
Clabburn, P. *The Needleworkers' Dictionary*, 1976
Howard, C. *20th-Century Embroidery in Great Britain*: – 1939; 1940–63; 1964–78; 1978–; 1983–6
Iklé, E. *La Broderie Mécanique 1828–1930*, 1931
Morris, B. *Victorian Embroidery*, 1969
Swan, S. Burrows *A Wintherthur Guide to American Needlework*, 1976
Synge, Lanto *Book of Antique Needlework and Embroidery*, 1986

KNITTING

Palmer, M. *Framework Knitting*, 1984–6
Rutt, R. *A History of Knitting*, 1987

LACE

Bury Palliser, Mrs *Lace*, 1902–1964–1975
Levey, S.M. *Lace, A History*, 1983

TAPESTRY

Gobel, H. *Wandtteppiche*, 1923–8
Standen, E. *European Post-Mediaeval Tapestries and Related Hangings in the Metropolitan Museum of Art*, 1985
Thomson, W.G. *A History of Tapestries*, rev ed 1973
Weigert, A. *French Tapestries*, 1962

CARING FOR TEXTILES

Clabburn, P. *Caring for Old Textiles*, 1984
Crafts Council (UK) *Conservators Handbook*, nd
Finch, K. & Puttnam, G. *Caring for Textiles*, 1977
Landi, S. *The Textile Conservator's Manual*, 1985

TEXTILE MACHINERY AND TECHNOLOGY

American Fabrics, (eds) *The Encyclopedia of Textiles*, 1976
Bagnall, W.R. *Textile Industries of the United States*, 1893
Benson, A. Warburton, *Looms and Weaving*, 1986–90
Benson, A.P. *Textile Machines*, 1983–87
Burnham, D.K. *Textile Terminology; Warp and Weft*, 1981
Bush, S. *The Silk Industry*, 1987
Clark, H. *Textile Printing*, 1987
Moncrieff, R.W. *Man-Made Fibres*, 1975
Storey, J. *Textile Printing*, 1974; Storey, J. *Dyes and Fabrics*, 1978
Walsworth, A.O. & Mann, J. de L. *The Cotton Trade and Industrial Manufacture 1600–1780*, 1931–65
Wingate, I.B. (ed.) *Fairchild's Dictionary of Textiles*, 1967

INDEX

TEXTILE MUSEUMS AND SOCIETIES

SOME MUSEUMS with notable textile collections.

AUSTRIA: Vienna, Schatzkammer, Kunsthistorisches Museum; Österreichisches Museum für Angewändte Kunst; BELGIUM: Brussels, Musées Royaux d'Art et d'Histoire; CANADA: Toronto, Royal Ontario Museum; FRANCE: Angers, Musée des Tapisseries; Lyons, Musée historique des Tissus; Mulhouse, Musée de l'Impression sur Étoffes; Troyes, Musée de la Bonneterie; Paris, Musée des Arts Decoratifs; GERMANY: Krefeld, Gewerbesammlung der Ingenieurschüle für textilweisen; Nuremburg, Nationalmuseum; ITALY: Milan, Poldi Pezzoli Museum: NETHERLANDS: Amsterdam, Ri-

jksmuseum; SWEDEN: Stockholm, Nordiska Museet; SWITZERLAND: Riggisberg, Abegg-Stiftung; UK: Edinburgh, Royal Scottish Museum; London, Science Museum, Victoria and Albert Museum; Manchester, Whitworth Art Gallery; Nottingham, Castle Museum; Paisley, Museum and Art Gallery; USA: Boston, Museum; Los Angeles, County Museum; New York, Metropolitan Museum, Smithsonian Museum of Art and Design, Cooper Hewitt Museum; North Andover, Mass., Museum of American Textile History; Washington, DC, The Textile Museum; USSR: Leningrad, The Hermitage; Moscow, State History Museum.

SOCIETIES: The Passold Research Fund,

c/o The London School of Economics, Houghton St, WC2 2AE publishes *Textile History*; The Textile Society of America, Hon. Sec. Milton Sunday, Cooper Hewitt Museum, New York; The Textile Society for the Study of Textile Art, Design and History, Hon. Sec. L. Brassington, 111 Greenfields Ave., Alton, Hants, GO34 2EW; Centre Internationale d'Etudes des Textiles Anciennes (CIETA), 34 rue de la Charité, Lyons, France.

ACKNOWLEDGEMENTS: We would like to record particular thanks to Simon Franses, Cora Ginsburg, Nedgeley Harte, and the staff at Spinks and the Department of Furnishing Textiles and Dress at the Victoria and Albert Museum, for their patient assistance.